IN THE MIDDLE OF IT!

Tools to Help
Preteen and Young Teen
Leaders and Parents

Jeff Rorabaugh

IN THE MIDDLE OF IT!

Tools to Help Preteen and Young Teen Leaders and Parents

Jeff Rorabaugh

IN THE MIDDLE OF IT!
Tools to Help Preteen and Young Teen Leaders and Parents

Copyright © 2018 by Jeff Rorabaugh and Illumination Publishers.
ISBN: 978-1-948450-22-5.

All rights reserved. No part of this book may be duplicated, copied, translated, reproduced or stored mechanically or electronically without the specific, written permission of Jeff Rorabaugh and Illumination Publishers.

Printed in the United States of America.

All scripture quotations, unless otherwise indicated, are taken from the NEW INTERNATIONAL VERSION. Copyright ©1973, 1978, 1984, 2011 by the International Bible Society. Used by permission of Zondervan Publishing House. All rights reserved.

The "NIV" and "New International Version" trademarks are registered in the United States Patent Trademark Office by the International Bible Society. Use of either trademark requires the permission of the International Bible Society.

Interior layout by Toney C. Mulhollan and cover design by Roy Applesamy of Toronto, Canada.

Illumination Publishers titles may be purchased in bulk for classroom instruction, teaching seminars, or sales promotional use. For information, please email paul.ipibooks@me.com.

Illumination Publishers cares deeply about using renewable resources and uses recycled paper whenever possible.

About the author: Jeff became a Christian while attending the University of Georgia in Athens, Georgia in 1985. He married his wife, Jennifer, in 1989. They have two adult children and live in Athens, Georgia. Jeff is currently the Executive Program Director of Camp Swamp, a year-round camp serving churches and communities in the Southeast. Jeff has served youth for over 25 years. He has been involved in the planning and leadership of **Camp Swamp** for most of those years. He holds a Bachelor degree in Chemistry from the University of Georgia and a Master of Science degree in Operations Management from Georgia State University. Jeff has worked with the likes of The Coca-Cola Company, Scientific Atlanta, Frito-Lay, and Power Partners holding various operations management positions.

ILLUMINATION PUBLISHERS

CONTENTS

INTRODUCTION
6

CONSTRUCTION AREA I
Bible Lessons
8

CONSTRUCTION AREA II
Bible Reliability
218

CONSTRUCTION AREA III
Character Studies
232

CONSTRUCTION AREA IV
Heroic Character
273

CONSTRUCTION AREA V
Rising Preteens
292

CONSTRUCTION AREA VII
Spiritureality
314

Introduction

First of all, thank you, thank you, thank you for your willingness to work with kids! You are an unsung hero in what can be a thankless and many times overlooked job. You are, I am confident, doing what Jesus would do: being with the children. This book was written with you and parents in mind. Yes, you are right: ultimately, the kids are what we both have in mind. (I know what you are thinking or you wouldn't be reading this book!) But without loving leaders—like you—and spiritual parents guiding them to become more like Jesus, preteens and young teens are open to a myriad number of life paths that lead people away from God; thus, you are the target audience for this book.

Consider the following:

- "It is funny how mortals always picture us as putting things into their minds: in reality our best work is done by keeping things out." —C. S. Lewis, *The Screwtape Letters*

- "Experts define adolescence as beginning with biology and ending with culture." —*Age of Opportunity: Lessons from the New Science of Adolescence*, page 47

Due to these sentiments, among many others, I am convinced that the preteen and young teen years are the most important in spiritual development. It is a time of great change and challenge in all facets of life. Physically, emotionally and mentally, it is the time of exploration and tryouts, yet still mixed with enough lingering fear and wonderment for guidance, prudence and godly love to be effective. Realistically, the kids are in the middle of trying to figure it all out...and dealing with a tough environment as their peers are doing the same, many with misguided or unguided attempts; it's like drinking water out of a firehose! But God knows and has a journey, a race, custom made for them. I believe you and I through the Word can give them a foundation and the character to run that race in a manner that prepares them for adulthood. I am always amazed at the growth and change that takes place from the time they enter this age until their exit; so much can be accomplished.

This book was crafted to offer you the tools, thoughts and ideas to instill in young minds and hearts the concerns and knowledge of God via his word and his Son, that they may be guided to greater spiritual, Jesus-like character. Understand, these are only tools and will only be as effective as your own sincerity and integrity in handling the content and focus therein. In the end, all our efforts are geared toward moving the kids forward to the image of Jesus and his spiritual culture. Practically, I hope this book takes a little bit of pressure off, as I know you are probably running around in the middle of your own life; may this book be a valuable and every-week tool to more productive service in his name. I look forward to somehow seeing the result. Perhaps we won't know the good we have done until heaven, when we will no longer be "in the middle of it."

Much love and respect,
—Jeff Rorabaugh

CONSTRUCTION AREA I
Bible Lessons

Indicates an action, game, activity or group session.

Indicates a question to ask aloud. This is important. You want kids to engage and to express what they are thinking. It is a key to growth.

Read the Scripture aloud. You want to saturate young minds with God's Word. It should be front and center in all your teaching.

#1. A Quart of Happiness

Quick Line Game: Have students get in order by what method you shout out: by age, height, birthday, letter of first name, shoe size, etc. To win the game, you had to be in the right order—sometimes that is how it is in life and your heart.

What makes you happy?
What makes your family happy?

{Divide into four groups and discuss the topics below. Have someone lead the discussion. Then rotate after 5 minutes.}

Group 1: Honor [Read Ephesians 6:2-3]
How do you honor your parents?
- Obey right away without complaining.
- Listen—look in their eyes.
- Love them unconditionally.
- Be open with them.
- Appreciate them.

How do your parents act when you honor them?
What is promised when you show honor to your parents?
- The result of respect is that it brings joy to you and your family for a long time.

Group 2: Pleasing God [Read 2 Corinthians 5:9-10]
How can we please God?
How do you feel when you don't do these things? Why?
Can you be happy when you feel bad or feel the impending doom of punishment?
- By pleasing God, you can be happy.

Group 3: Honesty [Read 1 Peter 2:1]
What is deceit?
- Means to lie, not quite tell the truth, paint an incomplete picture

How does deceit hurt your friends and family?
How does it make you feel to lie?

? Can you be happy when you feel that way?
- Being honest helps you and your family to be happy.

Group 4: Grateful [Read 1 Thessalonians 5:16-18]
? What are some circumstances where it is hard to be thankful?
How would you describe a thankful person?
Why did God say be thankful in ALL circumstances?
- Because he wants you always happy [v. 16]

Instruct each person to sit in the group describing which of the above characteristics they need to change the most.

> There is a story of a very large and jolly man that had a great feast for all the children of his town. He told the kids that he would provide all the food and the desserts, but they were to bring the best Kool-Aid, one quart each, and pour it into a 500-gallon vat. One of the kids thought his one quart couldn't matter that much in 500 gallons, so he got there early and poured one quart of water into the huge vat. All day long over 2000 kids poured their quart into the vat. In the evening the jolly man blessed the meal. He took his biggest cup to the vat and opened the tap; to his surprise, it was filled with water. See, each child thought that they were so insignificant that their one little quart would not matter, so ultimately the vat was only filled with water. This can be the same of you if you don't see how important your one little attitude is to everyone around you.

You must put your heart in the right order so you and others can experience true happiness. Become the characteristic that you chose and you will be adding Kool-Aid, not water.

#2. Signs of Learning

? What are signs used for?
Can you give some examples?

Spotted in a toilet of a London office:
TOILET OUT OF ORDER–
PLEASE USE FLOOR BELOW

In an office:
AFTER TEA BREAK STAFF SHOULD EMPTY THE TEAPOT & STAND UPSIDE DOWN ON THE DRAINING BOARD

Notice in a health food shop window:
CLOSED DUE TO ILLNESS

Seen during a conference:
FOR ANYONE WHO HAS CHILDREN AND DOESN'T KNOW IT, THERE IS A DAY CARE ON THE FIRST FLOOR

Message on a leaflet:
IF YOU CANNOT READ, THIS LEAFLET WILL TELL YOU HOW TO GET LESSONS

Spotted in a safari park:
ELEPHANTS PLEASE STAY IN YOUR CAR

Notice in a field:
THE FARMER ALLOWS WALKERS TO CROSS THE FIELD FOR FREE, BUT THE BULL CHARGES

In a laundromat:
AUTOMATIC WASHING MACHINES: PLEASE REMOVE ALL YOUR CLOTHES WHEN THE LIGHT GOES OUT

In an office:
WOULD THE PERSON WHO TOOK THE STEP LADDER YESTERDAY PLEASE BRING IT BACK OR FURTHER STEPS WILL BE TAKEN

Outside a secondhand shop:
WE EXCHANGE ANYTHING–BICYCLES, WASHING MACHINES, ETC. WHY NOT BRING YOUR WIFE ALONG AND GET A WONDERFUL BARGAIN?

On a repair shop door:
WE CAN REPAIR ANYTHING. (PLEASE KNOCK HARD ON THE DOOR–THE BELL DOESN'T WORK)

In a London department store:
BARGAIN BASEMENT UPSTAIRS

? What were some signs in the Bible?
- Rainbow
- Circumcision
- Blood on door frames in Egypt
- Gideon's fleece
- Sun retreating 10 steps

- Virgin birth of Jesus
- Jonah 3 days in the belly of a fish
- Notice on cross regarding Jesus as King of the Jews

? Why were they used?
- To warn
- To guide
- To direct
- To teach

I need some signs from you:

? What do you want to learn during this year in the middle school ministry?
How would you like our time each week to go?
What would make it a time of fun and learning?

Use this lesson as an introduction or at the beginning of the year (or semester) to come up with some ideas of what to do and to get the students engaged in creating their own ministry.

#3. Across the Quad

? What does the following quote mean?

"Give me a firm place to stand, and I will move the earth." —Archimedes

Today, we are going to talk about getting along, respecting our differences, and being unified.

[Read 1 Chronicles 11-12:2]
{Read this with lots of zeal and theatrics; have a running commentary to a make it rich and full of bravado. You'll have to practice!}

? What stands out to you about this band of warriors?
What strengths do you see?
What weaknesses would you expect?

{Check out all the different "-ites." They were all kinds of people with all kinds of characteristics. From all over and yet they were as one behind David.}

? How could David's group of mighty men be torn apart?
What does it take for people from different backgrounds to get along?
What challenges come with building tight friendships...ones you would die for?

[Read Ephesians 4:2-3]
? What does this say it takes to get along?
- Humility
- Patience
- Acceptance of each other
- Respect for each person's role

The right attitude! Look at the mighty men's attitudes: [1 Chronicles 12:17-18]

Read the story called "The Most Mature Thing I've Ever Seen" in the book *Chicken Soup for the Teenage Soul*, pages 266-269.

Change comes with the right attitude: one of helpfulness and unity, NOT betrayal and violence.

? What are you doing to be unified with people?
On what place will you take your stand so that you can change the world?
What "quad" will you cross to make a difference?

As you grow and develop convictions, I pray you stand for peace, helpfulness and unity!

#4. An All Nature-al Character

? What is one of the worst excuses you have heard to get out of something? Why do we use excuses?

What do you think about these excuses for missing school:
1. I understand everything and I don't want to get confused.
2. When I woke up someone had moved the school and I couldn't find it.
3. The dog ate our car...but my homework is safe.
4. My bicycle was out of gas and the bus turned green.
5. A fleeting case of violent death.
6. Dad said I could take the week off to visit Paris and the Eiffel Tower.
7. It gives me a chance to explore new educational opportunities.
8. Ignorance is bliss.
9. I like the challenge of turning in my homework not knowing the assignment.
10. People might think I care.

[Read Romans 1:18-20]

? Based on this, why would man need an excuse?
- To ignore God and his expectations

On what basis does God ignore our excuses?
- The evidence of nature

Instructions:
1. Get into seven groups.
2. Give each group a scripture and animal from the list below. Bring in some poster size images of each animal. Have them google search to find characteristics of that animal that describe God's character.
3. Have each group report on their findings.
4. Listed are some example facts for each animal that can supplement their findings, if necessary.
5. Conclude with the following:

[Read Matthew 6:26, 12:12] You are much more important to God than any animal. Don't you think he cares about the type of character you have? So much so that he made examples for you to look at so that you would be without excuse. You are the only being he has made in his image...now take advantage of what you see by becoming like him.

Animal: *Eagle*

Value: *Caring:* In the way it selflessly and lovingly cares for its chicks, the bald eagle teaches us the value of caring. In fact, the eagle shows us a glimpse of just how lovingly God takes care of us.

Scripture: 1 Peter 5:7– "Cast all your anxiety on him because he cares for you."

- » The parent protects its chicks from stormy weather by forming a shelter with its outstretched wings.
- » Young ones have brown feathers on their heads and don't develop the white head feathers until after five years.
- » It builds the largest nest of any other bird. The nest is called an aerie and takes several weeks to build. It is usually built on a cliff ledge or in a tree. Made of sticks and twigs, it can weigh two tons! One aerie was built in Ohio in about 1890. The same aerie was used every year until storms destroyed it in 1925.
- » Females are larger than the males. Males are about 2 1/2 feet long and weigh about 10 pounds. Females are about 3 feet long and weigh about 13 pounds. Its wingspan is 6-8 feet from tip to tip.
- » They mate for life and use the same nest each year. Both parents take turns keeping the eggs warm until they hatch 35 days later.
- » When the young hatch, both parents provide their food. After catching food for the chicks, parent birds tear up the meat into small enough pieces for the chicks to eat.
- » Parents teach chicks to fly by pushing them out of the nest. As the baby bird falls through the air, a parent bird swoops down underneath it, catching it safely on its back.

Animal: *Raccoon*

Value: *Cleanliness*

Scripture: Psalm 51:7 – "Cleanse me with hyssop, and I will be clean; wash me, and I will be whiter than snow."

- » Its Latin name, lotor, means "one who washes." They have been seen dipping their food into water to moisten it and to remove sand or grit from it.
- » They can use their hands as well as monkeys can. They pick up their food with their hands and then place it in their mouths.
- » Babies are called kits and are born after a 9-week pregnancy. Usually 3-4 kits are born in a litter. At birth, they do not have defined stripes on their faces.
- » They like to live alone. They can be temperamental and will often fight with

Tools to Help Preteen and Young Teen Leaders and Parents

their own family members as well as others of their own kind.
- » They are nocturnal animals coming out mostly at night. They do not hibernate in the winter. Those who live where it is warmer are active year-round. But those who live farther north do spend long periods of time sleeping in the winter.
- » They are excellent survivors. This is because they are willing to live near people and they eat many different things. Their diets include fruits, nuts, insects, reptiles, garbage, crops and small animals.
- » They grow to be 18-30 inches long and weigh up to 46 pounds.

Animal: *Porcupine*
Value: *Protection*: Certainly, God has shown us the value of protection in the example of the porcupine. God has given us an even better form of protection. Read the Bible verse below to find out what your protection is.
Scripture: *Psalm 91:1* – "For he will command his angels concerning you to guard you in all your ways."
- » What they eat depends on where they live and the season. They enjoy grass in the spring. They eat roots, shoots, berries, young leaves, nuts and flowers in summer. In the fall and winter, they eat conifer needles and tree bark.
- » A full-grown North American one has as many as 30,000 quills. It usually weighs 8-15 pounds. Large males have been known to weigh as much as 40 pounds.
- » The North American one does not see well. But it can hear and smell very well. It moves slowly, but it carries an arsenal of quills for protection.
- » They live alone. The female and male stay together only long enough to mate. A single offspring is born about 7 months later.
- » North American ones are nocturnal animals (meaning they sleep during the day and come out at night).
- » They are good swimmers because their quills have air inside them. This makes the quills act like a life jacket, keeping them afloat.
- » It takes 4 years for a North American one to be fully grown.
- » They cannot actually throw their quills when defending themselves. Instead, they hit their attacker with their quill-laden tails. Tiny barbs, like fishhooks, make the quills difficult to remove.

Animal: *Elephant*
Value: *Love*: Elephants teach us the value of love. With their loving family units,

elephants care for and protect each other. They stay together knowing that each part of their family is very special. And when one elephant in the family dies, the other elephants show their great love by grieving the loss.

Scripture: 1 Corinthians 13:4-7 – "Love is patient, love is kind. It does not envy, it does not boast, it is not proud. It is not rude, it is not self-seeking, it is not easily angered, it keeps no record of wrongs. Love does not delight in evil but rejoices with the truth. It always protects, always trusts, always hopes, always perseveres."

- They eat up to 500 pounds of grasses, fruits, and other plant life each day.
- They can drink up to 40 gallons of water at one time. During the dry season, they will dig for water in a sandy riverbed.
- They can walk at a steady speed of 5 to 5 1/2 miles per hour. (That's faster than a man can walk.) A herd can cover 50 miles in a single day.
- Herds are led by a mature female. Every member of the group is related to this leading "matriarch."
- They live in loving family units. They seem to have strong feelings for others in their family and even bury their dead with twigs and leaves. They also grieve, staying by the "grave" for many hours.
- A pregnancy lasts for 22 months (that's 13 more months than people!). When born, a calf weighs about 250 pounds. The calf will drink milk from its mother for two years.
- They become fully mature (an adult ready to mate) when they are 14-15 years old.

Animal: *Bengal Tiger*

Value: *Strength:* The strength of the Bengal tiger reminds us of our Source of strength. God gives greater strength than tigers to the weakest person who asks. Thus, you too may possess the value of strength, through God.

Scripture: *Psalm 138:3* – "When I called, you answered me; you greatly emboldened me."

- They eat about 65 pounds of meat each night.
- They are strong and can kill animals 2-3 times bigger than they are.
- They live alone. During mating, a male will remain in a female's home range for 20 to 80 days. Other than this, they are solitary and do not like to share their hunting ground. They mark their hunting ground by shredding the bark of trees and with strong-smelling urine.
- Their home range occupies from 17 to 20 square miles. Each one usually has

several dens in its home range and will use whichever is closest at the time.
- Their roar is so great that it can be heard up to a mile away.
- They usually have a reddish-gold fur coat. However, white fur is also a possibility.
- Unlike their domesticated counterparts, they enjoy water. Because they do not like excessive heat, they often lie in pools of water to keep cool. They are also strong swimmers.

Animal: *Hummingbird*
Value: *Hard work*: Through its tireless energy this little creature shows us the value of hard work. We cannot even count to 200 in one second, yet the hummingbird can beat its wings 200 times in that time. The tiny bird weighs only 1/10 of an ounce, yet it migrates a distance of 1,850 miles!

Scripture: *Isaiah 40:31* – "Those who hope in the Lord will renew their strength. They will soar on wings like eagles; they will run and not grow weary, they will walk and not be faint."

- In spite of their tiny size, they migrate more than 1,850 miles from the eastern United States to spend the winter in Central America.
- The mother makes her nest from leafy material held together with spider's webs.
- The ruby-throated variety has the least number of feathers ever counted on any bird.
- Before migrating, they store a layer of fat equal to half their body weight.
- During courtship, they beat their wings up to 200 times each second! And males fly back and forth in a perfect arc. (Normally their wings beat at about 90 times each second.)
- Because it takes so much energy to beat their wings so quickly, these birds must eat twice their body weight each day. They also must eat often, usually every 15 minutes.
- They are about 4 inches long with a 5-inch wingspan. They only weigh 1/10 of an ounce.
- They are as agile in flight as an insect. They can fly upside down or backward and even hover in ways that other birds cannot.

Animal: *Sun Bear*
Value: *Loyalty*: By choosing one life partner and staying with them until death, the sun bear teaches us about the value of loyalty.

Scripture: *Proverbs 17:17* – "A friend loves at all times, and a brother is born for a time of adversity."

- They are thought to be very smart. One was seen sticking his claw into a keyhole and turning it, after watching someone unlock the door with a key.
- You can find out how old one is by counting the enamel rings in its teeth (just like counting the rings in a tree trunk!), though it is not advised you try this yourself.
- They make a nest by bending and breaking tree branches about 10-20 feet above the ground. Here they sleep during the day. They come out mostly at night.
- They do not sleep in the winter like most others of their species. This is probably because it is warm where they live.
- It is hard to see one in the wild. They are very shy. The Malaysian people think the shy animal is friendly. Some even keep them as pets for their children.
- When one chooses a mate, it remains with the same partner for the rest of its life. A pregnant female will usually give birth to two cubs. The cubs stay with their mother for 1-2 years.

#5. Amazed and Astonished

? What amazes you?
What amazes you about the Bible?
What amazes you about Jesus' message?
How would you say people reacted to him?

[Read Mark 1:27, 10:24]
Jesus amazed people.

Read from *Jesus the Same*, "The Strength of Jesus," pages 41-45 (available at www.ipibooks.com), or create a fun, relatable way to convey and illustrate this character of Jesus.

Jesus' mere existence, being himself, either inspired or enflamed people—inspired because they were astonished with the man; enflamed because they opposed what he stood for.

Choose a partner. Answer this question: Which are you and what ways do you convey this characteristic?
Ask for volunteers to share their answers.

[Read Mark 10:32-34]
? Who was leading?
Who was following?

If you aren't either astonished or amazed, then you aren't getting personal enough with Jesus or each other.

> One of Denmark's leading sculptors had a burning ambition to create the greatest statue of Jesus ever made. He began by shaping a clay model of a triumphant, regal figure. The head was thrown back and the arms were upraised in a gesture of great majesty. It was his conception of Christ the King: strong, dominant. "This will be my masterpiece," he said, on the day the model was completed. But, during the night a heavy fog rolled into the area and sea spray seeped through a partially opened window of the artist's oceanside studio. The moisture affected the shape of the model so that when the artist returned to the studio in the morning, he was shocked to find a wounded figure. The droplets

of moisture that had formed on the statue created the illusion of bleeding. The head had drooped. The facial expression had been transformed from severity to compassion. And the arms had dropped into an attitude of welcome. The artist stared at the figure, agonizing over the time wasted and the need to begin all over again. But something came over him to change his mood. He began to see that this image of Christ was the truer one. Then he wrote at the base of the newly-shaped figure: "Come unto me."

We should all desire to know better and get closer to the man Jesus. Let him impact you for this life and prepare you for the one to come.

Don't let a church service or even a church camp be the only thing that gets you close to him: have daily Jesus-based faith, not event-based faith.

#6. Bad Company Makes Good Coffee

Opening activity: Divide into teams. Ask for one volunteer from each team. Tell the group of volunteers they have a secret job. Tell them to destroy whatever is built when they hear the key word. Ask each team to build something (house of cards, stack of cups, etc.) Say the key word. Watch what happens and then discuss. Which one was easier, to build or destroy?

[Read 1 Corinthians 15:33]

? What is bad company?
- Someone who cusses, gossips, is divisive, judgmental, a bully

? How would you define good character?
How does bad company go about corrupting good character?
What could you do to keep your character from being corrupted?

Here are two ways:
1. Change Direction

In the eleventh century, King Henry III of Bavaria grew tired of court life and the pressures of being a monarch. He made application to Prior Richard at a local monastery, asking to be accepted as a contemplative and spend the rest of his life in the monastery. "Your Majesty," said Prior Richard, "do you understand that the pledge here is one of obedience? That will be hard because you have been a king." "I understand," said Henry. "The rest of my life I will be obedient to you, as Christ leads you." "Then I will tell you what to do," said Prior Richard. "Go back to your throne and serve faithfully in the place where God has put you." When King Henry died, a statement was written: "The King learned to rule by being obedient."

? How would you describe the ordeal of being around bad company?
- Suffering

? Is suffering something to be happy about?

2. Change Convictions [Read Romans 5:3-4]

A young woman went to her mother and told her about her life and how things were so hard for her. She did not know how she was going to make it and wanted to give up. She was tired of fighting and struggling. It seemed as though just as one problem was solved, a new one arose. Her mother took her to the kitchen. She filled three pots with water and placed each on a burner on high. Soon the pots came to a boil. In the first, she placed carrots, in the second she placed eggs, and in the last she placed ground coffee beans. She let them sit and boil, without saying a word. In about twenty minutes she turned off the burners. She fished the carrots out and placed them in a bowl. She pulled the eggs out and placed them in a bowl. Then she ladled the coffee out and placed it in a bowl. Turning to her daughter, she asked, "Tell me what you see." "Carrots, eggs, and coffee," she replied. Her mother brought her closer and asked her to feel the carrots. She did, and noted that they were soft. The mother then asked the daughter to take an egg and break it. After pulling off the shell, she observed the hard-boiled egg.

Finally, the mother asked the daughter to sip the coffee. The daughter smiled as she tasted its rich aroma. The daughter then asked, "What does it mean, mother?" Her mother explained that each of these ingredients had faced the same adversity: boiling water. Each reacted differently. The carrot went in strong, hard, and unrelenting; however, after being subjected to the boiling water, it softened and became weak. The egg had been fragile. Its thin outer shell had protected its liquid interior, but after sitting through the boiling water, its inside became hardened. The ground coffee was unique, however; while it was in the boiling water, it had changed to something desirable. "Which are you?" she asked her daughter. {Bring in an example of all three for them to see.}

? How will you respond to bad company?

Personal illustration: I was in a group at work who were cussing up a storm; I asked them to stop.

Your choices:
- Boil until you are weak and soft,
- Boil until you are hard and unchangeable, or
- Boil until your character is rich and tasty.

#7. Be Like Bill

? How do you greet something that is going to be challenging and hard?
Is it good to suffer? Why or why not?

Tell me what you know about Cerebral Palsy (CP).
{CP is a debilitating condition that results from damage to the central nervous system which in turn causes changes in the brain. This can happen from pre-delivery occurrences such as infection or stroke; or during delivery when a lack of oxygen to the brain causes damage. The resulting brain damage causes physical effects such as the inability to walk or coordinate muscle activity, slurred speech and various physical deformities. CP affects about 0.1% of the population.}

? What challenges might a person with CP have?
How would you expect a person with CP to be treated by others?
What would your attitude be toward life if you had CP?

Watch Bill Porter 20/20 video:
https://www.youtube.com/watch?v.=i22oOqAeccE, 15 min.

What about Bill Porter inspires you?
? What are some of your situations in which Bill Porter's story encourages you?
Why is persistence and perseverance so important in dealing with these situations?
How do you get to be persistent and perseverant? Are you born with it or what?

Two things that produce persistence and perseverance:

1. [Read Romans 5:3-4] Suffering
Paul is talking about rejoicing because of hope. Hope is powerful. There have been scientific studies to show that hope, something you can neither touch nor see, is so strong it can actually produce chemical changes in your brain which affect your happiness and well-being. Then Paul tells how hope is created. Many of us don't really suffer, not like Bill Porter, but we do have things in our life, and will have more things as we get older, that are there to create character and hope. I hope you will look on some of your situations with a different attitude and will

make decisions to keep on going no matter how tough it seems and never give up doing what is right.

2. [Read Hebrews 10:23-25] Encouragement

Not only do we need to hold to the hope that suffering produces, but we need to help each other. Bill Porter needed other people; people to lace his shoes and fix his tie and button his cuffs. He allowed others to enter his life. He could have been prideful and said no, but instead he accepted help. Just like Bill Porter, we won't make it if we don't let other people encourage us and help us.

> *"I never thought my life had meaning, and I didn't live it as though it was important to anyone except those close to me. My message to everyone [who reads this book] is that your life is important, too. Think about each person you meet each day of your life and what effect you might have upon them for good or ill. It isn't always the big decisions that make a difference in our lives; more often, it's the little ones."*
>
> —Bill Porter

Most of us will never reach celebrity status, but your life can mean just as much, I dare say more, to someone else. Do the everyday things with as much courage and determination as Bill Porter, and your life will bring honor and glory and immortality to you and to others.

#8. Be Quick to Listen Slowly

Opening activity: Divide your students into three or four teams. Tell the teams they're going to compete in a listening competition. You're going to read a list of items then ask a question about it. They'll have about 30 seconds to come up with one group answer and write it down. Make sure they know they're not allowed to write anything down while you're reading the list.

1. I'm going to read you list of clothing. Listen carefully: boots, sweater, belt, swimsuit, hat, shorts, pants, socks, jacket, mittens, and scarf. How many of those items began with the letter S? (Sweater, swimsuit, shorts, socks, scarf)
2. I'm going to read you a list of pizza toppings. Listen carefully: Onions, pepperoni, pineapple, sausage, olives, green peppers, mushrooms, anchovies, ham, and bacon. What was the fifth topping? (Olives)
3. I'm going to read you a list of toys. Listen carefully: electric train, remote-controlled car, Barbie doll, Gameboy, Lego blocks, Chutes and Ladders, Light-Brite, tea set, Tonka truck, Matchbox cars, Beanie babies. How many of those toys require batteries? (remote-controlled car, Gameboy, Light-Brite)
4. I'm going to read you a list of names. Listen carefully: Robin, Teresa, Claude, Ken, Jim, Peter, Frank, Connor, Lisa, Brianna, and Kelsey. How many of those names have only two syllables? (Robin, Peter, Connor, Lisa, Kelsey)
5. I'm going to read you a list of ice cream flavors. Listen carefully: vanilla, chocolate chunk, rocky road, pistachio, peanut butter swirl, chocolate mint, butter pecan, cookie dough. What was the fourth flavor? (pistachio)

Why is listening important?
How can not listening cause problems for you?
Why is being a good listener such an important quality in a friend?

[Read Isaiah 65:24, Psalm 34:15-16]
Do you believe God listens to us? Why or why not?
How do you think he listens to us?
What difference does it make that he listens to us?

{Have everyone stand up. Tell them you're going to read descriptions of some listening situations. Indicate that one side of the room is for REALLY HARD and the other is for NOT HARD. After you read each item, they should move to one side of the room or the other or in between to show how hard or easy it would be for them to listen in that situation.}

1. You're watching your favorite TV show and your little brother wants to tell you about his pretend pet.
2. A close friend of yours is telling you a funny story; and you have one you want to share, but hers is really long.
3. Your mom is telling you about her junior high school, but you have to go to the bathroom really bad.
4. Some kid from school starts telling you what he did this past weekend. You really don't want to be seen with him.
5. A friend of yours is cautiously telling you about something you do that bugs him.
6. A friend is telling you why she's been kind of bummed lately, but she's whiny and her story is boring and stupid.
7. An elderly guy in your church is trying to tell you about the old days, but your friends are waiting for you down the hall.
8. A kid you know from school is telling you a great story, but he's up close and has the worst breath you've ever smelled!

[Read James 1:19]

How does it make people feel when we listen to them?
Who do you know that's a great listener?
What do they do that's so great?
How can you improve as a listener?

> Writer Charles Swindoll once found himself with too many commitments in too few days. He got nervous and tense about it. "I was snapping at my wife and our children, choking down my food at mealtimes, and feeling irritated at those unexpected interruptions through the day," he recalled in his book Stress Fractures. "Before long, things around our home started reflecting the patter of my hurry-up style. It was becoming unbearable. I distinctly remember after supper one evening, the words of our younger daughter, Colleen. She wanted to tell me something important that had happened to her at school that day. She began hurriedly, 'Daddy, I wanna tell you somethin' and I'll tell you really fast.' Suddenly realizing her frustration, I answered, 'Honey, you can tell me—and you don't have to tell me really fast. Say it slowly.' I'll never forget her answer: 'Then listen slowly.'"

#9. Be Strong and Very Courageous

Give me a few words to describe your thoughts or feelings so far about this year. What factors influenced your choice or words?

Tell a friend in one minute about what success looks like for you this year. What will it take on our part to achieve success as you defined it?

[Read Joshua 1:1-9]

? How did God describe success for the Israelites?
- Win every battle
- Take possession of land
- Prosperous
- Become a nation

? What in their recent history made a mockery of these promises?
- Doubt
- Fear
- Panicked when leader was missing
- Worshipped idols
- Got angry with God
- Wanted to return to slavery
- Wouldn't fight

This is what happens when you don't trust God.

[Read Joshua 1:10-2:24]

? What is different about this new generation?
- Willingness to follow
- Did not allow rebellion
- Were reminded of great things God did
- Decided to trust God
-

? What are the two things that will lead them to success?
- Being careful to do everything in the Book of the Law
- God's own presence

They had new leadership, an inexperienced army, and no chariots; however, they did have trust and obedience, and stick-to-itiveness.

Clarence Jordan was a man of unusual abilities and commitment. He had two PhDs, one in agriculture and one in Greek and Hebrew. He was so gifted he could have chosen to do anything he wanted. He chose to serve the poor. In the 1940s, he founded a farm in Americus, Georgia, and called it Koinonia Farm. It was a community for poor whites and poor blacks. As you might guess, such an idea did not go over well in the Deep South of the '40s. Ironically, much of the resistance came from good church people who followed the laws of segregation as much as the other folk in town. The townspeople tried everything to stop Clarence. They tried boycotting him and slashing workers' tires when they came to town. Over and over, for fourteen years, they tried to stop him.

Finally, in 1954, the Ku Klux Klan had enough of Clarence Jordan, so they decided to get rid of him once and for all. They came one night with guns and torches and set fire to every building on Koinonia Farm but Clarence's home, which they riddled with bullets. And they chased off all the families except one black family that refused to leave. Clarence recognized the voices of many of the Klansmen, and, as you might guess, some of them were church people. Another was the local newspaper's reporter. The next day, the reporter came out to see what remained of the farm. The rubble still smoldered and the land was scorched, but he found Clarence in the field, hoeing and planting.

"I heard the awful news," he called to Clarence, "and I came out to do a story on the tragedy of your farm closing." Clarence just kept on hoeing and planting. The reporter kept prodding, kept poking, trying to get a rise out of this quietly determined man who seemed to be planting instead of packing his bags. So, finally, the reporter said in a haughty voice, "Well, Dr. Jordan, you got two of them PhDs and you've put fourteen years into this farm, and there's nothing left of it at all. Just how successful do you think you've been?" Clarence stopped hoeing, turned toward the reporter with his penetrating blue eyes, and said quietly but firmly, "About as successful as the cross. Sir, I don't think you understand us. What we are about is not success but faithfulness. We're staying. Good day."

Beginning that day, Clarence and his companions rebuilt Koinonia and the farm is going strong today.

Not sure what is in store for you or for us this year. My bet is that we will have our battles to fight and heartland to take possession of...but no matter, let it be a year where we walk in righteousness and with great confidence knowing that God is with us, so let us be strong and courageous!

#10. Bible True/False Questions

Occasionally, its nice to have a change of pace and test the kid's knowledge of the word of God. A true/false test is a good assessment and the kids enjoy it.

1. There is an account of a talking camel in the Bible. [Numbers 22:21-35] FALSE
2. The Apostle Paul once spoke so long to a group of believers that one of his listeners fell asleep and then fell out of the third story window he was sitting in. [Acts 20:7-12] TRUE
3. Unicorns are mentioned as living in the Garden of Eden. [Genesis 1:24-25] FALSE
4. Jesus once spit on a man's eyes [Mark 8:22-26] TRUE
5. The Bible says that getting physically beaten can help you spiritually. [Proverbs 20:30] TRUE
6. The Bible says that women are saved by giving birth to children. [1 Timothy 2:15] FALSE
7. When the people of a Samaritan village refused hospitality to Jesus and his apostles, James and John got so angry that they called down fire from heaven and completely destroyed the village. [Luke 9:51-56] FALSE
8. There have been people who have met angels and did not know it. [Hebrews 13:2] TRUE
9. The shortest verse in the Bible consists of two words. [John 11:35] TRUE
10. Jesus knows the exact day of his Second Coming. [Matthew 24:36] FALSE
11. There was a race of people in the Bible called the Nephilim. It has been said that they were the offspring of angels and women and that they survived the Great Flood. [Genesis 6:1-4] TRUE
12. According to the Old Testament Law, a stubborn and rebellious son who does not obey his father and mother and will not listen to them when they discipline him shall be stoned to death. [Deuteronomy 21:18-21] TRUE
13. One of the tragedies that Satan used to test Job was that his sheep and servants were burned up by a fire-breathing dragon. [Job 1:12-19] FALSE
14. The Bible acknowledges the existence of aliens and commands that they be treated with equality. [Leviticus 19:33-34 NIV1984] TRUE
15. Jesus once told an entire church that he was about to vomit. [Revelation 3:14-16] TRUE
16. The Old Testament Law forbids tattoos. [Leviticus 19:28] TRUE
17. The existence of dinosaurs is mentioned in the Bible. [Job 40:15-24; Job 3:8,

Job 41:1, Psalm 74:14, Psalm 104:26, Isaiah 27:1] FALSE
18. Jesus commanded his disciples to drink his blood. [John 6:53-59] TRUE
19. There is mention of dragons in the Bible. [Revelation 12] TRUE
20. The name of God is mentioned more times in the book of Esther than any other book in the Bible. FALSE
21. Certain women in the Bible had to shave their heads before they could get married [Deuteronomy 21:10-13] TRUE
22. Whenever David's son Absalom would cut his hair, it would weigh over 5 pounds. [2 Samuel 14:25-26] TRUE
23. Jesus drove a Honda, but did not like to talk about it. [John 12:49] FALSE
24. David fought in a battle at Gath against a man with six fingers on each hand and six toes on each foot. [2 Samuel 21:20] TRUE
25. Jesus once told Peter that he would find money inside a fish. [Matthew 17:24-27] TRUE
26. There is no sin that God will not forgive. [Matthew 12:31-32] FALSE
27. John the Baptist's diet consisted of locusts and wild honey. [Matthew 3:1-4] TRUE
28. Gideon used a loaf of bread to defeat an entire army. [Judges 7:9-15] FALSE
29. Samson once ate some honey he found in the carcass of a dead lion. [Judges 14:5-9] TRUE
30. At his birthday party, Herod gave his stepdaughter the severed head of John the Baptist as a present. [Matthew 14:1-12] TRUE
31. There is no mention in the Bible of three wise men coming to see the baby Jesus. [Matthew 2:1-2] TRUE
32. There is no mention of Adam and Eve eating an apple in the Bible. [Genesis 3:1-12] TRUE
33. There was a famine in Samaria so severe that two women got into a dispute over cooking and eating each of their daughters. [2 Kings 6:24-29] FALSE
34. The word Christian appears more than any other word in the New Testament. [Acts 11:26; 26:28; 1 Peter 4:16] FALSE
35. An angel told the Apostle John to eat a scroll, and he did. It tasted pretty good, but it ended up making him sick. [Revelation 10:8-10] TRUE
36. Methuselah is the oldest man on record, living to the age of 696 years old. [Genesis 5:27] FALSE
37. Old Testament Law allowed the Jews to eat any kind of bird or flying insect. [Deuteronomy 14:11-20] FALSE
38. The Bible allows you to heap burning coals on your enemy's head. [Proverbs 25:21-22] TRUE

#11. Blazing Friendships

Opening activity: Divide the group into pairs partnering with someone they don't know. Have them sit facing each other. The only restriction is they cannot get up. Tell each pair they have three minutes and that is all you tell them. See what they do with the three minutes.

? What did you do with your time?
How did you feel when sitting across from someone you didn't know?
What did you have to do to make something happen while you sat across from each other?
What does it mean to be giving?
- To apply your focus to something or someone other than yourself

? In what areas of your life does giving apply?
» Helping poor or needy   » Contribution   » Midweek
» Presents   » gifts » Greetings   » Party
» Shelter   » place of rest   » Taxes, respect   » honor
» Time with family   » A relationship with God   » Siblings

Lots of areas take your effort to give. Let's talk about one area in particular: your friendships.

? Why is giving so vital for a great friendship?
What keeps us from giving?
What is insecurity?
- Feeling unsure of oneself; thoughts of inadequacy

? Is it wrong? Is it linked to a sin? If so, which one?
- Pride

[Read Proverbs 18:1]

? What does this teach you?
- Friendships are ruined by pride and selfishness.

? How can pride and selfishness disease a friendship?
- Not introduce yourself
- Always do what you want to do

- Not talk about tough issues
- Don't ask questions

? What other circumstances are hurt by selfishness?
So, what is the cure for this disease?

[Read Philippians 2:3-4]

? What direction and encouragement does this give you?

I have a unique vantage point as I observe your relationships. I get to see you in a variety of settings: here at midweek, at activities, in your neighborhoods, going to movies, hanging out, etc. There is one thing common in all these situations: you can benefit from this scripture. Some of you are so worried about what you will look like that you miss out on having a great friendship. Others of you are so busy promoting your own interests that you miss out on having a great friendship. Good sound judgment—all sound judgment—promotes unselfishness.

> One of the ancient kings of Persia loved to mingle with his people in disguise. Once, dressed as a poor man, he descended the long flight of stairs, dark and damp, to the tiny cellar where the fireman, seated on ashes, was tending the furnace. The king sat down beside him and began to talk. At mealtime the fireman produced some coarse black bread and a jug of water and they ate and drank. The king went away but returned again and again, for his heart was filled with sympathy for the lonely man. They became good friends as time passed. At last the king thought, "I'll tell him who I am and see what gift he will ask." So he did, but the fireman didn't ask for a thing. The king was astonished and said, "Don't you realize that I can give you anything—a city, a throne?" The man gently replied, "I understand, your Majesty. You have already given the greatest gift a man could receive. You left your palace to sit with me here in this dark and lonely place. You could give nothing more precious. You have given yourself, and that is far more than I could ever deserve."

Challenge: Promote the interest of someone else this week.

#12. Building an Incorruptible Character

? What are some of the corrupt things you have heard about lately?
How does someone become corrupt?
Could you become corrupt?
How can you keep from becoming corrupt?

[Read 2 Peter 1:3-4]

? How can you escape the pit of corruption?
- Through God's promises

? How do we get God's promises?
- Through God's own glory and goodness

? What are some of the things you need for life and godliness?

[Read 2 Peter 1:5-7]

We need a ladder to climb out and the following things define each rung. {Bring in a ladder with each of these on a rung.} Let's define each one. What is:

? Faith?
- Belief that God exists

Goodness?
- Moral quality to act godly

Knowledge?
- Mental awareness of the teachings of Jesus

Self-Control?
- Ability to align one's will and actions within acceptable limits

Perseverance?
- Never-give-up attitude

Godliness?
- Jesus-like character

? Mutual affection?
- Application of godliness to other people

? Love?
- The heart of godliness

? Why did Peter say to build in this manner?
Perhaps each one depends on the previous one. This could be a template to grow to be like God.

1. Can't please or obey God if you don't believe in him.
2. What good will it do to have a faith that your character can't support?
3. What good does all that knowledge do, if you don't have the goodness to put it into practice?
4. If you don't know the standard, how can you control yourself to be like it?
5. To control one's actions takes repetitive actions, which you can't quit on.
6. Whatever godly quality you persevere in will eventually become your own characteristic, giving you a hint of godliness.
7. Godliness replaces selfishness, which comes out in how you treat people.
8. The Bible says God is love. You must grow in all these areas to love.

? Why would God be so concerned about you possessing these qualities?

[Read Matthew 24:12]
Though this prophecy is most likely about the fall of Jerusalem in the first century, it is descriptive of the world at large: it will only grow more and more wicked. The only hope our world and you have is to grow to be more and more like God. Want to fix the world? Then we must fix the person. Can't do that if you don't possess and grow in these qualities. Many of you want to have great characters about which you and others can be proud. Find out where you are and make the choices necessary to be a young man or woman of character.

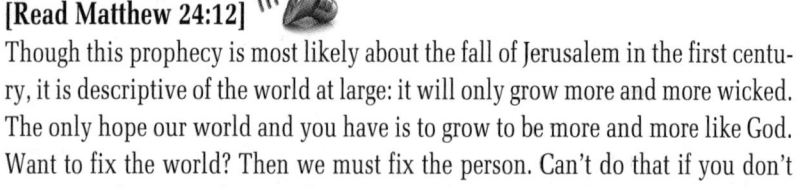

> "Freedom is useless if we don't exercise it as characters making choices…we are free to change the stories by which we live. Because we are genuine characters, and not mere puppets, we can choose our defining stories. We can do so because we actively participate in the creation of our stories. We are co-authors as well as characters. Few things are as encouraging as the realization that things can be different and that we have a role in making them so." –Daniel Taylor

#13. Convictions: A Life Sentence

Opening activity: Divide the group into boys and girls. The girls discuss what Elizabeth I meant by her quote, "Anger makes dull men witty, but it keeps them poor," and the boys discuss what Erica Jong meant when she said, "Gossip is the opiate of the oppressed." {Have a "preacher" for each group listen to the lesson and be ready to say what the group thought when asked—see below.}

? What is a conviction?
What are some issues about which people have convictions?
What are some issues about which people lack conviction?

? What do you think about the following statistics?
1. 74 percent of Americans would steal from those who won't miss it.
2. 64 percent will lie for convenience as long as no one is hurt.
3. 84 percent say they would break the rules of their own religion.
4. 81 percent have violated a law they felt to be inappropriate.
5. 30 percent say they would be willing to die for their God.
—As reported in *The Day America Told the Truth* (Prentice Hall, 1991)

? The word conviction derives its meaning from the word "convince," which comes from the root word *vincere*, which means "to conquer."

[Read 2 Timothy 3:10-15]
What was Paul trying to teach Timothy here?

? What helps you to "become convinced" about something?
- Bible
- People living the Bible
- Proven path
- Experiences
- Others' example and way of life
- Mistakes and bad choices

? When is it hardest to have conviction? Why?
- When much is against you because that is when your emotions take charge

"He who conquers his emotions has conquered the world."

What do you think are some useful convictions for someone your age? {Let them come up with several and then go over the following items.}

Here are two items I think you need to have convictions on:

1. [Read James 1:19-21] Anger—especially you boys.
It does not work. He says everyone—no one is exempt from this. Anger will keep you from a righteous way of life and it will keep out the Word. The meaning of "moral filth" in verse 21 is "ear wax." What happens if ear wax gets built up in your ear?
- The ear can't work as well.

Same with your heart. Don't make anger a pattern or it will cost you.

2. [Read Proverbs 26:20] Gossip—girls!
What does it really mean to gossip? The word gossip means "to grumble or complain." It reflects your heart, not the person's you are talking about. {Silence—let that sink in} You have got to understand this. I have heard more petty arguments and issues between you girls over silly stuff and then the talking begins—it happens in school too!—but I don't like it in here. Start with you and your heart and your fiery anger will die out. Don't let the gossip make you feel better about yourself; that's no different than what drugs do!

Boy Preacher: Tell the girls what you thought of Erica Jong's quote. {Oppressed heart}

Girl Preacher: Tell the boys what you thought of Elizabeth I's quote. {Keeps you poor}

#14. Cry Mercy: A Tale of Openness

Opening Skit: Get input from kids on what secret, if told to them by a friend, would put them in a dilemma as to whether or not they should tell someone. Use this idea in the following skit.

Scene: bus ride. The "secret-teller" tells his/her friend what the secret is and says not to tell anyone else. {Get some kids who can ham up the bus scene.}

? Ask the group: What are the friend's choices?

This happens not only between friends but also with you. Tonight's topic is openness.

? What is openness?
Is it important? Why?

Describe the person for whom openness is easy. {Odds are it will be the perfect person or no one, which is the point of the question.}

? Why is it difficult to be open?
What should we be open about?

[Read Proverbs 28:13]
? What should we talk about, according to this scripture?
- Sin
- Ungodliness
- Unconscionable acts

? What happens to you when you keep sin a secret?

[Read Psalm 38:3-4]
? How can you relate to David?
{Share about a time when you weren't open and how you felt, and what you felt when you opened up.}

? Which is worse: the pain from keeping a secret or the pain of telling the truth?

Talk about the Enron executive who committed suicide {or any current, relatable situation}

[Read James 5:16]

The Bible says to talk about your sins. This brings healing, which produces growth. A guilty person never grows or changes. They just keep running desperately trying to find a way out. The Bible teaches that the way out is to be open and renounce the secrets, then mercy comes and you will be free from your guilt. Think about how you feel when you don't tell the truth. Some of you tonight are feeling guilty about something about which you should be open. Learn from the Bible and from me...be open. Guilt serves no one but Satan! Being vulnerable is a key to connection with God and each other. Let's get open and get closer and freer.

#15. Discipling: A Key to Growth

We are going to do a Bible study on one of the most important lessons in life: DISCIPLING—it is the essence of growing.

? What is discipling?
Who needs discipling? [Jeremiah 17:9]
- We all do.

? What is the goal of discipling? [Colossians 1:28-29]
- To train you for life
- To train you to be like Jesus

After all, the more you are like him the better you will be.

? Who are the people in your life who disciple you?
- Parents
- Teachers
- Coaches
- Spiritual leaders
- God's Word (the Bible)
- The Spirit, etc.

? In what areas do you need discipling?

How would you describe your attitude toward discipling? Why?

[Read Proverbs 12:1]
? Why should your attitude be like this?

Your response to discipling (training) tells you everything about your attitude in growing and learning, and ultimately how smart you really are!

? What would your reaction be if I gave you some gold?

[Read Proverbs 25:12]
Your attitude should be the same with training and discipling; the more you

learn to desire it, the more you will grow.

[Read Jeremiah 17:10]
Bottom Line: What you become in life, and, ultimately, getting to heaven, will depend on how well you take training, correction, and education (discipling). If you are not willing to be trained, to take input from the people in your life, then you are being stupid—don't expect to be rewarded. Without discipling you will not, cannot, grow spiritually. Check your heart and your attitude about getting discipled and corrected! Invite it in your life.

#16. Distracted or Determined?

{Have the kids bring something that represents what they like to do. For example, one likes tennis, so they bring a tennis racket.}

Opening activity: Give each person a piece of paper and have them write down one thing in their life or character in which they would like to change or grow. Make a pile of the papers in front of the group.

? On a scale of 1-10, how sincere were you in wanting to change or grow?

Now, let's focus on some of your interests. Have each person tell the group what they like to do and then place their representative item on the pile of papers.

{The goal of this lesson is to see how quickly we can lose our focus. As the kids bring up their items be sure to stack the pile over the pieces of paper on which they earlier wrote.}

? What do you notice about the pile?
What happened to your goals?
Does this mean you weren't sincere?

[Read Luke 10:38]

? What can you tell me about Martha based on this verse?
- Friendly
- Kind
- Generous
- Sincerely wanted to help people

? What did she think about Jesus?

[Read Luke 10:39-40]

? What preparations do you think were necessary?
What was Martha's attitude at this point?
How can we display a similar attitude?

[Read Luke 10:41-42]
What was Jesus' response?
Why did he say "worried and upset"?
How does that relate to you being distracted from the decision you made to change?

Some of you are making unwise choices because of your worries or desires. You allow these to distract you and bury your desire to grow and change.

{Point at the pile} All the things on top are good and worthy, but beware: they can overtake the more important things.

{Have each person pick up their item and piece of paper holding one in the left hand and the other in the right hand. Now have them spend a minute evaluating and reflecting how they can find balance to reach their goal.}

#17. Do You Mind!

Opening activity: Show the kids the following pictures:

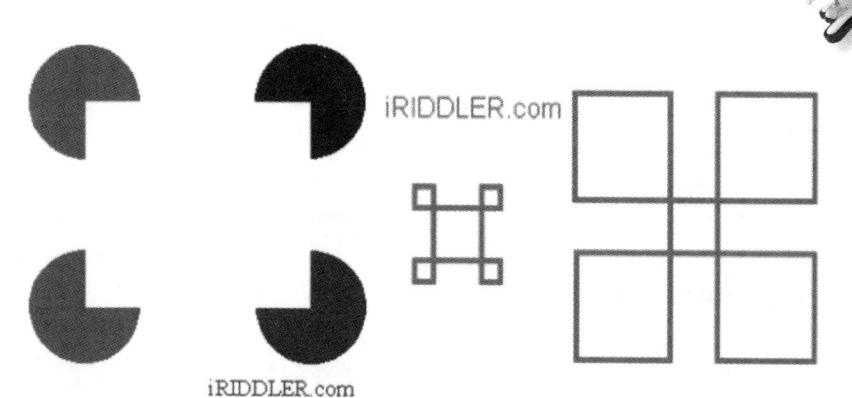

1. What do you see? {There is no square, but the circles make it seem like there is.}
2. {Color in the center squares yellow} Which yellow square is bigger? {They are the same but the surroundings make it seem they are not.}

? What do these two pictures teach you?
   - Not to be influenced by your surroundings

? How are you influenced by your surroundings?

Ask them this riddle: A horse is tied to a 15-foot rope and there is a bale of hay 25 feet from him. Yet the horse is able to eat from the bale of hay. How is that possible?
{The rope is not tied to anything, so the horse walks to the hay}

? What does this riddle teach you about yourself?
   - Make a lot of assumptions

? Funny how our brain makes a mental picture of things that aren't there or aren't true of the situation, which leads to many assumptions, hey?
How can assumptions be dangerous? Can you give me an example?

? How can your situation and assumptions affect your spirituality or sense of right and wrong?

? What weapon do you have that can deal with these situations and assumptions?
- Brain

[Read 2 Corinthian 10:1-5]

? What assumption was being made against Paul and others?
- We live in the world and by the standards of the world, therefore to do the right thing we must use the same weapons as the world.

? What are some of the worldly weapons you use to attempt to look right?
- Gossip
- Slams
- Lies
- Do what's "cool" dos (smoke, sex, etc.)
- Don't do what's "uncool" (be kind, good grades, etc.)

{Grab the picture with the yellow squares and say, "Isn't that the big squares making the center square look small?!"}

? What does the Bible say you have to use in order to do the right thing?
- Mind: "take captive every thought"

God gave you an incredible weapon against the foolish and sinful opportunities that are put before you. Your brain! It is a 3-lb supercomputer that has more connections than there are stars in the universe. It controls your emotions, your mood, how well you get along with others, your personality, everything about you. Is it no wonder he says to use it to take captive all the thoughts that are not good for you.

Let me tell you a story. {Retell Matthew 21:28-32 in your own words.}
There are some of you that need encouraging to do the right thing. You think you can't...well, stop and think that you can! Tell yourself that you can and then do it! God has given you the ability to make up your mind. There are others of you who need to be like the first son and change your minds. Stop and think; make a different choice or you may be wounded by the weapons of this world.

#18. Encouragement

Opening activity: Give each person a 3x5 card and have them do the following: write their name, write down the name of one person they want to encourage and write the encouragement. Collect the cards.

Tell me the most encouraging time of your life.
? What does the word encourage mean?
- To comfort or exhort; to build up, strengthen

? What are some of the most powerful things known to man?
Explain how encouragement can be powerful.

Tonight we are going to look at a story which displays the power of encouragement.

[Read 2 Samuel 19:1-8]
? Who was Absalom?
- David's son, who died

? Absalom died in battle—how would you feel if your son died in battle?
What was Joab so upset about that he went to the king and confronted him in this manner?
Why would Joab be so upset that David mourned for his son and ignored the men?
Does the timing seem right for David to go out and encourage the men?

First we must understand who Absalom is. Read [2 Samuel 15:1-12]
? Now what do you think of Absalom?

Next, let's understand some of the story.

[Read 2 Samuel 15:13-23]
Explain: David left Jerusalem under suspicion and much turmoil.

[Read 2 Samuel 16:13-14]
Explain: David's men stuck with David even under persecution.

[Read 2 Samuel 16:15-17]
Absalom plans his attack on David, his father.

[Read 2 Samuel 18:1-4]
- How did David's men treat David?
  - With respect and importance; willing to die for him

- Now, what do you think of about Joab confronting David to encourage the men?

- What can you learn from the story about the act of encouraging someone?
  - May have to offer encourage when you least want to.
  - Encouragement takes a selfless attitude.
  - The lack of encouragement can defeat an army.

David's lack of encouragement was about to defeat a whole army of men who were willing to die for him. They felt ashamed because the man whose life they had pledged to protect cared more about a traitorous son than for them. However, once David encouraged them they went on to win many battles. David's encouragement changed the face of the known world that day. Who knows that your encouragement couldn't do the same? My challenge to you is to encourage someone this week. The worst thing that most of us will have to overcome is embarrassment, not the death of a son. Find it within your heart to overcome even yourself to give something as incredible and powerful as encouragement. Let's begin your week by reading what you wrote.

{Read the encouragement written on the cards and have the kids guess who is being encouraged and who did the encouraging.}

#19. Especially Made

{This lesson was used to get our group ready to serve the participants of the Special Olympics. Perhaps it can be a model for something for which your group is preparing.}

? What does it mean to be special?
In what ways are you proven to be special?
If I said Special Olympics of Georgia, how does that change the meaning of the word special?
Should it change? Why or why not?

? What amazes you about how God made you?

Isn't it amazing that each part does what it is supposed to do!

What would happen if the different parts of your body decided not to get along and the eyes said to the ears, "I am better than you...please leave or go hang with the toes at least"; or the nose said to the fingers, "Why are you always picking on me?"

? Instead, what happens between the parts of your body?
- All the parts work together

[Read 1 Corinthians 12:14-25]
What causes the meaning of the word "special" to change when used in reference to the Special Olympics?
- By stereotype, they have become "the parts that we think are less honorable."

? Verse 25 says we should have equal concern for all of our parts. What do you think that means in light of the Special Olympics?

I think you will have a chance to learn and gain just as much if not more from this event than the athletes will. Remember the godly principle being taught here: that each person is special and deserves to be loved, honored, cherished and encouraged. That is what the event is all about.

Here are some comments from some of the athletes:
- » *"Cheering me on in the games is like cheering me on in life."*
- » *"My life would be sad if not for the Special Olympics."*
- » *"Your cheers give me self-confidence and self-esteem."*

{Finish the night by having the kids do something to prep for the event, i.e. make posters, prepare lunches, whatever it is specific for your group.}

#20. Famous Last Words

? What could the last words of a person mean?
- They reveal what is important to them.

Here are a few funny last words:
"How do you light this butaine stove?"
"What does this button do?"
"This bear is probably just hibernating."
"I'll get your toast out."

{Divide the group into seven teams. Explain that each team will receive one of Jesus' last statements. Each team will give what they think Jesus meant and why he said it.}

1. Luke 23:34 "Father, forgive them, for they do not know what they are doing."
2. Luke 23:43 "Truly I tell you, today you will be with me in paradise."
3. John 19:26-27 "Woman, here is your son.... Here is your mother."
4. John 19:28 "I am thirsty."
5. Matthew 27:46 "My God, My God, why have you forsaken me?"
6. John 19:30 "It is finished."
7. Luke 23:46 "Father, into your hands I commit my spirit."

{Be prepared through your own study to make comments on Jesus' words after each group gives their thoughts so that the kids will understand the words of Jesus and learn his heart. I have included some thoughts by a brother in my church.}

{Close it out by relating the power of last words and the merciful and compassionate heart that God has for you.} These are powerful impressions. What will be your last words? That all depends on the heart you develop in this lifetime.

The Utterances at the Cross

[Read PSALM 22:1-8]

It was after Jesus had been without sleep for 30 hours, deserted by his best friends, betrayed, ridiculed, beaten, flogged, spit upon, slammed over the head with a crown of thorns—after all this that Jesus was crucified. He spent six hours alive on the cross, gasping for breath, bleeding, yet he used his remaining energy to speak seven times. Let's look at what he said:

LUKE 23:34 – *"FATHER, FORGIVE THEM, FOR THEY DO NOT KNOW WHAT THEY ARE DOING."*
God had used a pagan governor to make his statement to the world: the sign over Jesus' head read "This is the King of the Jews." This is what they were doing with their king. Perhaps if their hearts had been softer, they would have at least attempted to find out what it was all about (like the thief on the cross next to him). Instead, some didn't care and cast lots for his clothing, others gave Jesus their "I told you so," because they never considered they might be wrong. Just as God the Father begins to witness the worst of sufferings inflicted on his Son, Jesus prays that God may remember why all this is happening: the reason for the crucifixion is forgiveness for those who repent and believe. If God were to count the crucifixion against us, we would have ceased to exist.

LUKE 23:43 – *"TRULY I TELL YOU, TODAY YOU WILL BE WITH ME IN PARADISE."*
Another reminder that forgiveness does not stop at the cross: at the last moment of his life, in excruciating pain, Jesus is concerned for the life of a repented criminal, and says the words that give him hope. It is never too late to turn back to God...but don't wait too long!

JOHN 19:26-27 – *"WOMAN, HERE IS YOUR SON.... HERE IS YOUR MOTHER."*
Joseph was probably dead. Jesus is the oldest son in his family. Per Jewish law, he is in charge of taking care of his mother. He is now entrusting that care to his best friend (rather than to one of his brothers, since they had not become disciples yet).

JOHN 19:28 – *"I AM THIRSTY."*
When it was all over, when everything else was done, Jesus makes a personal request, to satisfy his need, yet not without the purposeful intention of fulfilling Scripture (Psalm 22:15).

MATTHEW 27:46, MARK 15:3 – *"ELOI, ELOI, LEMA SABACHTHANI?"*
Again, Jesus fulfills Scripture, this time by quoting Psalm 22:1. His having spoken in Aramaic should have triggered in the mind of the Jews the rest of the passage in Psalms. The irony would then be: how can Jesus, the closest man to God that ever lived, who exemplified the perfect relationship with the Father, be "forsaken" by him at the last point in his life? There could only be one explanation: it wasn't his sin he was being forsaken for, it was everyone else's. ISAIAH 53 explains it all.
It was the Passover. The Israelites were supposed to be eating lamb; according to the Law, a firstborn, spotless lamb without defect that was sacrificed during Passover for the sins of the people. Jesus was that Lamb. He was laying down his life as a ransom for many.

JOHN 19:30 – *"IT IS FINISHED."*
Jesus has by now felt all the anguish, the pain, the guilt, the despair, the frustration that comes with sin, as if every single sin of every person in history came to haunt him all at the same time, just as he is enduring the worst physical pain of his life. And he had never sinned, so it was all new to him, all unusual. Like a baby who could barely talk, he was being punished without reason by a monster that didn't care and was enjoying it. Yet while Satan was enjoying it, Jesus and his Father were looking forward to the eternal victory: all sin would be paid for; humanity would now have a chance, no matter what Satan did. It was finished—the Scriptures were proven true; the love was shown complete.

LUKE 23:46 – *"FATHER, INTO YOUR HANDS I COMMIT MY SPIRIT."*
With a loud cry, Jesus said his last words, which are from Psalm 31:5. Both psalms quoted by Jesus on the cross talk about a man in distress, troubled by sin or by persecution, and oppression by sinful men. Both also talk about trusting God in times of anguish, regardless of the outcome, and about the saving power of God. The women, John, and maybe Peter, appear to have been close enough to Jesus at the cross to hear him say these words. The Scripture quotations must have jogged their memory and helped make the connection between the inexplicable event before them and the saving that God was doing. Now all that was left was the trust in God to be confirmed at the resurrection, proving God to be true, merciful and complete.

#21. A Father with Unmatched Shoes

Opening activity: Divide your group into teams. Explain that you will give the teams a series of clues to a famous dad. You'll give three clues, and each team will have to write down who they think the dad is. When all the rounds are finished, have the teams reveal their answers. Score as follows: 100 points for every dad guessed correctly after the first clue; 50 points after the second clue; 25 points after the third clue. {Feel free to use other dad figures.}

Round 1 Answer: Saul, father of Jonathan
1. I'm in the Bible. I'm in the Old Testament. I wasn't a very happy guy although I was a king.
2. I really struggled with jealousy. In fact, it just about drove me crazy when women sang about me killing thousands, but some other guy killing ten thousands.
3. I tried to kill my son's best friend, David. I chucked my spear at him and hunted him.

Round 2 Answer: Homer Simpson
1. Hi, I'm on TV! Woo-hoo!
2. I work at a nuclear power plant. I really, really like donuts.
3. I'm a cartoon with no hair, and my face is kind of yellow-orange. I'm famous for mess-ups and for saying, "Doh!"

Round 3 Answer: Mike Brady from the Brady Bunch
1. I was on TV back in the 1970s, but you've seen me on reruns.
2. I'm a pretty groovy dad, and I have three girls and three boys.
3. We're a blended family—and our house keeper is Alice.

Round 4 Answer: Barak Obama
1. I'm a politician, or at least, I was.
2. In fact, I was the president of the United States!
3. I was the first African-American President.

Round 5 Answer: Joseph, the earthly father of Jesus.
1. I'm another Bible dad, but I'm in the New Testament.
2. I was more of a stepdad. I was there when my son was born, but he's not

officially my birth son.
3. I was a carpenter.

[Read Luke 15:11-32]

Jesus gives us this story to help us catch a glimpse of God.
What kind of father do you think this guy is? {Push for a deeper answer than "a good one"}

? What did the father do to prove his love?
- He accepted the son back without an apology or an explanation for his actions. The father's love was given freely.

? What do we call that kind of love?
- Unconditional

? What did the son do to deserve the father's love?
- Not a thing!

? What are some examples from your life that would help you understand this kind of love?

? Why is it so hard to think of examples?
- This kind of love is not natural for humans.

? What are some examples that show how God unconditionally loves you?
Why do we have a hard time understanding this kind of love?
Which would help you be more spiritual, conditional or unconditional love? Why?

There is a story about a Chinese artist, a new Christian who wanted to paint the parable of the prodigal son. In his first attempt, he painted the father standing at the gate with his arms folded looking sternly down the road at a son coming. Another Christian explained to him that this was not the picture of our heavenly Father. "But most fathers are that way," said the artist. He was told that Jesus was trying to show what God was like with an unconditional love to those who come to him. He repainted the picture, and this time the father was running toward the son, his robes flapping in the wind, a look of joy on his face, and wearing two different kinds of shoes. When asked why, the artist simply replied that the father was so excited about reaching his son he grabbed the shoes nearest to him and ran, for he did not care if the shoes matched or not. All that mattered was that his son was now found.

God is only interested in loving you—this is what the Bible calls grace. Grace does not change with your response, and it does not care if the world misunderstands it; its sole purpose is to offer you unconditional love in the hope that you will return to the arms of God. Your fathers are trying their very best to be like this; honor them for that.

#22. Focus

NOTE: Do the Pre-class Prep exercise before reading any further. NO cheating! Pre-Class Prep for leader. Watch the Selective Attention Test Youtube video at this link: https://www.youtube.com/watch?v=vJG698U2Mvo and follow the instructions in the video. What were your results?

Opening activity: Before showing the video instruct students that you are going to test their ability to be focused so following the instructions on the screen. Show video. Afterwards, ask for answers. Give them the correct answer. Then ask how many saw the gorilla walk by. You may have to show it again to prove to some of them that there was actually a man in a gorilla suit.

? What kept your from seeing the man in the gorilla suit?
Were you doing something wrong?
Does this mean you weren't sincere?

? Who can tell me why Jesus told the parable of the soils?
What were the four types of soil?
- Hard, rocky, thorny and good

Let's discuss third soil of the parable—the thorny soil. [Luke 8:14]
? What does it mean to choke?
Why did Jesus pick thorns and not weeds?
What kind of things choke out or distract you from sincere goals or growing spiritually?
What needs to accompany sincerity to mature or grow more spiritual?

[Read Colossians 3:2]
"Set your minds." I think many of you are very sincere in wanting to make changes and grow in your character; however, you lack maturity. Jesus chose thorns because they are the hardest to remove. Thorns are not "bad"; they can be a source of protection, but they can also choke your desires out. All the "thorns" you mentioned are choking out your spiritual desires.

Some of you need to make some changes in your schedules, priorities, even your way of thinking—see the gorillas in your life, if you plan to change and grow.

Others of you need to set your mind on what you are learning and focus it toward change; you're are too focused on the gorillas.

Get other people (friends, parents, Bible) in your life to help you focus and to see the gorillas.

#23. From Manurity to Maturity

[Read Luke 14:34-35]

? What are some things that will keep your saltiness?
- Repentance

{Bring in a bag of manure from a garden supply store or an actual cow patty.}

What is this stuff? {Let them guess for a few minutes...they will obviously guess the cow patty.}

? What happens if you lose your saltiness?
- Manure pile!

? What does manure do in a garden?
- Helps a plant grow

? What might you call a "salty" person?
- Mature

You've got to mature. Repentance is a mature subject, and it's time that we talked about what it is and how to do it. I asked my 8-year-old daughter what repentance is and she said, "It's when you've done something wrong and you say you're sorry and change your heart." Even an 8-year-old knows what it is, just like most of you; however, the hard part is doing it.

{Make two signs, one with MANURE on it and the other with MATURE.}

? What's the difference between these two words?
- An 'N' and a 'T'

'N' = Nature

? What do I mean by your nature?
- A person's basic behavior

[Read Colossians 3:5-8]

? How many of you are aware that you have a sinful nature?

If you are not trying to change your sinful nature, i.e. stop disobeying, stop lying, stop looking at the pornography on the internet, stop gossiping, then you are not maturing and you cannot please God.

'T' = Think
? What does it mean to repent?
"To repent" in the Greek: *metanoeo*: to change one's mind or purpose or direction.
It takes your mind to repent—to stop what is natural, that is, your sinful nature, and to do what is right—to change your purpose.

Repentance is the key to going from "manurity" to maturity.

[Read 2 Corinthians 7:8-11]

? What does repentance look like?
- Begins with sorrow

Got to understand that you hurt God or someone else and it is wrong.
- Produces something

Much like the manure: you change the 'N' to a 'T' and begin to change your mind and become alarmed and eager to be different.
- Wants to make things right

Change of mind must include a change in the situation if at all possible.

[Read Luke 15:11-20]
Let's look at an example.
? Is there sorrow?
- Yes!

? Is there alarm and eagerness to be different?
- Yes!

? Is there a plan to make things right?
- Yes!

? How often do you sin?
- For most of us, every day!

? A better question is how often do you truly repent? Is repentance important to you? It is to God.

Repentance is a gift from God. [Acts 5:29-31]
Why would God give us repentance as a gift? Because it makes it special and therefore wants us to treat it special.

? Does repentance mean you have to feel sorry for yourself and host your own pity party?
- No

[Read 2 Corinthians 7:10, Luke 15:20]
Genuine repentance leaves no regrets. He got up and went, not wallowed!

This is how you need to respond. Many of you want to mature; to do so you need to repent. Some of you need to show it in here and definitely you need to show it to your parents. Don't wallow and feel sorry for yourself. That produces nothing; it's losing your saltiness and is not even fit for the manure pile. Instead, think! Change your mind and be like the man in Luke: be sorry, get eager to change, and make things right. Repentance is a gift to you, and God not only expects you to use that gift, but he thinks you can or he would not have given it to you. Now, let's go from "manurity" to maturity!

#24. The Fundamentals of Friendship

As kids arrive: Provide a nametag and a black or red marker. Have the kids write their names on a nametag. They can choose which color marker. Until you split up for the lesson, have all the workers pay "special" attention to the people whose nametags are written in black. Give gum out only to those people, talk with them, hug them, etc. Treat people with red nametags as lower-class citizens. *Now split up boys and girls.*

_____ BOYS – A Winning Team _____

Opening activity: On a sheet of poster board draw a football field as if it were in the middle of a stadium; give each person a 3x5 card and ask them to think of the person at a football game that best represents them in reference to their relationships with people in the middle school group. This could be a player or referee, a fan, blimp driver, owner, cameraman, etc. Have each person (or as many as time will allow) place their choice on the field and tell why they made that particular choice.

? What makes a great team?
What could you do to make this group a better team? {Make sure when they give their answer they say "*I can...* or *I will...*" It needs to be first-person kind of talk.}

[Read Galatians 2:11-14]
Describe the team that Peter and Paul were on. They were on God's team, which has all kinds of people.

? How did Peter cause disunity within this team?
- Caused a clique or a faction

Making a team takes effort. Doesn't happen naturally. In fact, our nature is to create cliques.

? **[Galatians 5:19-20]** Factions, disunity, CLIQUES are an act of the flesh—what we do naturally. To make a great team, you must do the opposite of your nature. What are some fundamentals to the game of football?
- Blocking
- Tackling, etc.

Tools to Help Preteen and Young Teen Leaders and Parents

Let's come up with a few basics to building friendships, just like blocking and tackling:

[Read Proverbs 17:17, 18:24] What basic element of friendship are these scriptures talking about?
- Loves at all times
- Sticks closer than a brother

Be devoted to the friendships you already have in here. Don't be a friend only when it suits your pleasure. Stick up for each other. Watch each other's back. That's what blocking is all about. Block for your friend even if you lose face.

[Read Proverbs 18:1] What basic element of friendship is this scripture talking about?
- A friend person looks at for you in an unselfish way

Be friendly. Tackle a new friendship. Invite someone you don't know very well to come over or go to the movies or just hang. Tackle/pursue their interest. You may be surprised and learn to like something else and enjoy yourself. Once this person has become a friend, don't forget to block for them as well.

What's the goal of every football team?
- To score more points and win the game

How will this team {meaning the group} win?
- By creating a place where 1) you can be accepted for who you are (blocked for) and 2) great friendships are made (tackles)

What clique did we create earlier tonight? How did it make those of you with red nametags feel? How many of you would like some help to keep people from feeling that way? I will help you with this by pointing out ways you can be better friends and reminding you to block and tackle.

> *There's a story of a man who had a neighbor who was trying to put a TV antenna on his roof in time so he could watch the upcoming Super Bowl, but he was having a terrible time. The man decided to give his neighbor a hand. He went over and took with him his best tools and soon had the antenna up. His neighbor asked him what he made with such fancy tools. The man replied, "Friends, mostly."*

The scriptures we've looked at tonight are tools that, if you actually use them, will help you to make great friends, will help this team become stronger, and will keep some of you from feeling what the red name-tagged people felt. It will help us become a winning team!

Challenge: Before you leave, give a ticket to two people that you've never had to your house.

GIRLS – Forever Friends

? What is a faction?
- A group within a group for the purpose of excluding

? What do factions or cliques do to a group?
- Disunify it

? What faction, what clique, did we have at the beginning of midweek tonight? How did it make you feel? Why?

[Read Galatians 5:19-20]
In these verses, God says factions or cliques are an act of the flesh—they are what we do naturally.

What factions could we or do we have in this room? (Point out how they are "natural" groupings.)
- 6th vs. 7th vs. 8th; by school; race; establsihed vs. new to the group

? What is the solution to factions and cliques?
- Each one deciding to be a friend to the other girls in here

The main thing I want to talk about tonight is how to be a great friend.

[Ruth 1]
? What could have kept Ruth and Naomi from being friends?
- Age difference (grade)
- Different culture (school)
- Different race

Tools to Help Preteen and Young Teen Leaders and Parents

? What are some characteristics you see that made Ruth a great friend to Naomi? Here are the three characteristics I've picked for us to focus on:

1) Unselfish [Proverbs 18:1]
? What does this tell you about being unfriendly?
- It is selfish.

Why?
? How was Ruth unselfish with Naomi?
- Stayed with her instead of returning to her family
- Moved to a strange country to help her
- Was more concerned with Naomi than herself

? What ways are you unfriendly or selfish in here?
- Not smiling
- Not responding when someone talks to you
- Being quiet all the time
- Not open to hanging out with someone you don't know very well

2) Expressive
Describe Ruth's words to Naomi.
- Beautiful
- Warm
- Expressive

? How do you think they made Naomi feel?

[Read Proverbs 22:11]
? How do your words affect your friendships?
What keeps you from being more expressive to others in here?

3) Devoted
[Read Proverbs 17:17]
? What does this verse tell you about friendship?
- A true friend is always there—even in hard, uncomfortable times.

? How is Ruth an example of this with Naomi?

? What are the comfort zones you need to leave to be a better friend to others?
- Being willing to hang with people who are different, have different interests
- When you are hanging, being willing to try new things the other person is interested in
- Being the initiator—don't wait for others to come to you

? Can anyone tell me the end of the story of Ruth and Naomi?
Ruth gets remarried to an awesome guy—Boaz.
She is no longer poor.
- She has a baby.
- Naomi gets taken care of by Ruth and her husband.
- Naomi gets to be a grandmother and have an heir.
- Ruth is one of Jesus' ancestors (her name is listed in Matthew 1).

God blessed Ruth, all because she decided to be a great friend to Naomi.

Challenge: Write an invitation to two people in this room you've never had to your house before and give it to them tonight.

#25. Generosity: The Greed Killer

Game: Chasing the Wind
1. Divide group into four teams (or whatever is best for your size group).
2. Put 20 pennies per team in a bowl/cup in front of the team.
3. Each player gets 15 seconds to run around and get one penny from the other teams.
4. A player cannot get pennies from any one team twice in succession.
5. After 15 seconds, players place the pennies they have collected in their pile.
6. A team is eliminated, if at any point in the game, they completely run out of pennies.
7. The winner is determined by being the last team to have pennies.

{Odds are that no team will win. This is the point. Have each team report how many pennies they have left.}

? What observations can you make about this game?
What are some examples in life that this game could represent?
- Chasing money
- Trying to be popular
- Being greedy

? What are some things we can be greedy over?
What is greed associated with?

[Read Jeremiah 6:13]
? What are the dangers of being greedy?
- Lying
- Manipulating to get what you want
- Sinful

? What is the cure for greed?
- [Luke 11:39-41] To give...be generous!
What are ways you can be generous?
- Time, attention, thoughts, opinions, ideas, money, things

? What situations expose a greedy attitude?

- Friendship (always doing what you want, something you own and won't let sibling play with, this class)
- Missions contribution, weekly contribution

Let me take a minute to teach you how to approach any situation where generosity is a prerequisite; this is referring to a monetary contribution, but I think you will see the principles of heart at work which can apply to any situation where a heart to give is needed.

[Read 2 Corinthians 8:1-4, 8, 12-14, 9:6-7]
In and out of reading this scripture, do a running commentary on the attitude the Bible is trying to get us to understand:
[V. 3] Give what you are able.
[V. 4] It is a privilege to give—we need it, God doesn't.
[V. 8] No one is making you give.
[V. 12] Give according to what you have.
[V. 9:7] Give what you want—what you think is generous.

> *A sobbing little girl stood near a small church from which she had been turned away because it "was too crowded." "I can't go to Sunday school," she sobbed to the pastor as he walked by. Seeing her shabby, unkempt appearance, the pastor guessed the reason; taking her by the hand, he took her inside and found a place for her in the Sunday school class. The child was so touched that she went to bed that night thinking of the children who have no place to worship Jesus. Some two years later, this child lay dead in one of the poor tenement buildings, and the parents called for the kind-hearted pastor who had befriended their daughter, to handle the final arrangements. As her poor little body was being moved, a worn and crumpled purse was found which seemed to have been rummaged from some trash dump. Inside was found 57 cents and a note scribbled in childish handwriting. It read, "This is to help build the little church bigger so more children can go to Sunday school." For two years she had saved for this offering of love. When the pastor tearfully read that note, he knew instantly what he would do. Carrying this note and the cracked, red pocketbook to the pulpit, he told the story of her unselfish love and devotion. He challenged his deacons to get busy and raise enough money for the larger building.*
>
> *The story doesn't end there! A newspaper learned of the story and published it. It was read by a realtor who offered them a parcel of land worth many thousands. When told that the church could not pay so much, he offered it for a selling price of 57 cents. Church members made large subscriptions. Checks came from far and wide. Within five years the little girl's gift had increased to $250,000.00, a huge sum for that time (near the turn of the century).*

Tools to Help Preteen and Young Teen Leaders and Parents

Her unselfish love had paid large dividends. When you are in the city of Philadelphia, look up Temple Baptist Church, with a seating capacity of 3,300, and Temple University, where hundreds of students are trained. Have a look, too, at the Good Samaritan Hospital, and at a Sunday school building which houses hundreds of Sunday scholars, so that no child in the area will ever need to be left outside during Sunday school time.

#26. Get Real!

Opening skit:
Parts:
Guy—asks girl on date; **Girl**—father owns restaurant; **Cashier**; **Server**.

Story Line:
After summoning up some courage, the young man finally asked her on a date. She suggested a great place she knew, and he took her there. It was more than he expected; a restaurant that was very glamorous and fancy. It was the kind of place where celebrities hang out, and everything was there. The evening was perfect, and they enjoyed being together. He assumed he was going to pay for everything, and had saved up some money just for this date. He wanted to make it very special; however, the fun stopped when the bill came. He almost got a shock; he didn't have that kind of money! He did not know how to tell her because he thought it would spoil things. From that time, he began to feel uncomfortable. He felt he had put himself to shame, and he began to sweat. "Is there something wrong?" she asked. "Just getting hot," he said, trying to hide the problem. Eventually, as the evening progressed, he wanted to disappear and never see her again rather than expose his problem. He excused himself, saying he wanted to check his wallet in the car. But as he stood up it fell from his jacket. Sweat became visible. When it was time to go he told her he would go to the cashier himself, hoping to leave quietly and never come back. But she insisted on coming along. She had really enjoyed herself and began to thank him for the lovely evening. The cashier recognized her and greeted her politely, calling her by name. Then she told him he did not have to pay anything because her father owned the restaurant.

Scene 1:
Guy [entering from stage right] "courageously" asks Girl [entering stage left] out for a date. She says yes and says she knows of a great place. He will pick her up at 8:00 p.m. [They walk off in separate directions.]

Scene 2:
[Seated at table at the restaurant] Guy talks about what a great place. Girl agrees. [Server enters]. They order. Make small talk as they wait for food. Food brought. Eat. More get-to-know-you talk. [This has got to be rather quick so we can get to point of the skit.] Check comes. [At this point, guy gets obviously worried about

Tools to Help Preteen and Young Teen Leaders and Parents

how he is going to pay the bill. Girl questions him to see if he is okay. Follow script above.]

Scene 3:
Time to go. Follow script above. Make it natural, not too funny. As they get up from the table to leave, freeze the scene and ask the first two questions below. After the discussion, resume the scene and finish with Cashier noticing Girl and calling her by name and saying he hoped the meal was satisfactory and that her father was away from the restaurant but he said don't worry about the bill. It was on the house. At which point, the guy will look surprised and relieved and the girl will say it is okay, my father owns the restaurant.

? How would you describe the guy's evening so far?
What do you think he will do?

{Finish scene}

? What would have made this guy's date more enjoyable?
- Being real

? What does it mean to be real?
What topics are hard for you to be real about?
Why is it hard for you to be real?
What suffers when you are not real?

[Read John 1:43-50]
? What strikes you about Nathanael?

? Why did Jesus compliment him as "an Israelite in whom there is no deceit?"
- Nathanael was willing to ask tough questions.

Some of you will not ask questions because you are afraid someone will think badly about you or that God will think badly of you. God already knows what you think. What he wants is honesty! Nazareth was known as a despised and despicable place. Nathanael knew this and was willing to question why the much-expected Messiah would come from there. I think many of you are not stronger in your belief of God because you aren't willing to say what you think about Jesus or question God's existence.

[Read Hebrews 11:6]

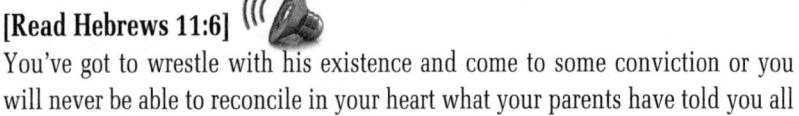

You've got to wrestle with his existence and come to some conviction or you will never be able to reconcile in your heart what your parents have told you all your life.

- Nathanael was willing to be the same in private as he was in public.

This is what he saw in Nathanael while he studied and prayed. Because of its shade, the fig tree was a good place to study and pray and commune with God. Nathanael must have been very open in his relationships. How can I tell? He was open with his friends. He wasn't worried about what they thought. I think some of you hurt your relationships because you aren't honest. You are immature and don't talk openly but in private and behind people's back. For example, some of you won't tell the truth to your parents. When asked why you lied to them about something, you say it's because you are afraid of punishment, but the real truth is that you don't like the way your dad or mom reacts. You don't like their anger and how it makes you feel, but you are afraid to tell them this because you think it's being disloyal. Why not tell them the truth and get over your fear of them. {This is an example among my kids; you may have a different one in your group.}

[Read 2 Timothy 3:10-11]

Challenge:
1. Get real with God. Ask him tough questions; tell him how you really feel and see if he doesn't prove trustworthy.
2. Get real with people you are close to. Talk about how you are feeling so that you can get help and be more secure and go to the root of issues instead of constantly having to make up lies or deceive yourself.

God will prove faithful and he will rescue you and reward your realness.

Memory Verse: 2 Timothy 3:10-11
You, however, know all about my teaching,a my way of life, my purpose, faith, patience, love, endurance, persecutions, sufferings—what kinds of things happened to me in Antioch, Iconium and Lystra, the persecutions I endured. Yet the Lord rescuede me from all of them.

#27. Getting Practically Personal

? How well do you think you have done to pull our group together?
What do you think is a next step to your growth?

? **[Read Mark 1:21-43]** A day in the life of Jesus
What strikes you about Jesus' day?
- Met lot of individuals' needs

? How would you characterize his interaction with individuals?
- Personal, one-on-one

? What are other ways he could have met all those needs?
- Blanket healing

? What do you think are some of the needs in this room?
What can we do to imitate Jesus' way to meet each other's needs?
- Get personal with each other

? How can we do this?

We need to get into each other's lives. Here are some practical ways you can help each other, told in story form:

> A WW2 story tells of how some soldiers brought the body of a dead friend to a French cemetery. The priest asked if the dead man had been a Catholic, but they did not know. The priest said that the man could not be buried in the graveyard. They men took their friend and buried him outside the cemetery fence. The next day they came back to see if the grave was all right, and to their astonishment they could not find it. They were about to leave in confusion when the priest came out. He told them that he had been so troubled about the event that he arose early in the morning and moved the graveyard fence to include the grave of the soldier who had died. **Move your fences. Make room in your schedules for people.**
>
> You can make more of an impact by becoming interested in other people than you can by trying to get people interested in you.
> **Stop being selfish and be interested in someone else.**

Sam Rayburn was Speaker of the House of Representatives longer than any other man in our history. There is a story about him that reveals the kind of man he really was. The teenage daughter of a friend of his died suddenly one night. Early the next morning the man heard a knock on his door, and when he opened it, there was Mr. Rayburn standing outside. The Speaker said, "I just came by to see what I could do to help." The father replied in his deep grief, "I don't think there is anything you can do, Mr. Speaker. We are making all the arrangements." "Well," Mr. Rayburn said, "have you had your coffee this morning?" The man replied that they had not taken time for breakfast. So Mr. Rayburn said that he could at least make coffee for them. **Do something people wouldn't expect you to do.**

Author and lecturer Leo Buscaglia once told about a contest he was asked to judge. The purpose of the contest was to find the most caring child; the winner was a four-year-old boy. His next-door neighbor was an elderly gentleman who had recently lost his wife. Upon seeing the man cry, the little boy went into this gentleman's yard, climbed into his lap and just sat there. When his mother asked him what he had said to the neighbor, the little boy said, "Nothing. I just helped him cry." **Feel what someone else is going through.**

Sir Edmund Hillary and his Nepalese guide, Tenzing Norgay, were the first people to make the historic climb of Mount Everest in 1953. Coming down from the mountain peak, Sir Edmund suddenly lost his footing. Tenzing held the line taut and kept them both from falling by digging his ax into the ice. Later Tenzing refused any special credit for saving Sir Edmund Hillary's life; he considered it a routine part of the job. As he put it, "Mountain climbers always help each other." **Do something for someone without expecting any repayment.**

Gestures often speak more eloquently than words. In his first season with the Brooklyn Dodgers, Jackie Robinson, the first black man to play major league baseball, faced venom nearly everywhere he traveled–fastballs were aimed at his head, the bases often had spikes in them to hurt him, the opposing dugouts and the crowds yelled demeaning words at him. During one game in Boston, the taunts and racial slurs seemed to reach a peak. In the midst of this, another Dodger, a Southern white player named Pee Wee Reese, called for a time out. He walked from his position at shortstop toward Robinson at second base, put his arm around Robinson's shoulder, and stood there with him for what seemed like a very long time. This gesture spoke in ways that words cannot describe: "This man is my friend." **Take a risk for someone.**

Bottom line: We need to grow in the depth of our friendships in this room.

Challenge: Take time each week to get closer to one other person in your teen ministry by putting one of these things into practice.

#28. Gifts for Godliness

{Set up a circle of chairs such that each chair is facing away from the center of the circle and place a slice of lemon or small piece of ginger in a sandwich baggie and put it under each chair. As each person arrives, blindfold them and take them to a chair putting their stuff on the floor in front of them. They cannot move around but only sit in the chair and wait for instructions. Once everyone is there and has had a few minutes to be in this rather unique setting, you may start. Begin with them staying blindfolded and sitting with their back toward you and listening to the scripture and answering your questions.}

[Read 2 Peter 1:3]

? What is a godly life? Is it something you should desire? Why?
What has God given you to help you live a godly life?

Here are three things that God has given you to live in a godly manner:

{Have them reach under their chair and taste what is in the bag. Have them take their blindfolds off, get their Bibles, and turn toward the middle of the circle.}

1. Friendships

? When we began tonight, how did you feel not being able to see or interact with people?
What did you think of the singing, or if your group didn't sing, the level of interaction of the group?
Why did it make such a difference not being able to see each other?

[Read Hebrews 10:24-25]

? What does this tell you about the role you play in each other's lives?

We need each other. You need someone in your life to help you. Imagine spending your whole life feeling like you did when you first came in...that's what it would be like and is like for some people who have no one to encourage them and spur them on.

2. Faithful instruction

? How did you feel before you tasted the lemon or ginger? How did it taste? Were you surprised?

? How does tasting a piece of ginger blindfolded relate to life?
- Dumb decisions and bad results

[Read Psalm 119:97-104]
? What did the Bible do for David that made him so proud of it?

The Bible will save your life or at the very least keep you from a bad, sour decision. You hold the words to literally live by—they will not fail you; they will keep you from harm. Put them into practice and see the result.

{Have them get out of the chair and sit on the floor in front or around you.}

3. Freedom
? How did it feel to get up?
What happens to you when you feel trapped and confined?

[Read Galatians 5:13-15]
? What is dangerous about freedom?
- Takes much responsibility

For example, driving: great freedom, but lives can be lost if not responsible

? What freedoms do you have?
- To choose
- To love
- To give
- To complain

? How does God suggest you use your freedoms?
- To be giving

? Isn't that godliness?

> *On Christmas Day 1968, the three astronauts of Apollo 8 circled the dark side of the moon and headed for home. Suddenly, over the horizon of the moon rose the blue and white Earth garlanded by the glistening light of the sun against the black void of space. Those sophisticated men, trained in science and technology, did not utter Einstein's name. They*

did not even go to the poets, the lyricists, or the dramatists. Only one thing could capture the awe-inspiring thrill of this magnificent observation. Billions heard the voice from outer space as the astronaut read it: "In the beginning God"–the only concept worthy enough to describe that unspeakable awe, unutterable in any other way. "In the beginning God created"–the invasive, the inescapable sense of the infinite and the eternal.

There are many amazing things on your horizon—let God create in you a great character by:
- » Remembering your friendships—they make your life full and fun.
- » Putting into practice God's faithful instructions through his word—they make your life safe and keep it from disappointment and disillusionment.
- » Using the freedoms you have for the benefit of someone else.

#29. God Is Like a Gift

? What's the best gift you've ever received? Why was it so great?
What's the best gift you've ever given? Why was it so great?
If you were going to get the ultimate gift today, what would you hope it would be?

{**Ask for two volunteers.** Once they're up front with you, pull out two gifts and set them on a table. One should be something cheap like a super-ball, or a pencil. The other should be something the students would actually want—like a whole bag of candy or a 12-pack of Coke. Whatever the gifts are, it needs to be totally obvious to everyone that the second one is more desirable. Tell your volunteers you're going to flip a coin to see who gets to choose a gift first. But before you do, explain that there's a little more to this. If they choose the first gift, it's theirs—no strings attached. But if they choose the second gift, they'll need to pay two dollars to get it. They can get the money from other kids in the room or out of their own pockets—it doesn't matter. Now flip a coin and let them choose. After both volunteers have returned to their seats, ask the following questions.}

? Which was the better gift?
What did you think watching _____ pay for the second gift?
What makes something a gift?

[Read Ephesians 2:8]
God tells us that our salvation is a gift from him—we didn't do anything to earn it, we can't buy it, and he won't take it back. But the Bible shows us that God is more than a gift-giver—he's actually a gift himself.

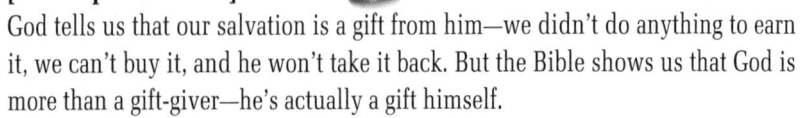

? How can you be a gift to someone?

Turn your room into a meter. Point to one wall and designate it the "extremely cool gift" wall. Point to the opposite wall and designate it the "totally lame gift" wall. Now read this list of ways you can be a gift and have the students move to one wall or the other, or somewhere in between, to show how they feel about each gift. When you're done, discuss their answers.
» Write an encouraging letter to someone who's not your best friend.
» Sit with a lonely kid at lunch.

- » Tell some kid you'll be nice to her if she pays you.
- » Do one of your brother's or sister's chores without expecting anything in return.
- » Tell your mom and dad you love them.
- » Clean your room, and then tell your mom about it 16 times.
- » Mow a neighbor's yard for free.
- » Visit an elderly neighbor.
- » Listen to a friend's problems while huffing, looking at your watch, and making it obvious that you'd rather be anywhere else.

Katie Fisher, 17, entered the Madison County, Ohio Junior Livestock Sale hoping the lamb she had for sale would get a good price. For months Katie had been battling cancer. She had endured hospital stays and been through chemotherapy a number of times. Before the lamb went on the block, the auctioneer told the audience about Katie's condition, hoping his introduction would push the price-per-pound above the average of two dollars. It did—and then some. The lamb sold for $11.50 per pound. Then the buyer gave it back, and suggested the auctioneer sell it again. That started a chain reaction. Families bought it and gave it back; businesses bought it and gave it back. Katie's mother said, "The first sale is the only one I remember. After that, I was crying too hard." They ended up selling the lamb thirty-six times that day, raising more than $16,000 in the process.

You can be a gift to someone. Don't spoil your gift by charging for it! Give freely and you will be like God!

#30. Great Moments

{This lesson was used as a follow-up to a HOPE Global Outreach. Use it as a model for a HOPE event in which your group has participated.}

Opening activity: Get 4 volunteers, two boys and two girls. Get four more volunteers to take buckets of water and towels, two boys and two girls. Pass out index cards to the remaining kids. Have the first group remove socks and shoes and have the second group wash their feet with wash cloths and dry them off (don't need to take too long, just get the idea across).

While the foot washing is taking place have the kids watching write down their thoughts and feelings on the index cards that were passed out. Once finished, have them turn in the cards.

? How did you feel getting your feet washed? {To the feet washees}
How did you feel washing their feet? {To the feet washers}

Read the responses on the cards (no names).

[Read John 13:1-15]
Explain that this was just before he was to be crucified and that this was a job that a slave performed. Jesus had a purpose for everything he did.

? Why did Jesus do this just before his crucifixion?
Why was Peter so upset?
What was Jesus trying to teach?
Would you consider this a great moment in Jesus' life? Why or why not?

Tell me about some of the ways you served [at a HOPE Global Outreach]. What did you do? How did you feel during it? How do you feel now?

[Read Acts 20:32-35]
This statement of Jesus is not written in any of the gospels, and yet Paul remembers it.

? Why do you think this statement made such an impression on Paul?

Tools to Help Preteen and Young Teen Leaders and Parents

Read story of the taxi cab driver, below.

It made such an impression on Paul because he knew that helping people and showing love would make great moments that give people happiness and fulfillment. The trick is to be ready, to be on the alert for these moments. They won't always be organized like the recent event. Most of them will come when you least expect it. You may miss the opportunity unless you are ready with a serving heart, a heart to make a great moment.

Because I drive the night shift, my cab often becomes a moving confessional. Passengers climb in, sit behind me in total anonymity, and tell me about their lives. I encounter people whose lives amaze me, ennoble me, make me laugh and sometimes weep. But none touched me more than a woman I picked up late one August night.

Responding to a call from a small brick building in a quiet part of town, I assumed I was being sent to pick up some partiers, or someone who had just had a fight with a lover, or a worker heading to an early shift at some factory in the industrial part of town.

When I arrived at 2:30 a.m., the building was dark except for a single light in a ground floor window. Under these circumstances, many drivers would just honk once or twice, and then drive away. But I had seen too many impoverished people who depended on taxis as their only means of transportation. Unless a situation smelled of danger, I always went to the door. This passenger might be someone who needs my assistance, I reasoned to myself. So I walked to the door and knocked. "Just a minute," answered a frail, elderly voice. After a long pause, the door opened. A small woman in her 80s stood before me. She was wearing a print dress and a pillbox hat with a veil pinned on it, like somebody out of a 1940s movie.

The apartment looked as if no one had lived in it for years. All the furniture was covered with sheets. There were no clocks on the walls, no knickknacks or utensils on the counters. In the corner was a cardboard box filled with photos and glassware. "Would you carry my bag out to the car?" she asked. I took the bag and then turned to assist her. She took my arm and we walked slowly toward the curb. She kept thanking me for my kindness. "It's nothing," I told her. "I just try to treat my passengers the way I would want my mother treated." "Oh, you're such a good boy," she said.

When we got in the cab, she gave me an address, and then asked, "Could you drive through downtown?" "It's not the shortest way," I answered quickly. "Oh, I don't mind," she said. "I'm in no hurry. I'm on my way to a hospice." I looked in the rearview mirror. Her eyes were glistening. "I don't have any family left," she continued. "The doctor says I don't have very long." I quietly reached over and shut off the meter. "What route would you like me to take?" I asked.

For the next two hours, we drove through the city. She showed me the building where she had once worked as an elevator operator. We drove through the neighborhood where she and her husband had lived when they were newlyweds. She had me pull up in front of a furniture warehouse that had once been a ballroom where she had gone dancing as a girl. Sometimes she'd ask me to slow down in front of a particular building or corner and would sit staring into the darkness, saying nothing.

As the first hint of sun was creasing the horizon, she suddenly said, "I'm tired. Let's go now." We drove in silence to the address she had given me. Two orderlies came out to the cab as soon as we pulled up. They were solicitous and intent, watching her every move. They must have been expecting her. I opened the trunk and took the small suitcase to the door. The woman was already seated in a wheelchair. "How much do I owe you?" she asked, reaching into her purse. "Nothing," I said. "You have to make a living," she answered. "There are other passengers," I responded. Almost without thinking, I bent and gave her a hug. She held onto me tightly. "You gave an old woman a little moment of joy," she said. "Thank you." I squeezed her hand, and then walked into the dim morning light. Behind me, a door shut. It was the sound of the closing of a life. I didn't pick up any more passengers that shift. I drove aimlessly, lost in thought. For the rest of that day, I could hardly talk.

What if that woman had gotten an angry driver, or one who was impatient to end his shift? What if I had refused to take the run, or had honked once, then driven away? I don't think that I have done anything more important in my life. We're conditioned to think that our lives revolve around great moments. But great moments often catch us unaware—beautifully wrapped in what others may consider a small one.

#31. He Is the Potter

{Give everyone a paper plate and a can of play dough (1/2 a can if a large group).}

[Read Isaiah 64:8]
God molds us into what we are...tonight you are going to play the part of the potter and mold some answers to two questions.

Use your play dough to answer the following question:

? What is your image of God?

{Have those that want to, share their creation and explain their answer.}

Again using your play dough, answer the following question:

? What do you think is God's image of you?

{Divide the group into teams of four or less. Have each team find a scripture which either describes God or describes God's view of them. Have each group read their verse to the rest of the groups. Have each worker read a verse or two on the same subject.}

[Read Zephaniah 3:14-17]
Regardless of what you think about yourself, God loves you and thinks you are awesome. Did you hear the scriptures about God? {Refer to some of the scriptures the kids found.} He is mighty, just, fair, perfect, loving, kind, compassionate, merciful, pure, etc.

Listen to how he feels about you: he rejoices over you. Tonight is an opportunity for you to hear what God has to say (and to have a little fun with our creativity or lack thereof) about us. Let God's word teach you tonight; let it inspire you and inform you so that you may be encouraged and be molded into the image that God chooses—an image of love.

[Read 1 John 4:19]
Many of you want to be loved but you must first know how to love, and to know

how to love, you must first understand God's love for you—it is total, unconditional, and all encompassing. After all, he is love.

Challenge: Come back next week and tell me five ways you saw God's love for you throughout the week.

#32. Herod Today, Gone Tomorrow

Tell me about a difficult decision you've had to make.
What are some things that make decisions difficult?
What makes a decision bad?
- Either the results or the heart behind the decision

? What are the results of a bad decision?

[Read Mark 6:14-26]

? Did Herod like John? Then why did he have him arrested?
What was the party like?
What did Herodias' daughter do?
What was Herod's reaction?
How did he respond to her request?

{Split the group into two teams. Assign a dynamic leader to each team. You play the role of King Herod. One of the teams is to advise you to kill John and the other is to advise against it. Give the teams five minutes to prepare, while you go and get your crown and robe. When the five minutes are up, have the teams take turns advising you on what to do. When the teams have exhausted their arguments, call the debate to a close and return to the Bible to find out what Herod does.}

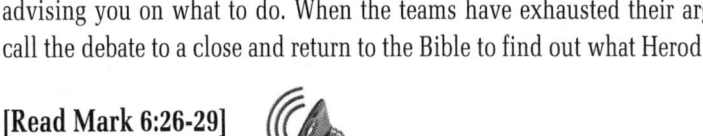

[Read Mark 6:26-29]
? Why did Herod kill John?
After killing John, what affect did this have on his character?
By killing John, Herod silenced the voice that was convicting him. How can you do that?

Bottom Line: You will have opportunities to make many choices this year. Don't be like Herod and give in to peer pressure and make a choice you will regret or that will bring you harm. Also, keep yourself from damaging your conscience, by making great choices, getting advice, searching the Bible for answers, and standing up for what is right.

One night an Arab had settled in for the night and had just fallen asleep when his camel stuck his head in his tent and explained that it was awful cold and asked permission to just stick his legs inside the tent to keep them warm. Granting him permission, the Arab went back to sleep. A little while later the camel woke him up a second time and asked permission to stick his head in. Again, permission was granted. This continued throughout the night until finally the Arab woke up to find the entire camel in the tent with him. When he told the camel that there just was not enough room in the tent for both of them, the camel suggested that the Arab might want to leave.

Your character and your conscience are something that will vanish if you don't treat them well. Just keep letting bad decisions into your tent and your character will be asked to leave; just be Herod for today and your character will be gone tomorrow!

#33. Hidden Treasures

Opening activity: There are two $1 bills hidden; if you find them, you can keep them. {give 5 minutes to search}
There are two $50 bills hidden; if you find them, you can keep them. {give 5 minutes to search}

[Read Matthew 13:44-46]

What word would you use to describe how you felt during the $50 hunt?
How was that different than the $1 hunt?
What parallels can you make about this and honoring God?
What word would you use to describe these two men during their treasure hunt?
What was the value of the treasure in the field or the fine pearl?
How could you tell their value?
What value does God have in your life?
How could someone tell?
What cheapens God's value in your life?
Why did these two men have to sell everything to get their treasure?
- Because they wouldn't have had enough to pay for them if they hadn't.
- It would have lowered the price and made them less valuable.

[Read Luke 14:25-33]

What happens when you don't give up everything?
What does it look like when you don't live as if you sold everything?
What does it communicate about your heart?

[Read Matthew 6:19-21, 24]

How you act and what you put your time into and what decisions you make tells everyone what you treasure.

You were running around here like fools looking for that $50, which will be spent in a few days and whose memory will be gone in a couple of weeks.
That's how it is with treasures: girls, boys, your ego, your sin, the Bible, God, church, teen ministry

Whatever you hide in your heart is what you treasure, and eventually you will sell everything you have and run around like a fool for it because it will have become so dear to you.

The question is: Does what you have hidden in your heart hold any spiritual value? You cannot serve both God and what the world treasures.

I challenge you to look at your life and re-evaluate: the things on which you have $50 price tags may only be $1 items and prove worthless to you; while those you have labeled cheap could prove eternally valuable.

#34. Honesty Is the Best Policy

Honesty Game: Break up into groups and give a deck of cards with various questions on them. {Use the Honesty Game Card Questions, below.} Have each person pick a card and answer, then watch the results.

? How did you feel answering some of these questions?
What made them hard to answer?
When I say someone has gotten honest, what do you think I mean? {Probably think that people have stopped telling lies; explain that we usually associate honesty with not telling lies, but honesty means saying what you think and feel, too.}

? Who comes to your mind when you think of honesty?
Why is honesty so important in your relationships?
How can lack of honesty affect your relationships?
How do you create a culture of honesty?

[Read Psalm 139:1-4]

? What are some things God knows about you?
- Favorite color
- Meanest thought
- Feelings
- Worst sin
- Greatest accomplishment

? In light of that, why does it make sense to be honest?
- Because he knows anyway and still loves you

He takes the good with the bad and keeps on loving us...that is amazing!

? What causes us to be dishonest?
- Fear of being wrong or thought of as silly
- Someone not respecting your thoughts/feelings
- Being labeled you for what you think

{This might be a great time to talk about a situation when something was hard for you to talk about to someone and the affects that had on you and your relationship with that person.}

[Read Psalm 101:7]

? How does God feel about being dishonest?
- No room in his house

Please get conviction on this so that you can expect honesty from yourself and others. God does not like it no matter what form—outright lies or just not saying what you think.

[Read Psalm 32:1-4]

? What happens when you hold things in?
- Waste away
- Hurts your confidence
- Plays with your mind
- You make up things the further you get from the event

? {Refer back to your example above, if necessary.} This verse is primarily talking about confessing sin, but isn't it true of unspoken feelings and conscience-stricken thoughts?

My overall plea to you is to be honest.

? By show of hands, right now how many of you can think of someone with whom you need to talk? How many of you need to get honest about some things?

Take this time tonight, if it's someone in here, and talk. If you are the one being talked to, listen with both ears. If they are not here, make a promise to yourself that you will talk this week. Resolve things and decide to be honest. This is the way of maturity. This is the way of God!

Once there was an emperor in the Far East who was growing old and knew it was coming time to choose his successor. Instead of choosing one of his assistants or one of his own children, he decided to do something different. He called all the young people in the empire together one day. He said, "It has come time for me to step down and to choose the next emperor. I have decided to choose one of you." The kids were shocked! But the emperor continued. "I am going to give each one of you a seed today—one seed. It is a very special seed. I want you to go home, plant the seed, water it and come back here one year from today with what you have grown from this one seed. I will then judge the plants that you bring to me, and the one I choose will be the next emperor."

There was one boy named Ling who was there that day and he, like the others, received a seed. He went home and excitedly told his mother the whole story. She helped him get a pot and some planting soil, and he planted the seed and watered it carefully. Every day he would water it and watch to see if it had grown. After about three weeks, some of the other youths began to talk about their seeds and the plants that were beginning to grow. Ling kept going home and checking his seed, but nothing ever grew. Three weeks, four weeks, five weeks went by–still nothing. By now others were talking about their plants but Ling didn't have a plant, and he felt like a failure.

Six months went by, still nothing in Ling's pot. He just knew he had killed his seed. Everyone else had trees or tall plants, but he had nothing. Ling didn't say anything to his friends, however. He just kept waiting for his seed to grow. A year finally went by and all the youths of the empire brought their plants to the emperor for inspection. Ling told his mother that he wasn't going to take an empty pot. But she encouraged him to go, and to take his pot, and to be honest about what happened. Ling felt sick to his stomach, but he trusted his mother was right.

He took his empty pot to the palace. When Ling arrived, he was amazed at the variety of plants grown by all the other youths. They were beautiful, in all shapes and sizes. Ling put his empty pot on the floor and many of the other kids laughed at him. A few felt sorry for him and just said, "Hey, nice try." When the emperor arrived, he surveyed the room and greeted the young people. Ling just tried to hide in the back. "My, what great plants, trees and flowers you have grown," said the emperor. "Today, one of you will be appointed the next emperor!" All of a sudden, the emperor spotted Ling at the back of the room with his empty pot. He ordered his guards to bring him to the front. Ling was terrified. "The emperor knows I'm a failure! Maybe he will have me killed!" When Ling got to the front, the emperor asked his name. "My name is Ling," he replied. All the kids were laughing and making fun of him.

The emperor asked everyone to quiet down. He looked at Ling, and then announced to the crowd, "Behold your new emperor! His name is Ling!" Ling couldn't believe it.

Ling couldn't even grow his seed. How could he be the new emperor? Then the emperor said, "One year ago today, I gave everyone here a seed. I told you to take the seed, plant it, water it, and bring it back to me today. But I gave you all boiled seeds which would not grow. All of you, except Ling, have brought me trees and plants and flowers. When you found that the seed would not grow, you substituted another seed for the one I gave you. Ling was the only one with the courage and honesty to bring me a pot with my seed in it. Therefore, he is the one who will be the new emperor!"

– From *"In the Garden with Jesus,"* a children's devotional written by Tiziana Ruff

Honesty Game Card Questions

Say one thing you notice about the person on your left.

What is the biggest lie you have ever told (or one of the biggest)?

Tell us about a situation in which you were reluctant to tell the complete truth.

Pick the person here whom you know best and say three words that describe your relationship to this person.

Tell us something that you think might surprise or shock us.

What are you like when you are by yourself?

Do you like what the person to your right is wearing?

Name three words which describe how a person might feel telling you exactly what they think.

Have you ever picked your nose and eaten it?

Have you ever wet the bed?

#35. Humility...It's Not a Weather Word

? What is sin? Give some examples.
Which sin does the most widespread damage?
Which sin do you think God hates the most? [Read Proverbs 8:13]
- God hates pride.

? What is pride?
Why does God hate it so much?
- It is the root of every sin.

For example:
- » Sex: "I deserve to have my pleasure and I should not worry about the consequences."
- » Lying: "I do not trust that God can work through the truth. I have more confidence in my ability to deceive and distort the truth."
- » Rebellion: "I know better than my leaders, and I can accomplish things by doing what I want to do."
- » Disobedience: "I know the Bible says this, but I have a better way."

The answer to pride is humility. We spend so much time on pride and what it is and isn't that we forget to talk about humility—what it is and it isn't, and how important it is.

Let's figure out what humility is:
{Split into manageable groups (five or fewer) and have half the groups answer question one and the other half answer question two. Have each group write on big sheets of paper and present their answers to everyone.}

? What is the wrong kind of humility?
- Wimp/pushover, yes-man, having no opinions

? What is the right kind of humility?
- Listening to input, getting help, taking correction, apologizing

[Read Philippians 2:3-8]
? What qualities of humility do you find in this passage?

- Selfless actions
- Thinking of others
- Finding positive things in others (no slams!)
- Considering others' interests ("What do they like?")
- Understand that we are nothing (Wow!)
- Obedience

[Read Psalm 149:4]

Why should this be important to you?
- Your salvation depends on it!

Most of you think that humility is a church thing or something your parents demand from you, something that you have to have in church or at home—wrong! Humility is a part of your character. As it is now, it is always with you—whether at church, at home, at school or when you go to college, live in your own apartment, and have your own job and family. Humility will be there or it won't! That depends on what you do today. It depends on how much you are willing to think less of yourself and more of God and others. Remember, your salvation depends on it and so do others!

#36. Hurry Scurry!

Opening activity: Get into groups of three or four and make a list of situations in which hurrying would be disastrous or ill advised. Have a person from each group report on the lists.

? What makes hurrying be the wrong thing to do in these situations?
What does hurrying typically communicate?
- Impatience, this is my time schedule, selfishness

[Read Isaiah 5:18-19]

? What does the phrase "woe to those" mean?
Why was Isaiah saying that to these people?
Many times we want things to happen on our timetable as if we were God, the sovereign one. Who are we to rush God about anything?

[Read John 11:1-45]

? What was Martha's response to Jesus when he finally made it to Bethany?
What was Jesus' response to her?
What was Jesus trying to find out by asking Martha if she believed?
When we want God to hurry what are we really saying to him?
- I don't trust you...I know what is best.

This is the alleged transcript of an actual radio conversation between a US naval ship and a Canadian maritime contact off the coast of Newfoundland in October 1995.
Americans: Please divert your course 15 degrees north to avoid a collision.
Canadians: Recommend you divert YOUR course 15 degrees south to avoid collision.
Americans: This is the captain of a US navy ship; I say again divert your course.
Canadians: No. I say again, you divert YOUR course.
Americans: THIS IS THE AIRCRAFT CARRIER USS LINCOLN, THE SECOND LARGEST SHIP IN THE UNITED STATES' ATLANTIC FLEET. WE ARE ACCOMPANIED BY THREE DESTROYERS, THREE CRUISERS AND NUMEROUS SUPPORT VESSELS. I DEMAND THAT YOU CHANGE YOUR COURSE 15 DEGREES NORTH, THAT'S ONE FIVE DEGREES NORTH, OR COUNTER-MEASURES WILL BE UNDERTAKEN TO ENSURE THE SAFETY OF THIS SHIP.

Canadians: We are a lighthouse; your call.

Who are we to think that we know what is best? God is the lighthouse for our lives. It is in our best interest to listen and wait for his direction.

#37. I See You...I Encourage You!

Opening activity: Play any game involving names. A favorite of mine is simply called the "Name Game." Divide group into two teams. Put an opaque sheet or blanket in between the two sitting teams. While holding the sheet/blanket up so no one can see over it, have one team member from each team come and sit in front of the sheet/blanket such that they are facing each other with the sheet/blanket in between them (they shouldn't be able to see each other). On a count of three, drop the blanket; the first person to say the other's first name wins a point for their team. Raise the blanket and repeat with new team members until a winner is declared by reaching 10 points—or whatever goal.

? Who can tell me what your name means?
How does it make you feel to have a name that means such?
How many people would you say you pass by each day?
How many do you say hi to or encourage in any way?

? Among the tribes of northern Natal in South Africa the most common greeting is the expression: Sawu Bona, which means, "I see you." The common reply is Sikhona, "I am here." It is an insult not to acknowledge people with this greeting.

? Why do you think they see it as an insult?
• They live under the spirit of *Ubuntu*, which is a frame of mind stemming from the saying "A person is a person because of other people."

? What do you think this means?
• You don't exist until someone acknowledges your existence.

? How does God show you this same line of thinking?
What one word could describe all of these things?
• Encouragement

? What does the word encouragement mean?
• It has several meanings: to harden one's heart, to establish one's character, to prepare, to make secure, to make firm

[Read Psalm 10]
God does see us [v. 14]. He shows us encouragement every day if only we will see it. We are made to need encouragement—why do you think peer pressure is

so effective?
- Because it gives encouragement, and this can be positive or negative [Psalm 64:5]

Each one of us needs encouragement—we need to be seen; to be acknowledged.

? How encouraged do you feel on a scale of 1-10?
In what area would you like to be more encouraged?
How can you help to encourage each other?

Once, when he was running for President, Abraham Lincoln received a letter from an 8-year-old girl who suggested that he grow a beard. In her opinion, Lincoln would stand a better chance of election if he grew one to hide the homeliness of his face. Lincoln could have been offended, but instead he answered her letter personally and thanked her for her suggestion, further adding that he'd like to visit with her when his campaign came to her area. On the day that Lincoln's campaign train was scheduled to pass through the town, practically the whole town was assembled at the station. There were the leading Republicans wearing their top hats, the shiny marching band, and the townsfolk in their finest attire. Almost everyone was there; all except the little girl, for she was left home. After all, her father reasoned, Lincoln would be interested only in the politicians and their speeches–the votes and the voters–not the attentions (or encouragement) of a little girl. It so happened, however, that as the campaign train approached the town it was forced to stop for repairs. Lincoln, not wanting to sit in the warm train, set off across the field afoot in search of the little girl's home. When Lincoln introduced himself at the door, the maid was speechless, but the little girl and her playmate, the maid's daughter, welcomed him as if they were expecting him. The two girls had been having a pretend party, drinking pretend hot chocolate out of their small teacups, and they invited Mr. Lincoln to join them. After a while, Lincoln said he must be going, thanked them for the party, and asked them how they liked his new beard. He then walked to the waiting train. When Lincoln boarded the train, it started on its way and went right through the town without stopping. Right past all the waiting dignitaries, politicians, loud playing band and flag-draped platform; right past ladies and gentlemen in their Sunday best, for Lincoln had not come to visit people who were putting on a show for his benefit. He had come to visit and say thank you to a little girl who just wanted to spend time with him and offered him some honest encouragement.

My challenge for you is to encourage each other...don't be fake or overly impressive, that is for your benefit, not your friends'. Keep it real and give real encouragement. Find out what the needs of your friends are and meet them with love and strength and kindness whether in word or deed—then and only then will you truly see and acknowledge them. Who knows, someone may dare to do the same for you!

#38. Image Is Everything

Opening activity: Divide the group into equal teams and seat them in parallel lines. Give each team a box. About 10 feet in front of each team, place a spoon and a pile of cotton balls. Explain that this is a race to see which team can bring the most cotton balls back to their box, carrying them in the spoon. However, each person on the team will have a different handicap: the first person may not use their left leg; the second, their right arm; the third, their right leg; the fourth, their arms; the fifth, their legs; the sixth, their eyes (blindfolded); and so on. Each person with their limitation should go to the pile of cotton balls, pick up the spoon, get as many cotton balls as possible in the spoon and bring them back to the box, return the spoon to the pile, and return to the end of the line. After everyone has gone, declare a winner by who has the most cotton balls.

In regard to how you look, what would you like to change about yourself? Most of these changes don't actually hamper our performances like the handicaps in the cotton ball game, but often we focus on them or other self-perceived deficiencies so strongly that we allow them to affect us as if they were handicaps.

How do these things affect you?
Why do they affect you?
- Because we compare ourselves to other people

[Read Genesis 1:26-27]
What does God tell you about yourself in this verse? You are made in God's and Jesus' image...Jesus may have had a big nose or big feet or (pick one of the things they wrote down), too!

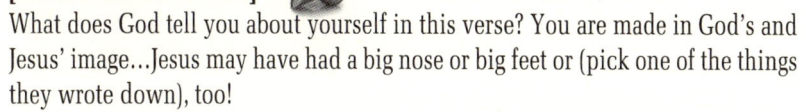

How many of you feel like you were made in God's or Jesus' image?
Who is more likely to think they are made like God, a four-year-old or you? Why? What happened in the last eight or nine years that a four-year-old would think that more than you?

This is what happened: The world has told you lies—that you aren't like God because you are not like a certain person; you have replaced the image of God with other people's image (fashion, model's, movie star's); other people's opinions of you have become more meaningful than God's opinion of you.

Let me show you what I mean. {Make a funny comment on how we're going to have a Bible study tonight to explain all the verses; it will lighten them up.}

[Read James 3:9]

? What is something that has been said that has negatively affected what you think of yourself?
Why would God call these things curses?
What does God see in your image?
Which would you rather have, God's image of you or people's image of you?
So, how do we begin to reclaim the image that God desires for you?

[Read Colossians 3:9-11]

? How does this verse teach you to renew your image to what it's supposed to be?
- Knowledge—learn God's image of you and let it renew your self-image.

Listen to what you are:
[Psalm 139:13-14] Wonderful – means amazing, unheard of, astonishing.
[Ephesians 2:10] Personal creation – would you make a machine that doesn't work? Neither would God!
[Isaiah 29:23-24] Inspiring – you can change the world and those around you.
[Luke 12:7] Valuable – "many" denotes all that there are.
[1 John 3:1-2] Called his child – "called" denotes "to name." He thought of you as a unique individual.

These are things, among many others, that describe you—God's image of you!

A worried mother wondered where her daughter was on the rainy schoolday afternoon. She should have been home by now. The rain was heavy, the thunder loud, and the lightning was bright. Finally, after a few anxious minutes she decided to put her coat on and look for her child. Out the door and down the street toward the school she went. As she turned the far corner of their street she spotted her daughter, walking slowly and smiling largely, toward home. The daughter spotted her mom and ran to her grinning from ear to ear. "Where have you been? Don't you know that it is lightning and you could be killed?" said the anxious mother. "But, mom," replied the wide-eyed little girl "isn't this neat? The puddles, the rain, the boom-booms, and besides, God is taking my picture!"

Like this little girl, look at things from a different perspective. Despite what others say or what even you might think, you are amazing. Quit listening to the thunder of the world and see yourself in a new light. See yourself as God sees you—an amazing, unique creation!

#39. Inside Out!

Opening activity: Break the group into small groups. Give each group one of the following personalities: conceited, insecure, worried, out of control, angry, or bad attitude. Ask each group to create a product or plan to cure their personality flaw. Have each group present their product or plan.

{Take a mental note as to how many deal with the outside or the inside.}

We all have an issue or two, and we are all looking for answers on how to deal with them. In the following verse, the Pharisees had an issue with some of Jesus' disciples.

[Read Mark 7:1-9]

? What issues did the Pharisees have with Jesus' disciples?
- Unclean
- Did not follow traditions

? What was Jesus' response?
- Rebuked their focus on traditions

? What's wrong with traditions?
- Can become more important than Bible
- Put emphasis on outside rather than inside

Describe ways we put more attention on the outside than the inside.
- Clothes
- Who we are seen with
- The Girl, The Boy
- Looking buff
- Acting cool and together
- Sex, drugs and rock 'n' roll
- Plastic smile: "Everything's fine."

[Read Mark 7:14-23]

? What is Jesus teaching you about dealing with your issue?
- You've got to get inside your heart.

By looking at what you do and how you are, you can learn much about your heart. Look at the products and plans to fix the issues I gave you. They deal with the outside and try to change the heart by changing the outside. {Or if they gave the inside plans, you can use the you-know-the-answer-so-why-do-you-still-insist-on-dealing-with-the-outside line of reasoning.} You must understand that the outside is shaped by the inside. Only when you understand this can you really begin to change your heart.

> *There was once a family from a remote part of the country, which was making their first visit to a big city. They checked in to a grand hotel and stood in amazement at the impressive sight. Leaving the reception desk, they came to the elevator entrance. They'd never seen an elevator before, and just stared at it, quite unable to work out what it was for. An old lady hobbled toward the elevator and went inside, and the door closed. About a minute later, the door opened and out came a stunningly good-looking young woman. Dad couldn't stop staring. Without turning his head, he patted his son's arm and said, "Go get your mother, son."*

You laugh, but when you start working on the inside, you will see a change that people will like even though they can't explain it.

#40. It's All Hearsay to Me

Catch Phrase: Students will need to listen to each other closely and listen for what's out of place in this activity. Divide students into pairs or groups and give each a unique, slightly odd secret phrase; for example, "three happy elves live in my basement." Give the groups time to plan a dialogue that incorporates the secret phrase once or twice. (Could incorporate a skit related to the topic, if you feel industrious.) When they've finished planning, let them perform the dialogue for the class. While watching, students try to guess the secret phrase and write it down accurately; they must also write how many times it was said. Give points to students who found the phrase and its repetitions. The student with the most points is the winner.

? What is the key to being successful in this game?
- Listening

? What is the difference between listening and hearing?
How can not listening cause problems for you?
Why is being a good listener such an important quality?
What makes it so hard to be a good listener?

We're going to read several scriptures about listening. Let's have some open discussion on each of them, and hopefully you will decide that it is in your best interest to be a good listener.

[Read Proverbs 1:1-6]
? What is the purpose of the proverbs?
What is the best way for you to gain something from the proverbs?
- To listen to them

? What are some characteristics of a listener?
- Wise, learner, adds to their knowledge, guided

[Read Proverbs 5:11-14]
? Who are your teachers?
What will happen to someone who ignores his teachers?

[Read Proverbs 12:15]
Tell me a situation where this scripture might be applicable.
? What is wrong with thinking you are right all the time?

[Read Proverbs 13:1]
? What is a mocker? How are they dangerous?

[Read Proverbs 15:31]
? What is a correction or rebuke; can you give me an example? Do you particularly like rebukes? How can they be life-giving?

[Read Proverbs 18:13]
? Describe a situation that this is talking about. What is so shameful about answering before listening?

[Read Proverbs 19:20, 27]
? What does verse 27 caution you about?

? How would you sum up listening and its importance to your life?

> *In 1929, Lady Astor won election to the British House of Commons (the first woman in history to do so). Endeavoring to make her mark in what had been exclusively a male preserve, she frequently interrupted other speakers. Castigated one day for such an infraction, Astor protested that she had been "listening for hours" before interrupting. "Yes," exclaimed an exasperated colleague, "we've heard you listening!"*

#41. It's All about Perspective

Opening activity: Place a glass half-filled with water in front of the group. Don't say a word and ask them to write down what they see. Have them read their descriptions out loud.

{Some will describe the glass as half full others will describe it as half empty.}

? What does this tell you about how we look at different situations?
Can you think of any situations where you may get differing perspectives such as the glass of water being half filled or half empty?

[Read 1 Corinthians 10:21-24]
? What is Paul trying to say?
Can you give me an example of something being permissible but not beneficial?
- Video games all the time
- TV all hours
- Too much time on the phone
- Too many sports
- Taking too many classes at once

Describe what would happen to a family if the dad did nothing but watch TV or the mom went to the mall every evening to spend time with her friends.

? What are some permissible but not beneficial things you find yourself doing?
Why aren't these things beneficial or constructive?
- Seeking your own good, not others'

? What do we call this?
- Selfishness

[Read Romans 12:9-13]
Paul has some bullets of advice, and the last one is to be hospitable.
? What does it mean to be hospitable?
How does the kind of selfishness we've talked about tonight affect a family's ability to be hospitable?
- Everyone gets into their world and does not give.

? How would a guest in your home know you were being hospitable?
- Greet them at the door
- Offer something to drink
- Be courteous
- Look them in the eyes
- Say goodbye

? Where do we develop the habit of not being hospitable?
- From the permissible things that we do over and over and yet are not beneficial when it comes to being giving to guests

Many of you need to check some of the things you do. You may be allowed to do them, but they may not be the best things to do. Some of you are disrupting your household because you think everything revolves around you and your hobby. This becomes your habit, and when people come over, you can't seem to find it in you to be friendly and giving to your guests.

Challenge: Ask yourself if there is anything you do to cause tension in your home or that doesn't make guests feel welcome, then ask your parents the same question. Sometimes life is about perspective, but it's not always about your own perspective. You may think it is okay to do something all the time, but really, it's not. Be open to another perspective and learn from it.

#42. It's More Than Just Eyesight!

What do you think is the most amazing part of the body?

{Give some facts about the eye. Perhaps invite an optometrist into the room.}

John 9
[Read vv. 1-5]

? What affect does this have on your view of "bad" things?

[Read vv. 6-12]

? How did this man regard Jesus?

[Read vv. 13-18]

? What happened for him to change his view of Jesus from a man to a prophet?

[Read vv. 18-27]

? What might the man be thinking, having been summoned a second time?
What was his view of Jesus now?
Why the change?

[Read vv. 28-34]

? What does this man think now?
What would cause him to defend Jesus so vehemently?

[Read vv. 35-36]

? What strikes you as odd about his response?
Then what was he defending when he was talking with the Pharisees?
Why did Jesus seek him out?

[Read vv. 37-38]

? Why did he worship Jesus?

? Where do you see Jesus on this continuum?

    Man => Prophet => Teacher => Truth => Lord

#43. Jesus Representin'!

{Give each person a paper plate and a can of play dough (or half a can if a large group).}

How would you finish the following? God is _____. Using play dough, make something that illustrates your choice to fill in the blank.

{Have each person present their creation.}

? How can we know what God is like?

[Read Hebrews 1:3]

? What does this say about the way we can know who and what God is?

? What emphasis does this put on believing Jesus is who he says he is?

[Read John 1:14]
Jesus came from the Father.
What did he bring with him?

? What do you want to know about Jesus so you can trust what he has to say regarding our list of topics?

Follow this study with the "Jesus Is True" lesson.

#44. Jesus Is True...Isn't He?

Game: Liar, Liar. Split the group into four teams. Each team will introduce one of their teammates. The object is to get the other team to guess whether the truth is being told about that teammate. Each team gets a point if they guess right.

? How can you tell if someone is lying?
- Eyes
- Body language
- Sometimes you can't

[Read Mark 14:60-62]
? What was Jesus claiming?
- To be the Son of God

? What stops you from believing this claim?
- Questioning whether he was a real person in history

Look at some facts:
» 27 New Testament documents refer to him.
» Early Christian writings of Polycarp, Origin, Eusebius, Iraneaus, Ignatius, Justin Martyr refer to him
» Non-Christian sources refer to him:
  o Cornelius Tacitus, Roman historian, AD 112
  o Flavius Josephus, Jewish historian, AD 37
  o Jewish Talmud
  o Encyclopedia Britannica uses 20,000 words to describe Jesus—more than Aristotle, Julius Caesar, Buddha, Mohammed or Napoleon. It states: "These independent accounts prove that in ancient times even the opponents of Christianity never doubted the historicity of Jesus."

- Popular opinion ignores Jesus and his teaching, so it must not be true.

? Would most people deny that Jesus' teachings are worthy and good? Then why do we ignore them? [John 18:33-38]
- Popular opinion rejects truth and moral living because people want to do their own thing.

? Do you agree?

However, this does not deny or nullify the existence of Jesus.

So, going back to the situation in Mark 14:

? What are the responses they could have had to Jesus' claim?
- Either true or false

? If false, what could they have called him?
- Crazy or a liar

First, let's focus on crazy:
? Based on what you know about Jesus, what makes it hard to believe he was indeed crazy?
How difficult was it to fool the other three teams with just one lie about someone on your team?
Do you think it is possible for Jesus to fool the world about something so serious as being the Son of God?

Now, in regard to him being a liar:
? How would you go about proving Jesus was a liar and not truly the Son of God?
- He said he committed no sin. Surely Judas would have caught him somehow! [See Matthew 27:4.]
- Would someone really be tortured and die for a lie?

? What evidence that we haven't talked about supports Jesus being a liar?

One historian wrote, "It would take more than a Jesus to invent a Jesus."
? What do you think of this quote? Agree or disagree? Why?

Again this historian writes:

"The hypothesis of imposture is so revolting to moral as well as common sense, that its mere statement is its condemnation. It was invented by the Jews who crucified the Lord to cover their crime, but has never been seriously carried out, and no scholar of any decency and self-respect would now dare to profess it openly. How, in the name of logic, common sense, and experience, could an impostor—that is a deceitful, selfish, depraved man—have invented, and consistently maintained from the beginning to end, the purest and noblest character known in history with the most perfect air of truth and reality? How could he have conceived and successfully carried out a plan of unparalleled beneficence, moral magnitude, and sublimity, and sacrificed his own life for it, in the face of the strongest prejudices of his people and ages?"

? What convinces you that Jesus is neither crazy nor lying?

? If not crazy or lying, then what must he be?
- Truly the Son of God!

#45. Just Do It

Call out some famous ad slogans and see if they can guess what product each represents:
"Capture the magic." – Kodak
"Plop, plop, fizz, fizz, oh what a relief it is." – Alka-Seltzer
"Think." – IBM
"Think different." – Apple Computer
"It's the real thing." – Coca-Cola
"Never let them see you sweat!" – Dry Idea
"What's in Your Wallet?" – Capital One Visa Card
and probably the most famous of all…
"Just do it." – Nike

? Why do companies use catchy slogans?
- Helps people remember their product

? What is an epitaph?
- Tombstone inscription in memory of the one buried there

Here are some epitaphs I found. See if you can guess whose they are:
"THAT'S ALL FOLKS! MAN OF 1000 VOICES." – Mel Blanc
"THE BOY BANDIT KING. HE DIED AS HE HAD LIVED." – Billy the Kid
"MY JESUS MERCY" – Al Capone
"Free at last. Free at last. Thank God Almighty, I'm Free at last." – Martin Luther King, Jr.

? What do ad slogans and epitaphs have in common?
- They describe what is unseen; tell you about something so you can determine if you want to invest or honor it

? What is the difference between an ad slogan and an epitaph?
- One is said at the beginning, the other at the end.

? How do people come up with ad slogans or epitaphs?
- Decide what they want people to know about the item (try to create its reputation), or communicate what was known about a person (report on their reputation)

Tools to Help Preteen and Young Teen Leaders and Parents

? What does the word "reputation" mean?
- The reported, public estimation of a person

? How does one build a reputation?
{Let them answer, then read the following verse}
[Read Proverbs 20:11] Your actions determine your reputation.

? What guides your actions?
- Your beliefs and convictions

It is the start of a new year and many people use this time to start over or start anew; companies do it with budgets, people do it with personal fitness, etc. I don't know whether you are thinking this way, but it may be the time to renew the reputation you have made or build the one you desire. Have you made decisions or said things you wished you could take back or acted in such a repeated manner that has gained you a regrettable reputation? Maybe you just want someone to know you for something.

? What are some necessary convictions for you to build a great reputation?
- Purity
- Honesty
- Integrity
- Generosity
- Loyalty
- Love
- Gratitude
- Humility
- Respectfulness
- Self-control
- Being encouraging, forgiving, and kind

? Sounds like the Bible, hey?

? What happens if you let your convictions slide?
- Your actions change accordingly
- You begin to make a reputation you may never lose.

If you want a great reputation, then make up your own advertising slogan or decide what you want said about you when you are not around (believe me people talk about you—you talk about me when I'm not around). Once you've decided, work backward by coming up with the actions, then deciding what convictions you must have to act that way; write those convictions on a piece of paper. Let those be your New Year's resolutions...and then **Just Do It!**

#46. Know Thy Maker!

Opening activity: Leader asks one person a question about that person. They answer and then ask someone else a question; they answer and ask someone else, and so on until everyone has answered or until time is up.

? What are ways you let people know about you?
[Read Romans 1:20] How does God let you know him?
- By what he has made

? What are some things that God made? {Let them list some and then talk about them.}

Elephant:
- » 19-24 feet long, 10-13 feet tall; 10k-14k lbs; tail 4 feet long, skin 1 inch thick
- » Trunk has 150,000 muscles
- » Eats 300-600 lbs of food and drinks 30-50 gallons of water per day
- » Pregnant 22 months and then gives birth to a 175 to 200-lb baby
- » Second to man in brain size versus body weight ratio; one of the smartest animals

? What does this teach you about God?
- God is big and awesome
- Clever and intelligent

Stars:
- » More stars than grains of sand on the earth—over one hundred billion trillion!
- » Closest one is 25 trillion miles away—there's a lot of room in space.
- » [Psalm 147:4] God calls each one by name.

? What does this teach you about God?
- He knows each part of his creation.

This means you: your name, birthday, favorite ice cream, day you will die... everything. He is intimate and yet huge.

Tools to Help Preteen and Young Teen Leaders and Parents

Water:
- » Every living thing needs water to live.
- » [Job 36:26-29] Water cycle to produce rain: evaporation => condensation => precipitation

? What does this teach you about God?
- God has a plan to sustain life

? He has a plan for you!

People:

? What unobvious characteristic of God can be learned from knowing yourself?
- He has feelings.

Consider the following:

[Read Zephaniah 3:17] – happy and delighted...singing over you!

[Read Ephesians 4:30] – saddened...at our disobedience.

A lady walked into a hat store to buy a woven hat for a special night out on the town. She wanted something original, so she chose an emerald-colored ribbon and asked the weaver to make her a hat immediately. Within fifteen minutes, he made the most beautiful hat she had ever seen. She asked, "How much?" He replied, "Five hundred dollars." The lady shouted, "For a piece of ribbon!" The man calmly unraveled the hat and responded, "You can have the ribbon for $5."

God longs for each of you to know him and so he has made, as Paul said in Romans, everything so that he can be clearly seen. You have the choice to see it as simple pieces of $5 ribbon or an elaborate creation made to give honor to its maker. I encourage you to open your eyes and look at the things God has made: the ant, birds, seeds, trees, sheep, goats, wind, rain, soil, etc. See your Maker in all of it that you might grow in your knowledge of God and in your respect for him.

#47. Leader=Servant

{When there is a change in leadership in the preteen and young teen ministry, use this lesson to let the kids get to know the new leaders, or you can use it for something else that is appropriate, such as preparing them for an upcoming change in the overall leadership of the congregation.}

Choose two or three volunteers. Have them choose a partner. Leave the partner in the room and take the volunteers away to each get a bowl, a wash cloth, and a towel. Have them return and wash their partner's feet in front of everyone.

Read [John 13:1-17] as they are washing each other's feet.

Ask the partners how they felt. Ask the volunteers how they felt. Ask the rest of the group how they felt as they watched.

? What was so amazing about Jesus washing their feet?
- This was a menial task usually done by a servant.

? Why did Jesus do it during the meal?
- No servant to do it before the meal, no one else offered, done deliberately to prove a point

? What was Jesus' point?
- That we should serve one another

? What role did Jesus play in the lives of the disciples?
- He was their leader and teacher.

? Who can tell me what the best definition of a leader is?

? What does Jesus' example tell you about the definition of a leader?
- A leader is a *servant* [Mark 10:35-45]

? What makes a great servant?
- Focuses on the needs of another

A leader is a *friend* [John 15:13-15]

? Why could Jesus, their leader, call them friends?
- He let them know him.

It is important that a leader be someone who is focused on the needs of others and who is not afraid to let people know him. With that, I would like our new leaders to come up and tell us a little about themselves. They are your servants, and I thought it would be great if they let you get to know them.

I want you to develop the conviction that the nature of a leader is to serve, not to be served as the world trains us to believe. That can easily be brought into and nurtured in the church, so be on your guard against it.

> *One Sunday morning a man came up to the evangelist after service and introduced himself. He said he worked with one of the members of the church and that this member had faithfully given him a tape of the sermons each week. They spoke for a while, but bottom line, he just wanted to say thank you to the evangelist because he didn't know anything about Jesus or the Bible before listening to the tapes, so he just wanted to meet him. He also brought a friend and wanted the friend to meet him. He looked at his friend and then turned back to the evangelist and asked, "What was your name again?" Later the evangelist was asked if it bothered him that the man forgot his name. The evangelist said, "I was thrilled. He simply remembered the message and not the messenger. Isn't that, after all, what's important?"*

Will a leader make decisions? Yes. Will he give direction? Yes, but it is all in the spirit of service, love, and deep concern for his friends—so much so that he would sacrifice his life (or even being remembered) for that of his friends, which was so vividly demonstrated by Jesus' death on a cross at the risk of no one caring or remembering. Read John 13:17 again: "Now that you know these things, you will be blessed [happy] if you do them"; i.e., the things that a servant does.

#48. Let Your Light Shine!

Opening activity: Turn off the lights. Light each one of the following items: match, flashlight, and halogen lamp. For each one, ask the group the following questions:
1. What is it?
2. What is its purpose?

In regard to intensity of light, how would you rank these three objects?
How do these items relate to you as an individual?
How do these items relate to you as a group?

What is the main characteristic that distinguishes each of these objects?
- The amount of light each one gives; otherwise they are basically the same

[Read Mark 4:21-24]
What is the purpose of light?
- To help us see

Why do you put a lamp on a stand?
- So the greatest amount of light can be given away

Jesus tells you to carefully consider what you hear.
What is it that he is trying to tell you in verse 24?
- That if you give, God returns the same amount plus more

{Get two volunteers. Give each a spoon attached to a broomstick or long dowel; tell them they are trapped and the only way to get out is to finish their bowls of crushed Oreos (or any other food). See what happens. The goal is for them to "escape" together by helping each other out—feeding each other.}

This exercise is based on a man's dream of heaven and hell: having a meal with a 6-foot-long fork and spoon, the difference between a starved group (hell) and a well-fed group (heaven) is whether you feed each other because your arms are too short to feed yourself.

What part of this can you control?

- Only the giving part

? What does Jesus mean when he says, "Whoever has will be given more; whoever does not have, even what he has will be taken from him"?

This passage, as with so many others, is about giving. Each one of you has the capacity to give. Not all of you are halogen lamps, the greatest givers, but all of you can give something. Some of you may only be a match, but how would one keep warm without a campfire or see without many candles lit? Some of you may only be a flashlight, but how would one walk in the dark or see on a dark trail? Jesus wants you to carefully listen because he knows the truth about giving: that if you give as much as you can, under any circumstance, God will give just as much in return and many times more! If you don't give, you will become so self-focused that love, peace, faith, and happiness will disappear, having been taken from you.

Do you want that? No, I didn't think you would... So, begin ways of giving in your homes, to your friends, for missions, in here, or at middle school activities. Everything you are a part of is impacted by how much you give, whether the recipients are thousands of miles away in another part of the world or in the next bedroom of your house.

#49. Liars Are Losers

Randomly divide your group into smaller groups of five or less. Explain to the kids that they will teach the lesson tonight. Handpick one of the groups (2-4 kids) to include several of your most honest kids, not necessarily your "leaders" or loudest kids. Except for the handpicked group, give each group of one the scriptures listed below:

Proverbs 12:19	Proverbs 12:22	Proverbs 21:6
Proverbs 26:28	Proverbs 16:13	Luke 16:10
Proverbs 10:9	Proverbs 11:3	Psalm 7:7-8

You may not have to use all of the scriptures; choose which ones will work the best for your group. Give each group 10-15 minutes to prepare a 2-3 minute presentation that will teach everyone else what their scripture means. They can teach it, preach it, and do a skit or anything creative; however, each person in the group must participate and the scripture must be read aloud.

While the groups are preparing, take the handpicked group aside and explain to them that you want them to be the last group to present by preaching about lying and being honest. Tell them that their scripture is Revelation 21:8. Ask them, "What do you think about lying?" "Do you like it?" "Why is lying wrong?" "What damage does lying cause?" "What happens if you continue to lie?" and other such questions. This will get their minds and their hearts thinking about what lying really means and the damage it does. Get them ready to preach—the better you prepare them, the better this will come across. Help them see this is their chance to say all the things they've wanted to say about and to liars! Fire them up! Your goal is to have people leave ready to change, to do whatever it takes to repent. Lying is a middle school thing because they are so worried about what people think about them and about getting into trouble. Satan has fooled them into believing that the truth will not set them free—help them see the light!

After the preaching, close out by saying, "You've heard the Word preached tonight. We'd be fools not to listen. Let me give you four practical ways to be honest: 1) Confess anything you've lied about and start tonight with a clean slate, 2) pray that you will tell the truth no matter how much it hurts, 3) don't tell half-truths or exaggerate, and 4) think! Think about the harm it will do to yourself and to others if you lie. If you are going to have enemies, have them because you are a person of integrity not because you are liar."

#50. Living in Harmony

? What is the definition of harmony?
- A pleasing mix of elements that form a whole; agreement of feeling

{Divide into groups. Being sure to involve each member, have each group create a representation of the meaning of harmony. Present each group's creation. Once finished, continue the discussion.}

? What is the opposite of harmony?
- Disharmony

? Which would you rather have, harmony or disharmony in your relationships? Why?

[Read Romans 12:16-18]
What kind of heart creates disharmony? {Draw them out. Ask probing questions. Ask for examples. Spend some time on this.}

?
- Prideful. How?
- Conceited. How?
- Disobedient. How?
- Selfish. How?

? How have you felt when you were treated in this manner?

[Read 1 Peter 3:8-9]
? What attitudes promote harmony?
- Sympathy, compassion
- Love
- Humility

What will you need to change to promote harmony with your friends and in your family? {Help them to identify the sin. It can most likely be boiled down to one of the four things above. Make a list of each person's sin.}

If you are going to have tight relationships among this group, you must be willing to have the kind of heart we discussed and change the thing that is written down.

? Is everyone willing to change? Would you like some accountability with this? If so, let me know and I will help you.

#51. Looking for Faith

{Hide $5 or $10 in the room and tell them that whoever finds it can have it. Make sure they don't destroy the room!}

Tell me about a time when you frantically searched for something.
How did you feel?
Why did you look for it so intently?

The Bible says that Jesus will come back one day.
What do you think he will look for?
- [Luke 18:8] He will look for faith.

What is faith? **[Read Hebrews 11:1]**
- Being sure of something

Describe ways we exercise faith in everyday life.
- Sit in a chair, start a car, expect the sun to rise

What does Jesus want us to be sure of?
What are the advantages of having faith? [Hebrews 11:1-4]
What are some ways you can measure your level of faith?

Three ways:
1. Worry [Matthew 6:25-34]
How can worry be a barometer of faith?
What do you worry about?
What can you do to relieve worry?

2. Obedience [Matthew 8:5-13]
How could Jesus tell the centurion was a man of faith?
How does obedience reflect faith?
When is it hardest for you to obey?

3. Tough situations [Matthew 8:23-26]
Why did Jesus say they had little faith?
How do you respond to situations you can't control?

Tools to Help Preteen and Young Teen Leaders and Parents

? How does fear rob your faith?
What situations challenge your faith?

? Does faith come naturally? Why not?
What are ways you can strengthen your faith?

> *Blondin lived from 1824-1897 and was a famous French tightrope walker and acrobat. His highest fame came in 1859 when he accomplished one of his greatest feats for the first time: walking a 1,100-foot tightrope suspended 160 feet above the waters of Niagara Falls. Blondin went on to walk across the falls several times, each time with a different theatrical flair. On one such high-wire walk Blondin crossed over the falls pushing a wheelbarrow. When he reached the other side, he asked the spectators if they believed he could do it again. Everyone cheered. Blondin then asked if they believed he could again cross the tightrope with someone in the wheelbarrow. Everyone cheered, believing that he could do it and wanting to see this incredible stunt. Blondin then asked for a volunteer to ride in the wheelbarrow. No one stepped forward.*

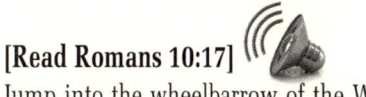

[Read Romans 10:17]
Jump into the wheelbarrow of the Word this week. Dig into your Bible. Think about scriptures that can help you. Put them in your mind and your heart. Faith must be developed, like muscles or your brain (learning math). It can't be done by anyone else but you.

#52. Making a Change

Opening activity: Have everyone get a partner and stand back to back with their partner. Have each person change three things about them (i.e. remove watch, untuck shirt, etc.). Turn and face each other and guess what the other person changed. Take five minutes or so to do this.

1. How many of you removed something to make a change?

[Read Matthew 5:27-30]
What is this talking about?
- Getting rid of sin

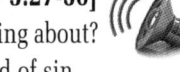

What is sin?
How does sin affect you?
What are some sins that get to you?

Find out which sin is dogging you and destroy it. Some of you would rather your whole body be thrown into hell than get rid of that one thing. Please don't be this person.

2. How many of you asked someone else what you could change?

[Read Ecclesiastes 4:9-10]
What is this teaching you?
What will it take for you to be this kind of friend?

Some of you don't have these kinds of friends because you won't let anyone be that close to you nor do you want to give that much. Please let someone help you.

3. How many of you kept the changes you made to yourself?

[Read Proverbs 26:11]
What does this teach you?
What will it take for you not to be a fool in regard to what you want to change?
- Friends that know
- Being fed up with it

Tools to Help Preteen and Young Teen Leaders and Parents

- Self-discipline

Some of you eat the same old throw-up over and over. Make changing a part of your character.

Isn't it about time to be serious about the changes you want to make? Change is not easy, but by cutting a sin out, asking a friend for help, and making lasting changes, you can be different by the end of this year (or month!). Let's go make a change!

#53. Mind over Matter

Game: Ship's Captain

You are the captain. The kids are the crew. Read to the crew your orders before starting the game. This gives them a chance to remember as many as possible. As you call out the orders listed below, eliminate people who don't follow orders. The idea is to see how many people have the mental capacity stay in the game.

ORDER	RESPONSE
To the ship	Run to the right.
To the island	Run to the left.
Hit the deck	Lie down on your stomach.
Attention on deck	Salute and yell, "Aye, aye captain!" Players may not move now until the captain gives the order of, "At ease." (I.e. even if the captain gives a different order such as "To the ship," the crew must remain at attention until told "At ease.")
Three in a boat	The crew must form groups of three and sing "Row, Row, Row Your Boat." Anybody who is not in a group of three is out.
The love boat	Crewmembers grab a partner and dance. Anybody without a partner is out.
Scrub the deck	Everyone on their hands and knees scrubbing.
Up periscope	Every player falls on their back and sticks one leg in the air. The last one is eliminated.
SHARK!	Everyone must run to a designated base (multiple bases can be used). The last player to the base is eliminated.
Sick turtle	Everyone falls onto their backs and waves hands and feet in the air.
Row the boat	Each player finds a partner, sits face-to-face, holds hands, and pretends to row a boat. Players who can't find partners or who are too slow are eliminated.

What does it take to be spiritual? {Make a list so the kids can see their answers. Circle the word "mind" if it is said; add it if not. (I wonder if they will mention it, which may serve to help disprove the fallacy that spirituality is an all heart-emotion-passion thing. Hmmm.)}

{Divide the group into two teams, and give each team a sheet of paper with the scriptures listed below. In 15 minutes, have them prepare an argument using the scriptures listed. The purpose of this is threefold: to get them to work together, to get them in the Bible (and the Bible in them), and to realize that they must think to be godly. Give time for each group to present their argument and then close out. {You may want to study this out for yourself and close with your convictions on the matter.}

Using one or more of the scriptures below as evidence, argue **FOR** this statement: *"It takes one's mind to be spiritual."*

1 Samuel 2:35	1 Samuel 15:29
1 Chronicles 28:9	2 Chronicles 30:12
Psalm 26:1-5	Psalm 64:6
Isaiah 26:3	Isaiah 26:3
Isaiah 46:8-9	Jeremiah 17:10
Lamentations 3:21-22	Ezekiel 11:5-6
Matthew 16:23	Luke 10:25-27
Luke 21:14	Acts 4:32
Romans 1:28-32	Romans 7:21-25
Romans 8:5	Romans 12:2
Romans 14:13	1 Corinthians 1:10
1 Corinthians 2:16	Ephesians 6:18
Philippians 3:19	Colossians 2:18

#54. No Slipup Here!

Opening activity: See how many people can guess who said the following slip-ups: {or find your own at www.slipups.com}
1. After Tiger Woods told her that he loved her music and had all her CDs, who said, "I don't follow tennis so I don't know much about you." [Christine Aguilera]
2. After the King of Jordan died, who said, "Oh, what a tragedy! He did so much for all the little children with his charity work, and it will be a big loss to the world of basketball." [Mariah Carey]
3. When asked, "What was the best thing you've ever read?" who answered, "You mean like a book?" [Justin Timberlake]
4. When speaking about education, who said, "Rarely is the question asked: Is our children learning?" ["George Dubya" Bush, quoted in Rolling Stone]

? What are some controversial issues today?
What makes them so controversial?
Would you say religion is controversial? Why?
What are some controversial religious topics?

[Read Mark 8:27-29] Jesus has been controversial for the last 2000 years.
? What makes Jesus so controversial?
- He claimed to be God, the Creator, the Almighty, the One and Only!

Let's look at this idea of Jesus being God.

Two alternatives: true or false
If false, two alternatives: knew it and lied, or didn't know it and was crazy.

LIAR?

? How could he be proved to be a liar?
If he were proven to be a liar, what else would he be?
- A hypocrite—not doing what he said told people to do

[Read John 8:42-47]
? If Jesus was a liar and a hypocrite, and was someone whom the religious leaders wanted to see fail, why didn't someone come forward and answer this question

and disprove everything he ever claimed to be?
- B/c they couldn't!

? Can you think of anyone you know who hasn't sinned?
- No. Everyone we know has sinned!

? Would you die for something you knowingly lied about?
- No, so maybe he didn't know he was lying and was a...

LUNATIC?
[Read Mark 3:20-21] His family thought that way.
[Read John 10:19-21] This was debated then, too.

? What do you think? Is he crazy?
Could he really do miracles if he was crazy?

? If not a liar or a lunatic, then what?
- He must be Lord.

? If he is Lord, then what choice are you left with?
- To accept or to reject the fact that Jesus is who claimed to be.

On the southbound side of Interstate 5 in Valencia CA, the home of Six Flags Magic Mountain, is a large Disneyland billboard with a single word dominating 75% of the space. The word? "Believe." That's the gospel message: believe. It is the same word, but with a different meaning. Disney is asking the public to suspend their disbelief for a time and enter into their enchanted kingdom for a day of recreation. They want us to pretend, for a time, that "make believe" is worth believing in. That is not the gospel message. God doesn't ask people to believe what isn't true; rather, he wants them to believe what is known to be true!

Many of you believe because that is what is printed on your billboard all your life—what you've been told to believe—but how many of you are actually checking it out? This truth has to be your conviction. People mess up what they say (as the examples we read show!) and what they do all the time. Yet Jesus, in 2000 years, has yet to be misquoted or found in any slipup column. Why? Because Jesus was, and is, the truth. No slipup here! I challenge you to check it out; if you don't, you may be missing out on the most amazing thing in life.

#55. Nothing Is Hidden

? Does a tree make a sound if it falls and no one is there to hear it? Why or why not?
Is sin wrong if no one is there to see it? Why or why not?

? What is sin?
What sins are obvious?
What are some sins that are not so obvious?

[Read Hebrews 4:12-13]
? Why do you try to hide sin?
What advantages are there to hiding your sin?

Let's look at an example of someone who tried to hide his sin.

{Briefly explain Joshua chapter six regarding Jericho and how they were to bring down the wall. [vv. 17-19] Highlight that God told them to completely destroy the city and to keep away from any of the devoted things. While explaining the context, emphasize this scripture; you might even have someone read it.}

[Read Joshua 7]
? [V.1] Why was God angry?
[Vv. 2-12] Did Joshua know about Achan's sin?
How did he find out?

{Explain verses 13-19 about the tribe-by-tribe thing.}
? [Vv. 20-21] What was Achan's sin?
How did Joshua discover it was Achan?

Like you, Achan thought he was getting away with something. He thought he could fool everyone around him...and he did! He also thought he could fool God...he did not. Neither can you! Let me tell you some things I know that you thought you kept hidden {fill in your own—these are my students'}: writing cuss words, gossip, and nasty things inside the front cover of your Bibles and journals; letters your parents have found in which you brag about having sex; lying to your parents about boyfriends or girlfriends; trying to sneak off; cussing at school and on the bus. There are things you're thinking about right now...things that will be uncovered sooner or later. Understand that you will be found out—nothing is hidden from God!

#56. OJT: On-the-Job Training

? What does OJT mean?
- On-the-job training

? What are some examples of OJT in the Bible?
- Joshua in Moses' tent [Exodus 33:11], Paul ("Go into the city and you will be told what you must do" [Acts 9])

Look at a famous one: Gideon [Judges 6:11-12]; God called him a mighty warrior.

Tonight, we are going to play some games and take a few minutes to learn from each one.

1. One Another
    a. First round: With two volunteers do the following:
        i. Spread a deck of cards on the floor in front of each one.
        ii. Tell them they are to put the cards in order from ace to king by suits.
        iii. Time them.
        iv. Fastest one wins a prize (gum, candy, etc.)
    b. Second round: With two teams of four do the following:
        i. Steps i-iii above
        ii. Fastest team wins

[Read 1 Thessalonians 5:11] We get better because of each other; always have someone in your life.

2. Strengthen Your Mind
    a. Write some custom license plates on a flip chart and see if the kids can guess what they mean:
        i. FASN8 = fascinate
        ii. KONX = connects
        iii. N4CMNT = enforcement
        iv. XNTU8THE+ = accentuate the positive
        v. W8R = waiter

[Read Romans 12:2] Renew your mind—put it to use. If you want to be more spiritual, you must practice thinking spiritually.

3. Listening
   a. Tell the group the following word problem. Repeat it only once. "You are driving a bus. You go east 12 miles, turn south and go 2 miles, and take on 9 passengers; then you turn west and go 3 miles and let off 4 passengers. How old is the bus driver?"
   b. Answer: the age of the person answering ("YOU are driving a bus.")

[Read Matthew 15:10, Mark 7:14] Quick to listen—someone tell me what this looks like. Listening is a key to getting spiritual.

You will find yourselves in many situations that are opportunities to get some training if only you will take notice. On-the-job spiritual training can happen every day.

I challenge you to find one thing per day where you can say, "Hey, this reminds me of what God would think or how Jesus would behave."

#57. On the Right Side of Mom

{Mother's Day lesson}

Opening activity: Have the group sit in chairs in a circle. Read the statements below and have the kids follow directions based on each statement.

1. Move one seat to your right if you said, "I love you" to your mom.
2. Move one seat to your left if you had an argument with your mom.
3. Move one seat to your left if you were told to clean your room.
4. Move one seat to your right if you helped with the dishes.
5. Move one seat to your left if you were grounded.
6. Move one seat to your left if you yelled at your mom.
7. Move one seat to your right if you discussed school problems with your mom.
8. Move one seat to your right if you talked with your mom privately.
9. Move one seat to your right if you helped cook a meal.
10. Move one seat to your left if you slammed your bedroom door.
11. Move one seat to your left if you lied to your mom.
12. Move one seat to your left if you have felt your mom was too busy for you.
13. Move one seat to your left if you argued with your mom about the telephone.
14. Move one seat to your right if you talked with your mom about a problem.
15. Move one seat to your right if you cried with your mom.
16. Move one seat to your right if you had a family devotional together.

If you ended up to the right of your original seat you had a positive week with your mom; if to the left, then it was a not-so-positive week; if you ended up in the same seat it was neutral.

? What is today?
- Mother's Day

? What kind of character does it take to make a great mom?
Do you think those characteristics are something she is born with?

{Divide into teams; have each team look up one of the following scriptures and write a word that describes God's character.}

Protective: 2 Thessalonians 3:3
Comforter: Isaiah 66:13
Accepting: Matthew 19:13-15
Compassionate: Isaiah 49:15
Patient: 2 Peter 3:9
Caring: 1 Peter 5:7
Sacrificial: Hebrews 10:5-10

Danny was born with no ears. He could hear all right, but he didn't have ears like normal people. All his life, Danny endured ridicule and rejection because of his deformity, but he learned to live with it. Thankfully, he had loving parents and a strong family to sustain him. When Danny was in high school, his doctor told him of a new procedure that made it possible to transplant ears from one person to another. That meant Danny could get new ears if someone who was compatible to him ever donated theirs. This was exciting news. After all, people donated body parts all the time—hearts, lungs, kidneys. But Danny soon found that donor ears were extremely scarce. Danny didn't give up hope, however. He knew that someday he would get new ears. He graduated from high school with honors and was accepted at a major university thousands of miles away. He kissed his parents goodbye and began his life as a college student. Again, though, he found it hard to make friends and fit in because of his lack of ears.

One day he got a phone call from his father. "Go to the hospital tomorrow, Danny. A donor has been found." The very next day Danny checked into the university hospital where doctors were ready to perform the surgery. A few hours later, Danny had new ears. When the bandages came off, Danny gazed into the mirror for hours. He finally had ears like normal people. For the first time in his life, he wasn't ashamed of the way he looked. He not only had new ears, he had a new life. Some time later, Danny received another phone call from his father. "Son, your mother is very ill," his father said. "She may not live through the night." Danny was on the first plane home. When he arrived, his father gave him the sad news that his mother had died. Together they went to the funeral home, where Danny was able to see his mother for the last time. He leaned over to kiss her cheek. Brushing her hair back from her face, he saw that she had no ears.

Think about the week you had with your mom and make changes this week to be on the right side if asked the same questions.

#58. Priceless

{Split into groups and discuss how much a human being is worth. Allow time to have each group report their values.}

In terms of a financial profile, if we could somehow break down the chemical composition of your body I could tell you your worth. You have within your body enough iron for a nail; enough sugar to fill a sugar bowl; enough fat for seven bars of soap (that may vary from person to person); enough lime to whitewash a chicken coop, enough phosphorous for 2,200 match heads, enough magnesium for the minimum daily dose of magnesium, and enough potassium to shoot a toy cannon, all mixed in with a little sulfur. Even in today's inflated market you are valued at only about $3.50.

? Why do people struggle with feeling worthless?
What would you tell a person who feels they are worthless?

[Read Luke 15:1-10]

? How much did the Pharisees and the teachers of the law think the people were worth?
What influenced their thinking?
What influences your determination of how much you are worth?
How does your way of thinking influence what you think other people are worth?

[Read 1 Timothy 2:1-6]

? What does this scripture (and the parables) teach you in regard to your worth to God?

> Back in 1957 a group of monks from a monastery had to relocate a clay Buddha from their temple to a new location. The monastery was to be relocated to make room for the development of a highway through Bangkok. When the crane began to lift the giant idol, the weight of it was so tremendous that it began to crack. What's more, rain began to fall. The head monk, who was concerned about damage to the sacred Buddha, decided to lower the statue back to the ground and cover it with a large canvas tarp to protect it from the rain. Later that evening the head monk went to check on the Buddha. He shined his flashlight under the tarp to see if the Buddha was staying dry. As the light reached the crack, he noticed a little gleam shining back and thought it strange. As he took a closer look at this gleam of light, he

wondered if there might be something underneath the clay. He went to fetch a chisel and hammer from the monastery and began to chip away. As he knocked off shards of clay, the little gleam grew brighter and bigger. Many hours of labor went by before the monk stood face to face with an extraordinary solid-gold Buddha. It is 10 ½ feet tall and weighs over two and a half tons. The statue is valued at $196,000,000.

Historians believe that several hundred years before the head monk's discovery, the Burmese army was about to invade Thailand (then called Siam). The Siamese monks, realizing that their country would soon be attacked, covered their precious golden Buddha with an outer covering of clay to keep their treasure from being looted by the Burmese. Unfortunately, it appears that the Burmese slaughtered all the Siamese monks, and the well-kept secret of the golden Buddha remained intact until that fateful day in 1957.

As you approach a missions contribution, I would like you to think of how much God thinks each person is worth: the price of a life. Get beyond the crusty outer layer and see people and yourself the way God does. I don't think he would give as a ransom his one and only Son or waste all that energy and resources, if he were not genuine in his care and love for you and others. Do whatever you need to do to get rid of the cover that blocks the real, valuable you! Let's see what you can do to make someone you may never meet feel the same way. I encourage you to talk with your family about a plan for missions.

#59. For Boys: From "Impure" to "I Am Pure"

[Read John 16:5-11]
Explain that Jesus is talking about God's spirit and this is one of the Spirit's roles.

- What is guilt?
- What affect does guilt have on you?
- What are some things that make you feel guilty?

I want to talk about purity tonight. It causes more guilt than most any other sin. It wrecks lives, marriages, homes, careers, and much more! And it all begins right now. What you practice now you will do later.

- What are ways middle schoolers are impure?
- What affect does it have on them?

[Read Ephesians 5:1-7]
- How much is a hint? Very, very little—so not even this much!
- Why would God take such a strong stance on impurity?
  - Improper
  - Selfish
  - Not what he wants
  - Abuse of others

Pornography:
» $20-billion-dollar-a-year worldwide industry.
» There are 100,000 porn sites on the web, with an estimated 200 new sites every day.
» Currently more than 50% of requests on search engines are for porn.
» 10,160 porn movies were released in 1999 alone.
» 70% of unmarried men and 55% of married men view porn once a month.
» There are more porn outlets today than there are McDonalds.
» More than 300 million X-rated videos are distributed each year.

- » Men are 543% more likely than women to view pornography.
- » According to Juniper Research, in 2017, over a quarter of a billion people viewed pornography on their mobile phone.
- » In 2012, Tru Research conducted a 2017 online interview with teens, age 13-17. 71% of teens reported having done something to hide what they do online from their parents.

Adultery:
- » The 1990 Kinsey Report states that around 50% of all married people will commit adultery.
- » 1 in every 4 persons who say they are Christians has committed adultery.
- » 1 in every 10 ministers has committed adultery.
- » In 68% of all divorces involved one party meeting a new lover over the internet.
- » In 56% of all divorces involved one party having "an obsessive interest in pornographic websites."

[Read 1 Thessalonians 4:3-8]

? What can you do to stay pure?

To go from impure to I am pure, you must add an 'A' between the 'I' and the 'M'. A is for Avoid.

? What does it mean to avoid?

A certain man wanted to sell his house for $20,000. Another man wanted very badly to buy it, but because he was poor, he couldn't afford the full price. After much bargaining, the owner agreed to sell the house for half the original price with just one stipulation: he would retain ownership of one small nail protruding from just over the door. After several years, the original owner wanted the house back, but the new owner was unwilling to sell. So the first owner went out, found the carcass of a dead animal, and hung it from the nail he still owned. Soon the house became unlivable and the family was forced to sell the house to the owner of the nail.

If you don't have the conviction to avoid impurity, something you regret will be hanging on your front door. It will force you to sell or move out! Gain conviction about being pure, about honoring God with your body and your thoughts. Avoid it all costs! Go from impure to "I am pure." Don't let it be a nail over your door.

#60. Purity for Girls

Tonight's class deals with something that is all around us, but it is something we rarely talk about.

? What is impurity?
Why is it so hard to talk about?
Why do we feel so guilty?

? What are some ways people your age are impure in everyday life?
- Lustful thoughts
- Flirting
- Movies/TV
- Internet
- Dirty jokes
- Music
- Clothes—the way you dress

? Why are people your age impure?
- Want to fit in
- Curiosity
- For attention

[Read Ephesians 5:1-5]
? What is God's attitude toward impurity?
{Touch on: dress (short shorts, tight clothes, too much skin), flirting, surfing the internet}

? What should we do with impurity?

[Read James 5:16]
? Who should you confess to?

Challenge: [Memorize and put into practice 1 Timothy 4:12.]
"Don't let anyone look down on you because you are young, but set an example for the believers in speech, in conduct, in love, in faith and in purity."

#61. Respect

{Have a good old-fashioned discussion about respect; set a tone of and ask for honesty and openness.}

Tell me one thing you are excited about regarding your time together as a middle school group.
What will it take to make our time together excellent?
What does respect mean?
Is it really necessary? Why or why not?
What makes it hard to do?
What does it take to be respectful?
Does it take perfection from the other person? Why or why not?
To whom is it the hardest for you to be respectful?
What are the benefits of being respectful?
How many of you struggle with being respectful? Do you want help to be more respectful? {Ask for a show of hands or a response from each person.}

1. Must begin by respecting God [Read Luke 11:14-28]
Jesus is teaching, and some woman blurts out a compliment; he reminds the crowd how to be truly blessed (or happy).

Why would Jesus give this answer?
- He must be convinced that it is the best way to live.

Some of you are learning that a respectful attitude is more rewarding, and some of you have yet to learn that.

It all begins with your attitude toward God. The level of respect you have for him determines your level of respect for everybody else.

Great example: NAME {pick someone from your group to hold up}

Pair up and discuss the following quote by Mahatma Gandhi: "You must be the change you want to see in the world." Get a few responses.

2. Must respect authority

? Who are the authority figures in your life?
- Parents [Ephesians 6:1-3]
    - #1 authorities and deserve your respect
    - Great example: NAME {pick someone from your group to hold up}
- Spiritual leaders [1 Thessalonians 5:12-13a]
    - Care for you beyond the obligations of parenthood
    - Great example: NAME {pick someone from your group to hold up}
- Governing officials (teachers, police, coach, etc.) [Romans 13:1-7]
    - Are there to bring order and to check unrighteousness; teachers are in government positions. Your attitude will not make them go away.
    - Great example: NAME {pick someone from your group to hold up}

? {Read the story of three brothers, below.} Which one will you be?

God is right, his way is right, and following him leads to a happier you. You must change your attitude in this area—remember Gandhi's quote? The Scriptures are clear on this subject. God gives you tough situations (i.e. teachers you don't like or people that are hard to respect) so that you can exercise and build up your character muscles. If you develop disrespectful patterns now, they will come back to haunt you, and you will regret not having developed a respectful character. Don't make that mistake.

The story is told about three brothers who started working at the same time for a fur company owned by an old friend of their father.

After working there for more than a year, one son was still receiving the same salary as when he started, and seemed to be unhappy with his job; the second son had received a raise; while the third son had received a very generous raise.

Curious about this, the father went to see his old friend, the president of the company and said, "Jim, my three boys all work for you, and I appreciate your giving them positions in your company. But I have a question. You pay one of them $2,500 a month, another $3,000, and the third $5,000. Why the difference?"

The president leaned back in his chair and was silent for a few moments. Then he answered, "Well, maybe I can show you why. Do you have enough spare time to wait around here for a while?"

"I can stay all day," the father said. "Well, I hope it won't take that long, but let's see." He picked up the phone and called the $2,500-a-month son and told him, "I hear the Ontario has just docked at the wharf, loaded with furs. Please go down there and see what cargo she's carrying and let me know."

About three minutes later the president's phone rang and the young fellow said, "I didn't have to go down there to get the information. I just telephoned them. They're carrying 1,500 sealskins." The president said, "Thank you."

He buzzed the next son, the $3,000 one, and said, "The Ontario has just docked. Will you please go down and see what she has on board and let me know at your earliest convenience?" About an hour later the phone rang and the son reported, "I just went down and checked the Ontario. She has 1,500 sealskins and some miscellaneous skins on board."

Then the president called the third son, the $5,000 one. He said, "The Ontario has docked," and told him the same story and made the same request. Four hours later the young man was back and came right to the president's office. He said, "Well, she had 1,500 sealskins on board and all are in good shape. I contracted to buy them for $25 apiece, and filled that order we had from one of our customers. He bought all of them from us at $40 apiece."

"The Ontario also had 500 red fox pelts. Of course, we don't handle red fox, but I knew someone who did, so I called him long distance and made a sale. That deal will net us about $6,000. There were also 39 mink skins on board. I went in and examined them. They're beautiful. Since you always like to handle the mink trade yourself, I took an option on them for the rest of today so I could report to you."

The president said, "Thank you. You did exactly right, and I'll check them out immediately." Then the young man left. Turning to the father, he asked, "Is your question answered?"

"Yes," replied the father, "the first one didn't even follow your instructions, the second did exactly what you asked, but the last one gave you his very best."

#62. The Resurrection Riddle
{Easter lesson}

Opening activity: Break into teams of 4 or 5 and hand out a page with 3 to 5 brain teasers or riddles and have the groups come up with answers. Don't give them the answers until the end of the lesson.

? What is significant about Easter Sunday to Christians?

? The resurrection of a dead person is sort of like a brain teaser or riddle—can it be answered? Is it possible?

? What does the word "resurrection" mean?
- Comes from root word for resurge, to live again

? Why is the resurrection of Jesus so important to Christianity?
What makes the resurrection hard to believe?

? What are some possible alternate outcomes other than he just came back to life?
- Jesus never died. {too many witnesses against this hypothesis.}
- Went to the wrong tomb.
- Body was stolen. Most likely of all; however, was it possible to pull off?

[Read Matthew 27:62-66]
The stone: [v. 60] "big" stone; Mark says the stone was exceedingly great.
The seal: Provided by the Romans, a rope across the stone fastened with clay
The sentries: Roman, not Jewish, so had no interest in what happened to the man inside; put more sanctity on a Roman seal than the philosophy of a risen savior

Bottom line: could not happen, in fact, by their own mouths it did not happen.
? [Matthew 28:11-15] Why else pay someone to be quiet?

Other Evidences

Grave Clothes:
? What would you expect to see if you walked into the tomb? [John 20:1-8]

They were laid out just as you would expect and consistent with the way he was prepared—powerful enough evidence to cause these men to change their belief about resurrection.

His Appearances:
? Over 500 people saw Jesus. Do you think a huge, far-impacting event could ever be kept a secret? Can you think of some examples?

His Enemies Kept Silent:
? If you hated all that someone stood for wouldn't you try to expose it as a lie?

Psychological Effect:
Countless years of transformed lives because of this event; the best example may be Jesus' own brother, James. [Matthew 13:55, John 7:5, Galatians 1:19]

Sociological Effect:
The birth of the church and its lasting impact on our world

Just like with brainteasers, there are always answers—you just have to think about them. The answer to our riddle is that Jesus did in fact rise from the grave.

Give the answers to the riddles to close out.

#63. Reverse Solarity

Opening activity: Set up four stations each with an "impossible" puzzle; can be brainteasers, riddles, or small handheld puzzles like the two rings or getting four little BBs in four holes, etc. Have small groups rotate through the stations. See how many puzzles are solved. Choose hard puzzles to make it a challenge.

? Thinking bigger than these puzzles: what are some other things that are labeled impossible?

Now, thinking of your life, what do you call impossible?

[Read 2 Kings 20:1-11]

? What happened? What was the miracle? What's the big deal about that?

[Read Joshua 10:1-15]

? What other events took place in order for the sun to stand still for a full day?

? How would you describe these two events involving the sun?
- Nothing less than miraculous—the whole solar system was frozen or reversed. That's incredible!!

Now think again about what you described as impossible.

? How does it compared to what happened in these two stories?

? What did Hezekiah and Joshua exhibit when making such "impossible" requests?

[Read Mark 9:14-29]

{Go over the situation.} Look at the man's attitude: "If you can." I wonder if he ever read what God did with the sun and if it crossed his mind that if God can do that, he can do anything.

? What was Jesus' reaction? With what tone do you think Jesus said. "If you can?"

[Read Hebrews 11:6]
Now, here is something that is impossible: to please God without believing in him and his power.

That's why Jesus responded the way he did: it was impossible for him not to believe in what God can do.

> *A young boy traveling by airplane to visit his grandparents sat beside a man who happened to be a seminary professor. The boy was reading a Sunday school take-home paper when the professor thought he would have some fun with the lad. "Young man," said the professor, "If you can tell me something God can do, I'll give you a big, shiny apple." The boy thought for a moment and then replied, "Mister, if you can tell me something God can't do, I'll give you a whole barrel of apples!"*

Take a minute by yourself to think about your impossible situation and ask, "Is this my attitude?"

#64. Rolling Your Eyes at Authority

Game: Sergeant Hotdog. Line everyone up at attention. They are to follow your orders completely: "No laughing, hands at your sides, no smiling, do everything I say. When I say hotdog, you say bun; when I say your, you say mama…" Keep making up orders and eliminate people who don't follow your orders completely, until you get down to the last one. Give a prize.

? What did you observe about the game?

[Read Mark 1:21-28]

? What about Jesus' teaching amazed the people?

? What was different about Jesus' teaching compared to the teachers of the law?
- Knew the truth
- Lived it
- Passionate for God's word and law
- Confident
- Expected a response; called for repentance

? Did anyone know that this man was demon possessed?
- Obviously not, or they would not have let him in the synagogue.

? What made the evil spirits in him cry out?
- Realized a man of authority was present

? Who are the authorities in your life?
- Parents, teachers, coaches, spiritual leaders

? Why do they have authority?

? What makes you cry out against authority?

? How should you respond to authority, especially your parent's authority?

[Read Hebrews 13:17]
How does obedience benefit you?
I have talked with many of your parents and watched many of your interactions with them. It is shameful how some of you respond to your parents. It is time for you to mature and realize that you are under authority. Even the evil spirits understood who was in charge and obeyed when they were given an order by Jesus to shut up. Why do some of you wait until your parents get upset before you will listen? This is of no advantage to you. Many of you worry about your parents being wrong. Don't! This verse says that they will answer to God for it—your only role is to obey.

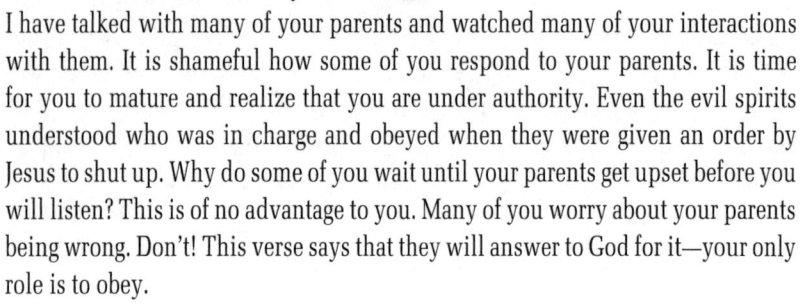

Challenge: Obey your parents the first time and see if your week isn't happier.

#65. Running Your Race

Opening activity: Show the video *Iron Man* or read the first five paragraphs of the chapter called "It Takes Two, Baby. Dick and Rick Hoyt" in the book *The Heart of a Champion for Kids*, pages 20-31, or go to http://www.teamhoyt.com/About-Team-Hoyt.html.

[Read Hebrews 12:1]
We've all got a race to run, a race marked out for us.

What was the race marked out for this dad?
How could this dad have responded to this race?

What race is marked out for you?
What choices do you have in regard to your race?
What do you feel as you face your race?

Some of you may have short races—something you want to accomplish this year. Some of you may be thinking about more eternal races—spiritual races. Either way, you have to face your race with the right heart and mindset. I have some suggestions as you face your race:

1. Focus
"Throw off everything that hinders and the sin that so easily entangles." Some of you want to have your cake and eat it too. You can't have worldly friends and expect to be godly. You can't have sex on the internet and expect to be pure. You can't have your mommy always wake you up and do everything for you and expect to have a great relationship with God. When are you going to grow up and be focused on something you want?

» If you want to be a great drummer, then have the character to focus on it and practice.
» If you want great grades, then have the character to do your homework.
» If you want to be spiritual, then have the character to focus on it: to get out of bed when the alarm goes off, to stop sinning, to make one spiritual goal and go for it!

Star Wars quote: "Your focus determines your reality."
—Qui-Gon Jinn to Anakin Skywalker

2. Friend

"The race marked out for us"; "surrounded by such a great cloud of witnesses"—you are not in this alone. You need to go public with the race you have chosen for this year or for this life; then and only then will you make it. If you don't have a best friend in this room, then you will not change a thing. That's what friends are for.

[Read Ecclesiastes 4:9-10]
Some of you won't let yourself have a friend.
Some of you won't open up to a friend.

Now, choose your friends wisely. You're saying, "What do you mean? I've got friends. Look at..." Yeah, but are they a part of the great cloud of witnesses or the hindrances and entanglements?

If you are going to run your race, you must have focus and you must have a friend.

Your race is yours alone. No one can run it for you. With the right focus and the right friends, you can run your race as one who will win the prize.

#66. Self-Control

Game: "Ask but Don't Tell." Four groups of 15 get into circles. Each person has 3 seconds to pass a question to someone by stating the question and using eye contact only. The person being asked can't answer the question, can't laugh or respond in any way for 5 seconds...or they're out! This game is about having self-control. Then that person repeats the process by choosing another person with eye contact only using a different question; no question can be repeated. If any response is made by the person being asked, they are out and the person who got them out asks someone else another question. The last one standing wins.

? What are your observations about the game? What is the key to succeeding?

[Read Titus 2:6]
? What does it mean to be self-controlled?

Give me examples of someone lacking self-control.

? What do you think about these people?

[Read 1 Peter 5:8]
? What is the devil prowling around looking for?
- A chance to pounce on you; for you to do something foolish

? What are some foolish things a person who lacks self-control might do?

{Use the following list. If one is said, turn to the scripture and look at what the Bible has to say about it.}
- Talk too much – Proverbs 10:8
- Talk about people – Proverbs 10:18
- Embarrass our families – Proverbs 11:29
- Snap back – Proverbs 12:16
- Don't seek advice – Proverbs 12:15
- Hotheaded and reckless – Proverbs 14:16
- Doesn't want to learn – Proverbs 15:14
- Mouths off – Proverbs 18:2
- Perverse mouth – Proverbs 19:1

- Fights, quarrels – Proverbs 20:3
- Thinks they're all that – Proverbs 26:12
- Picks fights; gives a hard time – Proverbs 27:3
- Arrogant, conceited – Proverbs 28:26
- Angry at parents – Proverbs 29:11
- Answers w/out thinking – Proverbs 29:20

Bottom line:
- » A godly character is one of self-control.
- » You are responsible for your own actions.
- » You cannot control what other people do and they cannot control you.
- » You are the final decision maker, not your parents, your friends, or your enemies...ONLY YOU!

#67. Tale of Two Sons

Opening skits:

Part 1
Scene: Jesus enters temple and begins to teach the people (the rest of the group) a parable. As he is talking, some chief priests and elders enter and interrupt him.

Jesus: "Now there was a farmer who went out to sow his seed. As he was scattering the seed…"

Chief Priest One: *[Walking in and interrupting Jesus]* "By what authority are you doing these things? And who gave you this authority?"

Jesus: *[turning to them]* "I will ask you one question. If you answer me, I will tell you by what authority I am doing these things. John's baptism—where did it come from? Was it from heaven, or from men?"

Elder: *[huddling them together]* "What do you think?"

Chief Priest Two: "If we say from heaven, he will ask, 'then why didn't you believe him?'"

Chief Priest One: "But if we say from men, what will the people say, for they believe John was a prophet."

Elder: "Why don't we say we don't know and see what Jesus does?"

Chief Priest One: *[breaking up the huddle and turning to Jesus]* "We don't know."

Jesus: *[Turning his attention back to the people he was teaching but directing his comment to the chief priests and the elders]* "Then neither will I tell you by what authority I am doing these things."

Part 2
Scene: Father is in the kitchen preparing his breakfast. Son #1 comes down and fixes a cup of coffee. Son #2 enters after son #1 leaves.

Father: [To son #1] "Your sister is coming home from the hospital this morning, and I can't be at the store today. Will you go and manage things until I can get there this afternoon?"

Son #1: "No, I can't, Dad. I made plans...besides, I don't like working at the store."

[Son #2 enters]

Father: "I have to pick up your sister from the hospital this morning, and I can't be at the store today. Will you go and manage things until I can get there this afternoon?"

Son #2: "Yea, no problem"

[Everyone leaves stage. Customer enters the store holding a list of supplies. Looks around but can't find what she needs.]

Son #1: "May I help you?"

{Have several kids perform part 1 of the skit.}

[Read Matthew 21:23-27]
The chief priests and elders confront Jesus because they don't understand who he is.

? What other ways could Jesus have answered these questions?
- "I am the Son of God. God gave this authority to me. Can't you believe because of the miracles I've done?"
- Got up in their grill: "Who are you to question me?"
- "Go away. Don't bother me with your questions."
- Ignored them.

? Why did Jesus answer their question with a question?
- Kept the attention on WHAT is important not on WHO is important.

By answering the way he did, he kept the focus on their heart.

Tools to Help Preteen and Young Teen Leaders and Parents

? What did this question reveal about their character?
- More concerned with themselves than with God's honor

{Ask the group the following question. Remind them to give careful consideration to the affect their answer will have on themselves and their friends. Ask it like Jesus asked the chief priests and the elders.}

? To make God proud of you—what do you think: no matter what or only when possible?
{Fill in what is appropriate for your group. I chose these because it fit.}

{Have several kids perform part 2 of the skit.}

[Read Matthew 21:28-32]

? Why did Jesus tell this parable to the chief priests and the elders?
Which son are they like?
Which son are you like? Stand up if you are like the first son; stand up if you are like the second son.

? Based on his actions, what can you learn about the second son's character?

? Why would the tax collectors and the prostitutes believe John before the chief priests and elders?
- They didn't worry about what people thought of them and they didn't get caught up in their own self-righteousness. They knew they were sinful and had nothing to lose in regard to their reputation.

? What did Jesus tell the chief priests and the elders they needed to do?
- Repent

You've got to repent of selfishness and people pleasing and seek God's approval. Be real! If you want to do what's right, then do it, no matter who is around you. If you don't, then at least have the guts and character to be the same. You worry far too much about what people think of you, when you should consider what God thinks of you. Don't be like the chief priests and the elders!

#68. Taming the Tongue

Opening activity: Divide everyone into five groups. Give each group one of the scriptures below and have them prepare a skit to communicate what the scripture is trying to prevent.

1. [Ephesians 4:29] Put downs/Slams/Discouragement
2. [Philippians 4:10-13] Complaining/Discontent
3. [Proverbs 11:13, 16:28] Gossip/Slander
4. [Ephesians 4:31-32] Anger with parents or siblings

{After each skit, read the scripture and preach the lesson to be learned. Take about 2-3 minutes between each skit to do this. The goal is to get across how impacting the tongue can be. If you have time, close out with James 3:3-6. Otherwise, encourage them to use their tongue wisely and for a noble purpose.}

"When we put bits into the mouths of horses to make them obey us, we can turn the whole animal. Or take ships as an example. Although they are so large and are driven by strong winds, they are steered by a very small rudder wherever the pilot wants to go. Likewise, the tongue is a small part of the body, but it makes great boasts. Consider what a great forest is set on fire by a small spark. The tongue also is a fire, a world of evil among the parts of the body. It corrupts the whole body, sets the whole course of one's life on fire, and is itself set on fire by hell." —James 3:3-6

Challenge: Say something good to someone each day of the next week and keep a record of what you say and who you say it to. Bring this record in next week.

#69. Temptation? What Temptation?

{Before class, place two $5 or $10 bills somewhere in sight in the same room where you will have this discussion. Watch to see if someone turns them in or keeps them.}

? What is the show *Temptation Island* all about?
Which temptations are being promoted?
What temptations do you face?
- Drugs, alcohol, lust, greed, deceit, laziness, anger, selfishness, gossip, slander

? What situations bring about these temptations?
When are there no temptations?
- There are very few times! Temptations are something we have to deal with.

? What is the definition of the word "temptation"?
- Wanting to do something you know you shouldn't

Does temptation equal sin?
{Have everyone participate in a debate to see: have them stand on the right side of the room if they believe temptation is a sin; or stand on the left side of the room if they believe temptation is not a sin. Give each side two minutes to prepare three arguments for their side. The right side is correct, but this shows that this is a confusing issue.}

[Read Matthew 4:1-11] Jesus was tempted.
[Read Hebrews 4:14-15] Jesus did not sin.

? What do these scriptures teach about temptation and sin?
- Not the same; Jesus was tempted yet he did not sin!

? What does this say about the possibility of avoiding sin?

? How can we resist temptations?
- Think of something else.

- Think of scriptures.
- Use self-control.
- Ask if this will do me any good.
- Set a goal not to sin.
- Do the opposite of the sin.
- Think: how will God feel if I do this?

[Read 1 Peter 5:8]
BE:
- Sober minded
- Alert, ready
- Firm

{Tell everyone you placed some money in the room. If it was turned in, publicly praise the person(s) who turned it in. (In fact, you could give it to them; after all, the Bible does say God rewards our righteousness.) Ask them if they were tempted to keep it and if they felt guilty for feeling tempted. If the money is kept, don't make a spectacle of the "keeper," but talk about the decisions it took to keep the money. Ask that the person give it back privately; if they don't come to you right away, go to them in private to ask for it back.}

Some of you feel guilty because you are confused, but temptation is not sin; no one goes to hell just because they were tempted, only because they continue to sin! Recognize the difference between temptation and sin, and decide not to sin by being alert and self-controlled.

#70. Tenacity: The Never-Give-Up Kind of Character

Opening activity: Have everyone in your group pair up. Give each pair one of the logic problems (see below). Tell them that they have the whole time tonight to work on their problem. Have some candy bars or some kind of prize for those who finish.

Once you get the feel that they are starting to give up, get their attention and have the following discussion:

- What does the following Chinese proverb mean? "The man who moved the mountain began by carrying away small stones."

- What does it mean to be tenacious?
  What does it mean to be persevering?
  How do you get a tenacious or persevering character?
  How can perseverance help you right now?

[Read Galatians 6:9]
- When are you most likely to give up?
  What causes you to give up?

[Read Galatians 6:7-8]
- What does it mean, "A person will reap what they sow?"
  How does this encourage you to persevere?

You are one of three types of people: those who do not want to be godly, those who want to be godly, and those who aren't sure. For those of you who do not want to be godly, I hope you change your mind, because God cannot be mocked and you will reap what you sow. For those who want to be or aren't sure, keep doing what is right, for you will reap a harvest if you only persevere. Decide to neither give up nor to allow yourself to be persuaded to give up.

Some of you are trying or have tried to change things in your life—keep at it, begin again! The mountain will move if you just keep moving one small stone at a time. The struggle will be worth it.

Now go back and finish your problem and win the prize!

BURNING ROPE
There are two lengths of rope. Each one can burn in exactly one hour. They are not necessarily of the same length or width as each other. They also are not of uniform width (may be wider in the middle than on the end), thus burning half of the rope is not necessarily 1/2 hour. By burning the ropes, how do you measure exactly 45 minutes' worth of time?

THE MAN WITH THE HAT
There are four men standing in front of a firing squad. Two of them (nos. 1 and 3) wear black hats and two of them (nos. 2 and 4) wear white hats. They are all facing the same direction and between no. 3 and no. 4 stands a brick wall (see diagram). So, no. 1 can see nos. 2 and 3, no. 2 sees no. 3, no. 3 sees only the wall, and no. 4 doesn't see a thing. The men know that there are two white and two black hats. The commander of the firing squad is willing to let the men go if one of them can say what color hat he is wearing. The men are not allowed to talk. The only thing they may say is "I'm wearing a white/black hat." If one of the men knows which hat he is wearing he must tell it and all men will be free. Which of the men can be 100% sure what color hat he's wearing?
=>
I II I I
1 2 3 4

THE FAMILY REUNION
At a family reunion were the following people: one grandfather, one grandmother, two fathers, two mothers, four children, three grandchildren, one brother, two sisters, two sons, two daughters, one father-in-law, one mother-in-law, and one daughter-in-law. But not as many people attended as it sounds. How many were there, and who were they?

GOOD BARGAIN
Two strangers from different parts of America both build similar apartment buildings in their hometowns. By chance, they both forget an important part of their project. They each, once again by chance, call the same national hardware store and order the missing items. The prices they are quoted are as follows: one will cost them $2, two will cost them $2, twelve will cost them $4, and a hundred and forty-four will cost $6. What was the item they needed?

GRAIN SILOS
Three grain silos have the following capacity: A) 8000 kilos, B) 5000 kilos, and C) 3000 kilos. A is full; B and C are empty. Can you, without weighing, put 4000 kilos in silo A and 4000 kilos in silo B?

Answer Key
BURNING ROPE
ANSWER: If you light both ends of one rope, it will burn in exactly 1/2 hour. Thus, burn one rope from both ends and the other rope from only one end. Once the one rope (which is burning from both ends) finally burns out (and you know 1/2 hour has elapsed), you also know that the other rope (which is burning from only one end) has exactly 1/2 hour left to burn. Since you only want 45 minutes, light the second end of the rope. This remaining piece will burn in 15 minutes. Thus, 45 minutes will have elapsed.

THE MAN WITH THE HAT
ANSWER: No. 1 may see two hats of the same color, in which case he knows for sure he is wearing the opposite color, speaks up, and the group is spared. If he sees a white and a black hat in front of him, he cannot tell what color hat he is wearing, so he keeps his mouth shut. Because no. 1 does not say anything, no. 2 knows that no. 1 must see a black and a white hat. No. 2 therefore knows that he wears a hat the opposite color of the one he sees that no. 3 is wearing; he speaks up and the group is saved.

THE FAMILY REUNION
ANSWER: There were two little girls and a boy, their parents, and their father's parents, totaling seven people.

GOOD BARGAIN
ANSWER: The people in the puzzle both forgot to add address numbers to their buildings. If each individual number cost them $2, then One (the number 1) will cost $2...and so forth. The number one forty-four is three digits (1, 4, 4.), and so costs 6 bucks.

GRAIN SILOS
ANSWER:
A 8 5 5 2 2 7 7 4 4
B 0 0 3 3 5 0 1 1 4
C 0 3 0 3 1 1 0 3 0

#71. The Big Picture

We're going to do a Bible study about two parallel stories, the 9/11 attack and Jesus' death.

{Imagine your group as a compass. At the end of the discussion for each phase, move to the designated point on the compass so that they will get the feel and the visual of another "state of being."}

Phase I: Confident {south}
What was the state of mind of the employees in the Twin Towers before the attacks in regard to being attacked?
- Confident, good life, no fear

How do you think the disciples felt when they were around Jesus?
- Confident, powerful

They had been taught [Isaiah 9:6-7] and did amazing things [Luke 10:17].

Phase II: Shock {east}
How did the nation respond to the 9/11 attacks?
- Shock

How do you think the disciples responded to their king being killed and with his death all the hopes of restoring the Israelite kingdom?
- [Luke 24:13-21] They had thought he was going to redeem Israel. They were sad and shocked that this wasn't working the way they thought it was supposed to.

Phase III: Fears & Doubts {north}
What do you think the citizens of New York felt days after the attack? Why?

[Read John 20:19]
What were the disciples feeling?
- Fear

Tools to Help Preteen and Young Teen Leaders and Parents

Why?
- Afraid that it wasn't over; of what would happen to them for being associated with Jesus

? What happens to your faith when you fear?
- Doubt

Phase IV: Faith {west}
? Could this happen again?
- Nobody really knows.

[Read John 20:24-28]
? How did Thomas react?
- Wouldn't believe until saw the evidence, then he exclaimed, "My Lord and my God!"

Nobody knows what will happen to our lives each day. Neither could the disciples. Jesus dying on the cross was a catastrophic event in their life and in their political ideas. They didn't see how this fit into the big picture. Use the picture book by Tana Hoban, *Take Another Look*.

? How did the cross fit into the picture?
- Redemption was indeed Jesus' purpose—just not the way they thought!

? What are some godly purposes this event may have?
- Save people, more people studying the Bible, have a godly confidence {at this point move to south position again}

No matter what, God has a plan.

[Read 2 Thessalonians 3:1-3]
We live in a world of evil, among faithless people who will resort to such acts as September 11, 2001, but he is faithful and will protect you. Believe that! He is faithful! I want you to feel safe, not shocked; be faithful, not fearful. I want you to have confidence in God's faithfulness, the right kind of confidence—because he sees the big picture!

#72. Two Builders

Opening activity: Use decks of cards and have a contest to see which team can build a house of cards using the most number of cards.

[Read Matthew 7:24-27]
What does the house represent?
- Our lives

When it comes to your life, what are some differences between building on rock and sand?
What point is Jesus making in this passage?
What does the sand represent and how do people base their lives on it today?
- Money, other people's opinions, feelings and emotions, traditions and habits, possessions

What does the rock represent?
- The practice of God's word

Practically, how can we build our lives on God's word?
- Read it, obey it

What are some things that keep us from building on the rock of God's word?
- Ignorance, laziness, peer pressure, too busy

In many earthquakes, many of the people who died didn't know they were living right above a dangerous geological fault. Or they knew, but they were too busy or too lazy to do anything about it until it was too late. Right now, WHAT are you building your life on?

[Read Luke 12:16-21]
What do you notice about this builder?
- 11 times in just 4 verses, he says I, me, my, or myself.

Is this man lazy?
- No!

Tools to Help Preteen and Young Teen Leaders and Parents

? Then what is his problem?
- He is building toward the wrong goal.

Tell me about a time when you worked very hard to achieve something, only to find out it wasn't all you had hoped for.

? How are people greedy and self-centered today?
In v. 21, what does it mean to be "rich toward God"?
- To give God your time, money, and priority

? What excuses do people make who are not rich toward God?

CONCLUSION: Today we've looked at two builders. The first had the wrong foundation. His house collapsed during the first crisis, the storm. The second had the wrong goal. He lost his life because he was not rich toward God. Build rightly—you are at a stage in life where it will pay off later in life.

#73. The Choice of Unbelief

? What are the five senses?
What are things you can't detect with those five senses?
- Gravity
- Viruses
- Love
- Dinosaurs
- Wind
- Electrons
- Electricity
- Satan
- Germs
- Hope
- Fear
- Future
- Milky Way Galaxy
- Internet

? Are they real?
How do you know?

[Read Hebrews 11:6]
? What does this verse teach you?

? What must you do before you can please God?
- Believe he exists

{Have the kids close their eyes. Ask for honesty, and then ask for a show of hands of 1) how many do not believe God exists or 2) doubt if he exists. Make a mental note of whom; it could be useful later.}

Despite all the evidence, some of you don't believe God exists or at the very least you wonder about him. In order to help, I would like to invite those that do believe God exists to share one piece of evidence as to why you believe he exists. {Have them stand and give their evidence.}

? How has God rewarded someone you know who has earnestly sought him?

[Read Romans 1:18-20]

? What does Paul mean when he says, "People are without excuse"?
- The evidence is overwhelming and very plain to see that God is real.

? What excuses do people have for not believing God exists?

? Why would they come up these excuses?
- So they can please themselves and not God

Bottom Line: There is no reason why we shouldn't believe in God. The evidence is clear, if only we will look around and see it. Even though you have much to learn about him, I believe that deep down in your hearts, you believe that God does exist. Some of you seventh and eighth graders are learning that sin can be pleasing for a short time; that pleasing yourself feels good. BUT pleasing yourself comes at a high price: hurting yourself or others, hardening your heart and conscience, dealing with the wrath of God. You sixth graders learn from the older ones. I am telling you this because I have talked with people who told me that they weren't sure if they believed God was real. That concerns me, but I believe they would rather deny God and please themselves than deny themselves and really live. Don't you make the same mistake!

#74. The Good, the Bad, the Ugly

{Discuss the following question: "Why do bad things happen to good people?" Include in the discussion an example or two of the things that happen and whether or not you would use different adjectives to form the question.}

? [Read Mark 10:17-18] How does this scripture alter the question?

? So now the question becomes, "Why do bad things happen to people?"

? How do you determine whether something is bad or not?

{Read the story entitled "The Woodcutter's Wisdom" (below).}

? How does this story alter the question?

? So now the question becomes, "Why do things happen to people?"

? How would you answer *this* question?

? Was the cross a bad thing that happened to a good person?

Most times we answer by saying "Yes, but it was for the good of many" and so forget that for Jesus it was a terrible calamity. Yet look at how he faced this terrible situation. [John 19:10-11, Matthew 26:39].

? What does Jesus' attitude communicate to God?
- That all things work for the good of those who love him, that God is sovereign

? How does this encourage you to face "things that happen to people?"

The bottom line in is that God is indeed sovereign and who are we to understand the mind and ways of God (Romans 11:33, Isaiah 55:9, Daniel 4:35). When we do our own thing, it often turns "ugly" because of our lack of wisdom and understanding; however, he who adheres to Psalm 9:10 and Romans 8:28 will be all right no matter what things happen. It doesn't mean we have to like what happens or that we can't show emotion toward what happens, just that we have to trust that God knows what he is doing.

The Woodcutter's Wisdom

Once there was an old man who lived in a tiny village. Although poor, he was envied by all, for he owned a beautiful white horse. Even the king coveted his treasure. A horse like this had never been seen before–such was its splendor, its majesty, its strength. People offered fabulous prices for the steed, but the old man always refused. "This horse is not a horse to me," he would tell them. "It is a person. How could you sell a person? He is a friend, not a possession. How could you sell a friend?" The man was poor and the temptation was great. But he never sold the horse.

One morning he found that the horse was not in the stable. The entire village came to see him. "You old fool," they scoffed, "we told you that someone would steal your horse. We warned you that you would be robbed. You are so poor. How could you ever hope to protect such a valuable animal? It would have been better to have sold him. You could have gotten whatever price you wanted. No amount would have been too high. Now the horse is gone, and you've been cursed with misfortune." The old man responded, "Don't speak too quickly. Say only that the horse is not in the stable. That is all we know; the rest is judgment. If I've been cursed or not, how can you know? How can you judge?"

The people contested, "Don't make us out to be fools! We may not be philosophers, but great philosophy is not needed. The simple fact that your horse is gone is a curse."

The old man spoke again. "All I know is that the stable is empty, and the horse is gone. The rest I don't know. Whether it is a curse or a blessing, I can't say. All we can see is a fragment. Who can say what will come next?"

The people of the village laughed. They thought that the man was crazy. They had always thought he was fool; if he wasn't, he would have sold the horse and lived off the money. But instead, he was a poor woodcutter, an old man still cutting firewood and dragging it out of the forest and selling it. He lived hand to mouth in the misery of poverty. Now he had proven that he was, indeed, a fool.

After fifteen days, the horse returned. He hadn't been stolen; he had run away into the forest. Not only had he returned, he had brought a dozen wild horses with him. Once again, the village people gathered around the woodcutter and spoke. "Old man, you were right and we were wrong. What we thought was a curse was a blessing. Please forgive us."

The man responded, "Once again, you go too far. Say only that the horse is back. State only that a dozen horses returned with him, but don't judge. How do you know if this is a blessing or not? You see only a fragment. Unless you know the whole story, how can you judge? You read only one page of a book. Can you judge the whole book? You read only one word of a phrase. Can you understand the entire phrase?

"Life is so vast, yet you judge all of life with one page or one word. All you have is a fragment! Don't say that this is a blessing. No one knows. I am content with what I know. I am not perturbed by what I don't."

"Maybe the old man is right," they said to one another. So they said little. But down deep, they knew he was wrong. They knew it was a blessing. Twelve wild horses had returned with one horse. With a little bit of work, the animals could be broken and trained and sold for much money.

The old man had a son, an only son. The young man began to break the wild horses. After a few days, he fell from one of the horses and broke both legs. Once again the villagers gathered around the old man and cast their judgments.

"You were right," they said. "You proved you were right. The dozen horses were not a blessing. They were a curse. Your only son has broken his legs, and now in your old age you have no one to help you. Now you are poorer than ever."

The old man spoke again. "You people are obsessed with judging. Don't go so far. Say only that my son broke his legs. Who knows if it is a blessing or a curse? No one knows. We only have a fragment. Life comes in fragments."

It so happened that a few weeks later the country engaged in war against a neighboring country. All the young men of the village were required to join the army. Only the son of the old man was excluded, because he was injured. Once again, the people gathered around the old man, crying and screaming because their sons had been taken. There was little chance that they would return. The enemy was strong, and the war would be a losing struggle. They would never see their sons again.

"You were right, old man," they wept. "God knows you were right. This proves it. Yours son's accident was a blessing. His legs may be broken, but at least he is with you. Our sons are gone forever."

The old man spoke again. "It is impossible to talk with you. You always draw conclusions. No one knows. Say only this: Your sons had to go to war, and mine did not. No one knows if it is a blessing or a curse. No one is wise enough to know. Only God knows."

#75. The Great Wall of Character

Game: Ask but Don't Tell. Four groups of 15 get into circles. Each person has 3 seconds to pass a question to someone by stating the question and using eye contact only. The person being asked can't answer the question, can't laugh or show any response for a time of 5 seconds. Then that person repeats the process by choosing another person with eye contact only using a different question; no question can be repeated. If any response is made by the person being asked, they are out and the person who got them out asks someone else another question. The last one standing wins.

? What made the game hard?
What does it take to be successful in this game?

? What are some recent convictions or decisions you made that you will carry through the school year?

? What will be some of the greatest opposition to these convictions or decisions?

? How will you stand firm in your conviction or decision?

[Read Philippians 3:17-4:1]
? What does Paul teach you about standing firm?
- Remember another's example
- Keep your mind on spiritual things
- Remember heaven or God's teachings
- Do what Jesus would do

The Great Wall of China is a gigantic structure that cost an immense amount of money and labor. When it was finished, it appeared impregnable. But three times the enemy breached it—not by breaking it down or going around it. They did it by bribing the gatekeepers. Dr. Harry Emerson Fosdick, in referring to this historical fact, had this to say: "It was the human element that failed. What collapsed was character, which proved insufficient to make the great structure men had fashioned really work."

#76. The Heart of a Warrior

{Give your thoughts on the Special Olympics. Describe the athletes.}

? Let's say we were going to start a new country with our group here tonight and we wanted to choose a leader. How would you describe the kind of leader you would want?

? What strikes you about the way the athletes were just described compared to the way you described this leader?

? How would you describe the person whom God would choose to be our king?

[Read 1 Samuel 16:1-6]
? Why would Samuel assume that Eliab was the chosen one?
- Tall, good-looking, etc.

Tell about a time when you judged someone by appearance.

[Read 1 Samuel 16:7-13]
? If the Lord does not look at the things we look at then what does he look at?
- The heart

? What about the heart?

Let's see what qualities of David are worthy of imitation.

{Recap in a fun, captivating way 1 Samuel 17:1-31. This is up to the time when Saul calls David to him because he has been saying he would slay Goliath.}

[Read 1 Samuel 17:32-37]
? What quality do you see in David that you would like to imitate?
In what ways do you find yourself being told you can't do something?
What are some of the Goliaths in your life?

172

[Read 1 Samuel 17:38-51]

? What mistake did Goliath make when he saw David?
- He looked at his outward appearance.

? What gave David victory over Goliath?
- God was with him.

? How can God be with you?
- By doing right [Psalm 37:25]

He practiced with his sling so much that it took only one stone. What is one skill you can develop to help you overcome your Goliath? Work on that until it takes only one stone to kill your Goliath. You may have to go through a lot of bears and lions before you can kill Goliath, but don't give up!

In a book called *The Decline and Fall of the Roman Empire*, a Roman emperor is quoted:

> "I have now reigned above 50 years in victory or peace, beloved by my subjects, dreaded by my enemies, and respected by my allies. Riches and honors, power and pleasure, have waited on my call, nor has my felicity [happiness] been kept from any earthly blessing. In this situation, I have diligently numbered the days of pure and genuine happiness which have fallen to my lot: they amount to 14 days! O man, place not thy confidence in this present world!"

I urge you not to grow up always looking and trusting in what you can see... working on the outward appearances. Instead I urge you to focus your eyes on the heart. Special Olympic athletes show us more than what is apparent. Now, it is your turn. What will you show the world? Your friends? Your family? Each other? Your Goliaths? I hope you will show them more than the mere appearances. I hope you will show them the heart of a warrior.

#77. Invincible

Def.: In-vin-ci-ble
Adj.: incapable of being conquered, defeated, subdued
Orig.: *in* (not), *vincere* (to conquer)
Syn.: bulletproof, impassable, impregnable, indomitable, insuperable, inviolable, invulnerable, irresistible, powerful, strong, unassailable, unattackable, unbeatable, unconquerable, undefeatable, unsurmountable, untouchable, unyielding

The word "invincible" is most associated and applied to combat, war or conflict situations.

Rest assured there is conflict happening across the globe. In fact, there are currently 40 wars involving or in 45 countries according to one source. {Check online for updated numbers.}

No one yet has proven to be invincible; for instance, here are war statistics for the US, the most powerful country in the world: {Read some statistics of US war casualties.}

Sound very convincing?

There is one who is invincible, and he is God.

Two of God's invincible attributes:

1. His Plans
[Acts 5] Gamaliel tells them they might be fighting God.

Tell you what happened to a city that wanted to fight God.

City of Tyre
[Ezekiel 26:3-8, 12-14] {written around 586 BC—have the kids underline the following phrases or write them on an easel for everyone to see.}
[V.3] many nations
[V.4] bare rock
[V.5] out in the sea, place to spread fishnets
[V.12] throw your stone, timber and rubble into the sea

[V.14] never be rebuilt

King Nebuchadnezzar was in power three years after this prophecy—ruler of the known world.
Tyre was arrogant and ungodly, on the edge of the ocean. "Nothing can get us... we are safe."
King Nebuchadnezzar put Tyre under siege, which lasted 13 years.

? Ask: What is a siege?

> » At the end of 13 years, Tyre relented and when Nebuchadnezzar broke down the gates, most of the people relocated to an island a half mile off the coast. The mainland city was destroyed in 573 B.C. The city of Tyre (out on the island) remained a powerful city for couple hundred years.
> » 240 years later, Alexander the Great wants to access the city as a port; Tyre says no so he lays siege to it; he uses Tyre's mainland rubble, stones and timber to make a causeway out to the island. Tyre tries to stop him, but with superior naval forces Alexander overcomes the city and kills 8,000 and enslaves 30,000 more.
> » 50 years later another king attacks what little of Tyre is left.
> » In the 11th, 12th and 13th centuries, crusades were fought in the region, and finally after 1,600 hundred years Tyre is no more.
> » Great location for a city, yet no city has ever been built there to this day.
> » In fact, the local fishermen dry their nets on the rocks of Tyre.

? Why go through all this when talking about plans?
- God is true to his word.

Nothing can overcome his plans. His plans can be seen in his promises to you. There are over 7,900 promises in the Bible regarding every aspect of life:
> » He will supply all your needs. [Philippians 4:19]
> » You will not be tempted beyond what you can bear. [1 Corinthians 10:13]
> » All things work for the good of those who love him. [Romans 8:28]
> » Promises for when you are depressed, lonely, obedient, courageous

[Read Psalm 33:11] God's plans are invincible—bulletproof, impassable, impregnable, indomitable, insuperable, inviolable, invulnerable, irresistible, powerful, strong, unassailable, unattackable, unbeatable, unconquerable, undefeatable, unsurmountable, untouchable, unyielding.

2. His Love

Grandpa's grandson, Jeffrey, was crying in his crib because he was put in there as part of a timeout. Jeffrey kept crying, "Out papa, out!" Grandpa replied, "I can't because you are in trouble." Jeffrey cried all the more. Finally, because he wanted to be with Jeffrey so much, he did the only thing he could: he climbed into the crib with him.

[Read Romans 8:35-39]
Nothing can overcome God's love for you—no discipline, no distance

[Read 1 John 4:8]
God is love. It's not what he does; it's what he is.

[Read Hebrews 1:3]
Jesus is the exact replica of God.

? How did Jesus live his life?
- [John 8:46] Can anyone prove me guilty of sin?
- [2 Corinthians 5:21] Sinless
- [Matthew 26:59-60] nothing false, no law broken

? He lived invincibly—a perfect life. Don't you think if there was one little piece of evidence that could take him down, they would have found it?

[Read Isaiah 43:1-7]

At the end of time, billions of people were scattered on a great plain before God's throne. Most shrank back from the brilliant light before them. But some groups near the front talked heatedly–not with cringing shame, but with belligerence: "Can God judge us? How can he know about suffering?" snapped a pert young brunette. She ripped open a sleeve to reveal a tattooed number from a Nazi concentration camp. "We endured terror...beatings...torture...death!" In another group an African-American boy lowered his collar. "What about this?" he demanded, showing an ugly rope burn. "Lynched...for no crime but being black!" In another crowd was a pregnant schoolgirl with sullen eyes. "Why should I suffer?" she murmured, "It wasn't my fault he raped me." Far out across the plain there were hundreds of such groups. Each had a complaint against God for the evil and suffering he had permitted in his world. How lucky God was to live in heaven where all was sweetness and light, where there was no weeping or fear, no hunger or hatred! What did God know of all that man had been forced to endure in this world? For God leads a pretty sheltered, "invincible" life, they said.

In response, each of these groups sent forth their leader, chosen because he had suffered the most: a Jew, an African-American, a child from Hiroshima who was horribly deformed from radioactive waste, an Ethiopian mom who lost her family to a machete. In the center of the plain they consulted with each other. At last they were ready to present their case. It was rather clever. Before God could be qualified to be their judge, he must endure what they had endured. Their decision was that God should be sentenced to live on earth–as a man! Let him be born a Jew. Let the legitimacy of his birth be doubted. Give him a work so difficult that even his family will think him out of his mind when he tries to do it. Let him be betrayed by his closest friends. Let him face false charges, be tried by a prejudiced jury and convicted by a cowardly judge. Let him be tortured. "At last, let him see what it means to be terribly alone. Then let him die. Let him die so that there can be no doubt that he died. Let there be a great host of witnesses to verify it." As each leader announced his portion of the sentence, loud murmurs of approval went up from the throng of people assembled.

And when the last had finished pronouncing sentence, there was a long silence. No one uttered another word. No one moved. The rage that blinded them had been replaced with understanding, for now they could see that the invincible had allowed himself to be treated equally with themselves. Each stood silent, enveloped in the plan and love of their God.

God is invincible and yet gives up his invincibility to win you over. His plans and his love are invincible.

#78. The Lamb of God

{Pass out copies of Lamb-O-Rama (below) and pens. Read through the instructions and make sure everyone understands them. Give the starting signal and let them go at it. Give a prize to the first one done.}

? What were lambs used for in the Old Testament, other than the things that lambs are normally used for, such as food and wool?

[Read John 1:29]
In the Bible, John sees Jesus approaching and says, "Look, the Lamb of God, who takes away the sins of the world!"

? Why do you think John would say that?
Why is Jesus referred to as the Lamb?
Why do you think they call Jesus *the* Lamb, instead of just a Lamb?
- » Because God is perfect, there's a price to be paid for sin. In the Old Testament, this was done with animal sacrifices.
- » Lambs were pretty commonly used for sacrifices.
- » When Jesus died on the cross for our sins, he became the last sacrifice for sin ever needed. We can have a relationship with God because of Jesus' sacrifice.
- » That's why Jesus is called the Lamb.

? What difference does it make that Jesus was slain for you?
- Forgiveness of sins
- Relationship with God
- Entrance into heaven

? How can that fact impact your life on a daily basis?

[Read Titus 2:11-12]
Living a godly life is a privilege given to you by the humility of the Lamb of God.

LAMB-O-RAMA

Complete these items in any order that you want, but you can only get the initials of each person once.

Shearing Time
Lambs and sheep often get their coats shaved off. Find someone who's willing to pull out a strand of his or her own hair and give it to you.
Have that person initial here: _____

Mary's Tune
Get in a group with two other people and sing "Mary Had Little Lamb" all the way through as loud as you can.
Have them both initial here: _____ _____

Counting Sheep
Sometimes when people can't sleep, they count imaginary sheep jumping over a fence. Act like a fence and have someone jump over you five times.
Have that person initial here: _____

Leg of Lamb
Get with one other person. Tie your left leg to their right leg and walk around the room twice.
Have that person initial here: _____

Bleating Chorus
Get with two other people and sing "Baa-Baa Black Sheep" all the way through in sheep voices (baa-baaing).
Have them both initial here: _____ _____

Good Shepherd
Get with two other people. Have them both get on their hands and knees and follow you around the room one time while they repeat "baa-baa."
Have them both initial here: _____ _____

Bo-Peep
Stand on a chair and yell, "Where are my sheep?" When you can find someone willing to be your lost sheep, have them come over to you.
Have that person initial here: _____

#79. The Lazarus Factor: An Attitude to Change the World!
[Christmas lesson]

What attitude change would most affect the world?
What attitude would you most like to change about yourself?

[Read Luke 16:19-21]
? What is the rich man's attitude?
What affect does living in luxury have on you?
How is Lazarus feeling?

[Read Luke 16:22-28]
? How is the rich man feeling?
What regrets might he be having?
Who is more in need now, Lazarus or the rich man?

? How does this story relate to you?

[Read Luke 16:29-31]
? What is God communicating to you based on how this story relates to you?

? This story is all about attitude: being giving is an attitude of noticing another's feelings. Some of you are waiting for some miraculous sign or until you become a Christian to love and give. If you aren't doing it now, what makes you think that some E.T. encounter is going to change you?

? How many of you have a Christmas list? Good, what are you giving? See, when we hear "Christmas list" we automatically think of what people can get us. I do! What if we start thinking of a Christmas list as what we can give to others? That's the attitude we need to take into this holiday season.

#80. The Others

Opening activity: Have a contest where all the kids stand up and start talking to each other. Without telling the kids what is going on, have leaders go around the room and tap those on the shoulder that say "I," they are to sit down; they are out. See how long it takes. Leaders must be quick...this shouldn't take long. Time how long it takes and once done tell the kids.

Now repeat the game telling the kids what got them out; it should take a little longer. Award a prize to the last one standing.

Compare the first round with the second. How were they different?
What was the one rule instituted?
How did this impact the second round?
Which seemed more natural? Why?
What does that tell you about yourself?
Based on this, what do you think God would have to say to you right now?

{Read the following verses and discuss what this means to them.}
[Read 1 Corinthians 10:24]
[Read Ephesians 4:29]
[Read Philippians 2:3-4]
[Read Hebrews 13:16]

Split into groups of three and discuss how you can apply these scriptures to what you will do in the next seven days.

[Read Galatians 6:9-10]
In the next seven days:
- » You will have the opportunity to help someone.
- » You will have a chance to do a task without being asked.
- » You will have a chance to push through feeling uncomfortable and self-conscious.
- » You will have a chance to encourage someone.
- » You will have a chance to say something unpopular yet right and truthful.
- » You will have to make a choice between what you want to do and what needs to be done.

» You will have missed or taken each one of the above opportunities.

There was a boy who got his hand caught inside an expensive vase. His upset parents applied soapsuds and cooking oil without success. When they seemed ready to break the vase as the only way to release the hand, the frightened boy cried, "Would it help if I let go of the penny I'm holding?"

What will help you have a great time in the next seven days is to let go of yourself and think about others.

Challenge: do this for seven days; no matter what you are involved in, whether it is hanging with friends, watching your little brother or sister, going to a dance, or by yourself...remember "the others" in your life.

#81. The Perfect Time to Change

_____ Girls' Section: What Women Want _____

? What would be a perfect situation for you?
Isn't it interesting how you picked outward things?
Can you think of a time in history when everything was perfect?

[Read Genesis 2:4-25]
1. The Perfect World

? What arguments could be made for Eden being the perfect situation for Eve?
- Didn't have to work for food
- No children to tend
- No rainy days (God had not made rain yet)
- No extreme temperatures (i.e. sunburn, snow—hey, they were naked!)
- No fear from animals or dangers
- No peer pressure
- No concern about looks
- No guilt
- No fear of death
- No doubts about God—he was right there with them

2. The Perfect Woman

? If this was so perfect, why did Eve want more?
So, where is the battle for perfection fought?
- The heart

3. The Perfect Heart

? If perfection can only be obtained by way of the heart (because we know that clothes, better looks, or a fancy house can't do it), how can your heart overcome or battle: pride, selfishness, gossip, cliques, deceit, and criticalness?

[Read 1 Timothy 4:7-8]
? What does it mean to train?
What happens when you train physically?
- Your body gets stronger.

? What happens when you train yourself to be godly?
- Your heart gets stronger; you get a little closer to perfection.

When you begin training, you change what you do; you replace one routine with another.

? What can you replace these sins with?
Pride
Deceit
Cliques
Gossip
Selfishness
Criticalness

? When is training done?
- Never; if you quit training for something, you quit being that thing.

Practical application:
Write down one thing you want to change.
Write down how you will train yourself this week, that is, what you will replace that sin with.

_____ Boys' Section: What Men Want _____

? What would be a perfect situation for you?
Isn't interesting how you picked outward things?
Can you think of a time in history when everything was perfect?

[Read Genesis 2:4-25]
1. The Perfect World
What arguments could be made for Eden being the perfect situation for Adam?
- Didn't have to work hard for food
- No children to protect
- No rainy days (God had not made rain yet)
- No extreme temperatures (i.e. sunburn, snow—hey they were naked!)
- No serious dangers (animals, enemies, etc.)
- No political adversaries

Tools to Help Preteen and Young Teen Leaders and Parents

- No guilt
- Top of the food chain...got to name the animals
- Following God was not confusing or unreal (could see God in the garden)
- No fear of death

2. The Perfect Man
If this was so perfect, why did Adam want more?
So, where is the battle for perfection fought?
- The heart

3. The Perfect Heart
If perfection can only be obtained by way of the heart (because we know that clothes, better looks, or a fancy car can't do it), how can your heart overcome or battle the following: selfishness, laziness, lust, greed, respect, and lying?

[Read 1 Timothy 4:7-8]
What does it mean to train?
What happens when you train physically?
- Your body gets stronger.

What happens when you train yourself to be godly?
- Your heart gets stronger; you get a little closer to perfection.

When you begin training, you change what you do; you replace one thing with another.

What can you replace the following characteristics with?
1. Selfishness
2. Laziness
3. Lust
4. Greed
5. Disrespect
6. Lying

Practical application:
Write down one thing you want to change.
Write down how you will train yourself this week, that is, what you will replace that sin with.

#82. The Verdict

? What do you think about the US court system?
What are some of the crazy lawsuits you have heard about?
- Woman suing MacDonald's because she claims a hot pickle burned her chin and ruined her life and marriage
- Man suing a tattoo parlor because of a misspelled word that he misspelled
- Lawsuit of the families of two pilots, who weren't licensed, who were killed while flying under a low-lying bridge

{Bring in a stuffed animal and sit it on a chair in front of the group.} We are going to hold court today. We live in a country where it is illegal to be spiritual or to have any characteristics that resemble God or his Bible. The punishment is death. {Tell the group that they are in a court of law. Pick six (or however many) people to be the jury. You are the judge, and they are the witnesses. Put the witnesses into teams of two or three and give them 10 minutes to ready their testimony. During this time, each team of witnesses is to prepare themselves by picking one godly characteristic that describes the stuffed animal or that they saw the stuffed animal doing. Tell them they must show that this characteristic is illegal by showing the court it is in the Bible, which is the rulebook on spiritual and godly living. After all the testimony is given, have the jury deliberate and give a verdict.}

{Once the verdict is read, ask the group, if they were on trial for being godly, would they be found guilty. Would they be found guilty of respect, encouragement, honesty, not gossiping, reading their Bibles, serving, being thankful, praying, etc.? Use the ones they used against the stuffed animal.}

[Read 2 Timothy 3:14-15]
Let's not forget what we learned. Continue in it. You know it is right, and it will make you wise and full of faith. Never give up on what you know is truth. Always, at any point in your life, be found guilty of being like God.

#83. The Voice of Compassion

{This lesson was used to prepare our group to be giving at the Special Olympics.} Everyone close your eyes and think of a time when someone helped you...a time when you didn't expect it. In one word, how did you feel after they helped you?

[Read Hebrews 1:1-2]
The Bible says God used to speak to us (meaning all people) through the prophets. Now, he speaks to us through Jesus. Who do you listen to today...parents, friends, TV, or the latest ideas? Maybe you only trust yourself because you don't trust anyone else, even God or Jesus. Verse 2 says that Jesus made the universe. He thought it and spoke it into existence. What is it he made? Let's take a look {hold a grape in your hand}

Because the universe is so big, it can be better understood by scaling it down so that the earth would be the size of a grape; that is taking the earth from an 8,000-mile diameter to about half an inch in diameter. Here are some facts based on this scaled-down universe:
1. In true terms, the moon is about 250,000 miles from the earth. In our scaled-down universe, it is about 16 inches away.
2. The sun is about 93 million miles away. In our scaled-down universe, the sun is about the size of a giant beach ball—about 4 feet across—and would be about 490 feet from the grape (earth).
3. The largest planet, Jupiter, is actually 400 million miles away and is about 800,000 miles wide. In our version, Jupiter is about the size of a grapefruit and is a little less than half a mile away.

This is all within our solar system; now let's go beyond our solar system:
1. The nearest star, other than our sun, is about 4 light years away. Light travels at 186,000 miles/second, so the nearest star is a stinkin' long ways! In our scaled-down universe, the nearest star is a mere 24,000 miles away. If you want to know the actual distance, multiply 24,000 by 1 billion. WOW!
2. The galaxy we're a part of, the Milky Way, which is about 100,000 light years wide or 56,000,000,000,000,000 miles (yes, 15 zeros; is that zillion?). In our scaled-down universe, our galaxy is only 55 billion miles wide.
3. The Great Andromeda Galaxy, our sister galaxy, and part of our "local group," is two million light years away or 19,000,000,000,000,000,000 miles. The light we now see from this galaxy left there about the time humans first appeared on Earth. In our scaled-down universe, it is about one

trillion miles away.
4. So, if the earth were the size of a grape:
    » The moon would be 16 inches away.
    » The sun would be 163 yards away.
    » Jupiter would be just under a half mile away.
    » The nearest star would be 24,000 miles away.

Now, let that sink in...
Jesus made all of it. If you were on that grape, you would be .00000007 of inch (that's seven hundred millionths of an inch). You would have to be seen with an electron microscope.

God is big! You are nothing! Why would he have a reason to speak to you? Why would he even notice you? And yet, look what the Maker of the universe does:

[Read Mark 1:40-42]
{Describe leprosy.}

? How would this leper feel?
- Unwanted
- Not loved
- Unnoticed
- Forgotten

Much like you could feel to God in his big universe. Much like some of the athletes in the Special Olympics.

? And yet, how does Jesus treat this gentleman?
- With compassion
- Heals him
- Touches him
- Gives him his life back

What you hear is the voice of compassion. Even 2000 years later, you still hear the sounds of love and giving ring through the air. I hope you will realize that all that you have and all that you are is a result of God's compassion. It's the result of him not overlooking you in all that he made; of him not forgetting you or comparing you with everything else he has made. God and Jesus are real, and so is their love and compassion for you.

I am asking you to speak to the athletes weekend with the same voice—the voice of compassion. Reach out to them and give to them. Look past the things that make you uncomfortable but don't look past the people.

#84. T.I.G.H.T.

[Read Romans 12:9-18]
Our goal for this year is for this group to be close, to be unified—across grades, across gender, within grades and within gender. It will take five things:

Trust [vv. 9-10]
Trust is a result of sincere love.
Trust is essential in building devotion and loyalty.
Trust is the ultimate way to honor another person.

In Harmony [v. 16]
Definition: A pleasing combination of the elements that form a whole
Pride will destroy harmony.
Judgmental attitudes will keep us from being a pleasing combination.

Giving [vv. 11-13]
Never be lacking in, keep your, serving the, be joyful in, patient in, faithful in, share with, practice this...all action verbs with an understood you.
This group will be as good as you make it.
Each of you has something special to give—decide what it is and give it. If you are not sure, ask me.

Heart (real) [v. 16]
"Do not be proud." Got to be real with each other.
Definition of proud: holding too high an opinion of oneself
This attitude will keep you from being honest and from being yourself.
We all have our quirks...that's okay—it's what makes this group awesome!

Truth [v. 17]
The Bible is truth. Be careful to do what is right, and then you and this group will be known for it.
The Bible will be our standard and with it, if we are willing to make it such, we will be close or T.I.G.H.T.

Be committed to being tight.

#85. Trustworthy

Opening activity: Divide the group into pairs. If there is an odd number have a threesome. Each pair is to choose a leader and follower. Give a blindfold to the follower and written instructions to the leader. The leader is to follow the instructions exactly as written for each of the three activities:

1. Without touching them, direct the blindfolded person to jump off the stage.
2. Without touching them, lead the blindfolded person outside and have them sit on a bench or on the grass. Give them an unwrapped chocolate kiss. Have them unwrap it and put it in your mouth to eat.
3. Without talking, have the blindfolded person walk into the building and then crawl back to the room and have a seat on the floor in front of the stage. Sit quietly until everyone returns.

? How did you feel as you went through the exercise?

? If you were the one blindfolded, what would the others have to do to earn your trust?

? How do these things relate to your relationships in this group?

? What qualities do you think a trustworthy person should have?
- Loyal, keeps a secret, truthful, no embellishing or coverups, responsible, has your best interest at heart, genuine, sincere, goes the extra mile

[Read Proverbs 18:24]
? How is the friend in this scripture trustworthy?

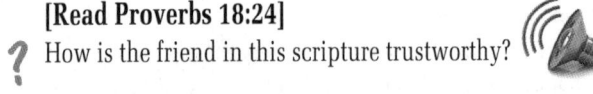

? How will you need to change to be a friend like this to the people in this group?

Unless you learn how to be trustworthy, you will be a person of many companions but no real friends. Listen to the things said here today about what we all want in our friends and be that kind of person. Change what you must in order to be trustworthy.

#86. Turning Up the Heat

{This will be a very interactive lesson. The goal is to get them to think about the scriptures and to communicate one overall theme: having a giving heart.}

{Before the lesson, assign one person for each of the following scriptures:
6th graders – 1 Thessalonians 2:8, Acts 4:32
7th graders – Acts 4:36-37, Luke 10:34-35
8th graders – Luke 6:43-45, Matthew 6:2-4}

{Explain to them that, when they are asked, they will stand and read the scripture and teach everyone what they think it means. Talking to them beforehand will give them a few minutes to prepare something. For smaller groups, you can assign these on the fly.}

Have everyone turn to Matthew 24:12-13. Explain that each person is to read it silently and when one of them is ready, explain what it means. {For smaller groups, you read the scripture and ask for explanations.}

? Is this scripture fact or opinion?
- Fact—Jesus said it!

How does that make you feel—not what you think, but what you feel (happy, glad, sad, mad, depressed, worried, anxious, etc.) and why? {Tell them what you feel. *It makes me feel worried and fearful, which makes me want to be real protective with my heart and pull back from people so I won't get hurt.*}

Some of you are going to read a scripture and teach it to us. As you are listening to them, be prepared to tell what the overall theme of these scriptures is.

{Go in the following order.}
6th graders – 1 Thessalonians 2:8, Acts 4:32
7th graders – Acts 4:36-37, Luke 10:34-35
8th graders – Luke 6:43-45, Matthew 6:2-4

? What is the overall theme?
- Having the heart to be a giver

{Read Matthew 24:12-13 again.}
Remind them that this is fact, not fiction, and of the feelings they had about this promise. Though it was about the fall of Jerusalem in the first century, it could be the case today.}

? How does having a giving heart secure your standing place?

Bottom Line: We live in scary times, and they are going to only get scarier because wickedness will increase. Our tendency is to not give because we don't want to get hurt or stabbed in the back or taken advantage of. What's funny is that either choice, to give or not to give, brings about the same feelings. You decide whether or not you want to "turn up the heat"; whether or not you want to be saved.

Now take time to pray about all that was discussed; pray about something that struck you; and pray to be a giver. Anyone who wants can pray. I will close it out in a few minutes.

#87. Unhandcuff Me!

Game: Prisoner Relay. Divide into teams of 5-10 people. Give each team a kickball and a pair of handcuffs. Have half of each team go to the other side of the room. Handcuff the first person's hands behind their back. When the "go" is given, have the handcuffed person pick up the ball and carry it to their teammate on the opposite side of the room. They cannot kick the ball. It must be carried. Once on the other side, place the ball in front of their teammate; have the teammate remove the handcuffs; have someone else handcuff the teammate; and this person picks up the ball and carries it across to another teammate, and so forth until everyone has been handcuffed and carried the ball. The first team to finish is the winner.

{Give the lesson while handcuffed. It is a constant reminder of being bound. At the appropriate time take off the cuffs. These make a great visual—have fun with it.}

What made this game difficult?
How does this game relate to your life?
What kind of things "handcuff" our relationship with God?

I want to talk about openness or being real.

[Read John 1:43-50]
Why does Jesus say there is no deceit in Nathanael?
What does it mean to be open?
- Be real
- Talk about thoughts and feelings
- Same on the outside as the inside

What keeps us from being open?
How does being open affect your relationships?
How does it affect your relationship with God?

[Read John 8:31-32]
What does the truth set you free from?
What are some examples of how the truth has set you free?

The truth—being truthful, being real—is very freeing. This is a great promise from God: that if you will not just believe in Jesus or the Bible but be truthful and open, and push through the pride or shame to be real and be yourself, you will be free from all the things you mentioned. Some of you want to have a relationship with God and, in fact, are working on it. Be open with God and other people; and ignorance, guilt, loneliness, shame, lying, insecurities, and the like will not handcuff you. You will be happier and more confident!

#88. Are You Up to the Task?

What is the most difficult thing that you have ever attempted?

[Read Genesis 6:9-13]

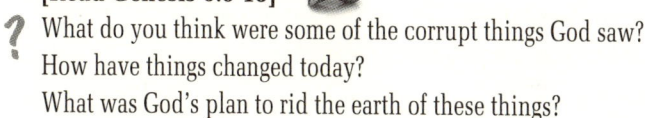

? What do you think were some of the corrupt things God saw? How have things changed today?
What was God's plan to rid the earth of these things?
- Flood—total destruction

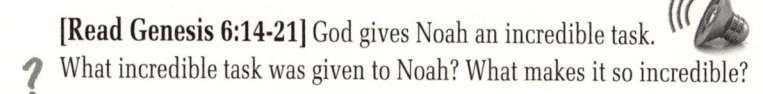

[Read Genesis 6:14-21] God gives Noah an incredible task.

? What incredible task was given to Noah? What makes it so incredible?

? What did God do to help Noah complete his task?
- Knowledge of how to build something
- Gave detailed instructions

? What are some of the difficult things God has asked you to do?
- Live with conviction
- Stand up for what is right
- Repent of sin
- Treat people fairly
- Be pure

? What has God given you to help you complete these tasks?
- Knowledge of evidences
- Truths of the Bible
- Jesus' life and sacrifice
- Friends
- Promise of heaven
- Fear of hell

? What temptations do you think Noah faced while building the ark?
- To compromise on the size of the boat {Hydraulic engineers use the ratio 12:2:1 today for the best stability; thus, changing the dimensions could have been fatal.}
- To doubt whether the flood would happen

- His neighbors must have ridiculed him
- Family probably started complaining
- To grumble against God because of the personal sacrifice involved in building the ark (giving up his home, Sunday afternoon naps, etc.)

? What temptations do you face today?
- To compromise on God's word
- To doubt the Bible
- To doubt whether judgment will really take place
- To be discouraged by ridicule
- Not to learn the Bible—ignorance does not make hell blissful

? How does the story end? [Genesis 6:22]

[Philippians 3:16] attained => has come to

? Noah completes what has come to him; what he knows to do. Each one of you is going to be given a task one day to test your convictions; to test what you know. Who will be stronger, you or the crowd; you or your selfish desires; you or your doubts; you or the world?

> *There is an old story of an eagle that, on an early morning during the spring thaw, soared high above the forest looking for something to eat. As he followed the course of a river he looked down and spied a small rodent, trapped on a piece of ice that had broken free and was floating downstream. Seeing an easy meal, he swooped down, landed on the ice, killed the mouse and began to eat. As he continued his meal, he saw that his perch was rapidly approaching a waterfall, but determined to finish eating and thinking he would rise into the air and to safety at the last moment, continued his course. As the ice neared the falls, the eagle finished his last bite. Satisfied with his breakfast, he spread his mighty wings and attempted to rise skyward as the chunk of ice tipped over the edge. While enjoying his meal, however, he had failed to notice that the warmth of his feet had caused his claws to become embedded in the ice. Try as he might, he could not dislodge them and free himself from what had now become the burden that would carry him to his death on the rocks far below.*

If you don't develop the character and heart now you will be like this eagle: meaning to fly high, rising to each honorable task, but you will be stuck in bad patterns and fall and do something you regret—not doing what you knew to do. Don't let that happen! Work on your convictions so that you can be up to the task. Put into practice the knowledge that you have already attained.

#89. What a Colossal Character!

{**Goal of the lesson:** to inspire awe of Jesus and foster interest in the book of Colossians. Give some background.}

Occasion and Date: Written by Paul around AD 61-63 while in prison in Rome. The letter is in response to Epaphras' visit to Paul telling him about a dangerous heresy making headway in the church. Epaphras was put in prison as well (Philemon 23). The heresy seems to have been a mixture of Greek, Jewish, and Oriental religions calling for the worship of angels as intermediaries between God and man, and insisting on the strict adherence to certain Jewish requirements to the point of asceticism (unusual or extreme self-denial in an attempt to get close to God); all as a part of the gospel of Christ.

Theme of the book: The Deity and All-Sufficiency of Christ

{Play some audio files of random sounds and have people guess what is making each sound. Perhaps a contest among teams.}

? What are some sounds that you hear every day?
What kind of sound does faith make?
What kind of sounds are you known for?

Read Colossians Chapter 1

? What did Paul hear regarding their love?
What did Paul and Timothy pray for on behalf of the people?
- Knowledge of God's will and to live a worthy life and please him

? What pleases God?
- Bearing fruit in every good work

? What is that?
- Growing in the knowledge of God

? How do we do that?
- Strengthening to have great endurance and patience

? How and why?

- Joyfully giving thanks

? For what and why?

? What is an epithet?
- A word or phrase expressing some quality or attribute

? What are some about Jesus?
- Image of the invisible God
- Firstborn over all creation
- By him all things were created
- Before all things
- In him all things hold together
- Head of the church
- Beginning and firstborn among the dead
- All his (God's) fullness dwells in him
- Reconciler of all things

? How do verses 21-23 impact you?

? How does this motivate you to please God and live a life that is worthy of the him?

Think of what we are in all that God has made. Think of all that Jesus is, and yet, we were given the gift of life through Jesus' death. He is God! He is supreme! Everything we have is due him and because of him. We are so far from giving God and Jesus what is due them. We struggle to fathom this concept—maybe this is why Paul referred to it as a mystery, but no longer. Paul is making it clear who Jesus is—that all of God's attributes are found in him, making him worthy of worship, praise, and dedication…and your attention and interest. I encourage you to read the whole book and see why Paul was so juiced about Jesus.

#90. What Are the Odds?

{Skip the missions contribution questions if they don't apply.}

? What is happening this Sunday?
- Missions contribution

? What will be done with the money?
Why such a big deal over this?
- Because God is real and Jesus is the Messiah and we want people to know!

? What comes to your mind when you hear the name Jesus?
Which is talked about more freely, Jesus or God? Why?
Is it easy to believe Jesus is who he says he is? Why or why not?

[Read John 5:39-40]
The context is the Jews are mad that Jesus claimed to be "equal with God" [vv. 17-18]

? What do these two verses imply about the OT?
- They were written about him being the Messiah.

Some of you are studying or have plans to study when you get older, but that will not save you. Just knowing the Scriptures is not enough. You must believe that Jesus is who he says he is: the Son of God who takes away your sins and is worthy to be followed and imitated.

? What is a messiah?
- A savior

? What makes it hard for you to believe that Jesus is the Messiah, the one talked about in the whole OT?

The OT contains the history of the ancestry of Jesus and has over 330 direct prophecies about him.

? Can you name one?

Let's look at just eight out of the 330-plus:

Let's look at just eight out of the 330-plus:
{Split the group in half and choose ahead of time which half will read which scripture. Have one half read the OT reference and the other half read the NT fulfillment. Print out the scriptures and hand them out to facilitate this part. Don't let this part drag.}

Prophecy	OT Reference	NT Fulfillment
1) Born in Bethlehem	Micah 5:2	Matthew 2:1
2) Preceded by Messenger	Isaiah 40:3	Matthew 3:1-3
3) Enter Jerusalem on a donkey	Zechariah 9:9	Luke 19:35-36
4) Betrayed by a friend	Psalm 41:9 – "lit., 'the man of my peace'; he who salutes me with a kiss of peace," as Judas did.	Matthew 26:49-50
5) Sold for 30 pieces of silver	Zechariah 11:12	Matthew 26:15
6) Money thrown into god's house and used to buy a potter's field	Zechariah 11:13	Matthew 27:5-7
7) People shook their heads at Jesus	Psalm 109:25	Matthew 27:39
8) Hands and feet pierced and crucified with thieves	Psalm 22:16,	Matthew 27:26, 38 {The type of death pictured in Isaiah and Psalms did not come under the Jewish system until hundreds of years after this was written.}

These are only eight of 330-plus prophecies, and yet they are specifically mentioned in the account of Jesus. Now what if these accounts weren't true? Don't you think someone opposed to Jesus being the Messiah would have come forward and said these are lies? Well, where are they? They aren't to be found, because it is true. Some are even proven outside the text of the Bible by other historical writers—but that's a whole other lesson.

The odds of just eight prophecies being fulfilled in one man is 1 in 1017 or 100,000,000,000,000,000. An analogy to understand this number: take this many silver dollars and lay them on the state of Texas. They would cover the whole state 2 feet deep. Now make a nick in one of the coins and stir the whole mass of coins. Blindfold someone and tell them to find the marked coin.

{If applicable} This is why we are having a missions contribution, because Jesus is the Messiah. It is truth. and the world needs to know that there is hope and a way of life that is beneficial for this life and the one to come. It is our way of giving to people whom we will never meet.
{Read or tell the following story.}

The Reflection

There were once two men, both seriously ill, in the same room of a great hospital, which was quite a small room, just large enough for the pair of them—two beds, two bedside lockers, a door opening on the hall, and one window looking out on the world. One of the men, as part of his treatment, was allowed to sit up in bed for an hour in the afternoon (something that had to do with draining the fluid from his lungs), and his bed was next to the window. But the other man had to spend all his time flat on his back—and both of them had to be kept quiet and still. This was the reason they were in the small room by themselves, and they were grateful for peace and privacy—none of the bustle and clatter and prying eyes of the general ward for them.

Of course, one of the disadvantages of their condition was that they weren't allowed much to do: no reading, no radio, certainly no television—they just had to keep quiet and still, just the two of them. They used to talk for hours and hours—about their wives, their children, their homes, their former jobs, their hobbies, their childhood, what they did during the war, where they had been on vacations—all that sort of thing. Every afternoon, when the man in the bed next to the window was propped up for his hour, he would pass the time by describing what he could see outside. And the other man began to live for those hours.

The window apparently overlooked a park with a lake where there were ducks and swans, children throwing them bread and sailing model boats, and young couples walking hand in hand beneath the trees. And there were flowers and stretches of grass and games of softball, people taking their ease in the sunshine, and right at the back, behind the fringe of the tress, a fine view of the city skyline.

The man on his back would listen to all of this, enjoying every minute of hearing about how a child nearly fell into the lake, how beautiful the girls were in their summer dresses, and then an exciting ball game, or a boy playing with his puppy. It got to the point that he could almost see what was happening outside. Then one fine afternoon, when there was some sort of parade, the thought struck him: Why should the man next to the window have all the pleasure of seeing what was going on? Why shouldn't he get the chance? He felt ashamed and tried not to think like that, but the more he tried, the worse he wanted to change. He'd do anything!

In a few days, he had turned sour. He should be by the window. He brooded and couldn't sleep, and grew even more seriously ill—which none of the doctors understood. One night, as he stared at the ceiling, the other man (the man next to the window) suddenly woke up coughing and choking, the fluid congesting in his lungs, his hands groping for the button that would bring the night nurse running. But the man continued to stare at the ceiling. In the morning, the day nurse came in with water for their baths and found the other man dead. They took away his body, quietly, no fuss.

As soon as it seemed decent, the man asked if he could be moved to the bed next to the window. They moved him, tucked him in, and made him quite comfortable, and left him alone to be quiet and still. The minute they'd gone, he propped himself up on one elbow, painfully and laboriously, and looked out the window. It faced a blank wall.

There will be people who will not get to see what you see; who will be staring at a blank wall. Your sacrifice will help people see more than they ever thought they could.

– Taken from *Growing Deep: Exploring the Roots of Our Faith*, by Charles R. Swindoll

#91. Who Do You Think Jesus Is?

What do people you know say about the Bible?
What do they say about Jesus?
What do they say about the church?

[Read Luke 9:18-20]
Why would Jesus ask this question?
How is this question relevant to you?
Why would there be such conflicting reports as to who Jesus is?
- Not many people take the time to get to know him or his teachings.

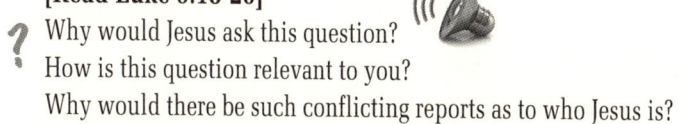

Why?
- Too set in their own way
- Afraid to change
- Preconceived notions
- Don't have their own convictions

How can you make the same mistake?
- I don't get to do anything because of that church.
- That church makes my life more difficult.
- God is a mean God...all he does is punish people.
- God can't be nice or else all the bad things wouldn't happen.
- Jesus is too good to be true.
- Jesus can't relate to me; the Bible can't really make me happy.

What is so dangerous about making these kinds of assumptions?

Jesus was very misunderstood because of the many assumptions people made. This caused people to doubt his upbringing, question his relationship with God, and misinterpret his purpose.

[Read John 7:14-18]
What does Jesus say to do in order to really understand what his expectations are?
- Put his teachings into practice

? What does he mean by verse 18?

I did this lesson because some of you talk bad about the church and about your parents—the advice they get, the decisions they make, the direction they give you. You get attitudes and slam them, sometimes publicly but most times secretly. You are like these Jews: you just want Jesus and his teachings to stop messing up your life. My conviction is that they are just what you need; however, that's my conviction. You learn about Jesus' teachings, put them into practice and find out for yourself. Stop insulting your parents when all they are trying to be are men and women of truth. Would you rather have hypocritical parents who say one thing but do another? I bet not! Stop cursing the church, which is just trying to honor God in a godless society. If you have constructive criticism, speak openly and humbly to a leader and watch it change. If not, then you make some changes yourself. "If you can't change the situation, change your perspective." Others listen to this junk because they don't have the conviction to stand up for truth. Be a young man or a young woman of truth—believe in truth and then stand up for it. "Happiness exists when the things we believe in are consistent with the things we do."

#92. Wisdom vs. Folly

Opening activity: Divide the group into teams of three. Have one person from each group sit at one end of the room blindfolded. Ensure that the blindfolded person can't hear. Instruct the other two that they are to give the blindfolded person directions to a certain object in the room; however, one of the two is to give correct directions and the other one is to give incorrect directions, and they are not to tell the person blindfolded which of them is telling the truth. The person must figure that out on their own. Give them 5-10 minutes to see which team can get to the object.

? What did you think of the game? What made it difficult?
For those of you who were blindfolded, how did you know who to listen to? How did you make your decisions?
For those of you giving the directions, how did you feel while you were talking?

We are going to look at two people tonight who are trying to get your attention.

[Read Proverbs 9:1-6] {Have them close their eyes as you read
? What came to your mind as you listened to me read this?

[Read Proverbs 9:13-17] {Have them close the eyes and read with venom.}
? What came to your mind as you listened to this one?

? Who are the two women?
- Wisdom and Folly

? How are the two women alike?
- Both call from the highest point in the city.
- Both call out to the simple.

? Who are the simple?
- Simple means someone naïve or easily persuaded.

? How are they different?
- Wisdom is more together; Folly sounds like a loose, undisciplined, out-

205

there girl.
- Wisdom gives a promise: "You will live"; Folly does not.
- Wisdom makes sense: "ways of understanding"; Folly is contradictory, sounds too good to be true—stolen water is good? Secret food?

? In the game that we played, how could the blindfolded person tell the difference between the people giving the directions?
- By the result

However, you may end up in a place you don't want to be, and by then it is too late. Better yet…take the blindfold off so you can see.

? As a young person, what are some of the tough decisions you have to make? {For each thing that they bring up ask the following question.}
What are some things that could help you see better to make that decision?

[Psalm 119:130] Wisdom is found in God's word, the Bible. There are scriptures for every question.

A woman and a man are involved in a car accident. It's a bad one. Both of their cars are demolished, but amazingly, neither of them is hurt. After they crawl out of their cars, the woman says, "So, you're a man… That's interesting. I'm a woman. Wow, just look at our cars! There's nothing left, but fortunately we are unhurt. This must be a sign from God that we should meet and be friends and live together in peace for the rest of our days." The man replies, "I agree with you completely. This must be a sign from God!" The woman continues, "And look at this, here's another miracle… My car is completely demolished, but this bottle of wine didn't break. Surely God wants us to drink this wine and celebrate our good fortune." Then she hands the bottle to the man. The man nods his head in agreement, opens it, drinks half the bottle and then hands it back to the woman. The woman takes the bottle, immediately puts the cap back on, and hands it back to the man. The man says, "Aren't you having any?" She replies, "Nah. I think I'll just wait for the police."

There will be all kinds of decisions that you must make. My challenge to you is to practice now to rely on good judgment by using the Bible to give you the light you need to see where you are going—or like this man, you will be caught in a situation you don't want to be in when the police come.

#93. Working under Pressure

{Do the Solomon Asch Conformity Experiment (Google it) with the group, using the two sets of instructions below. Be sure to prepare most of the group beforehand to choose the shorter line (to be "confederates" as described in the online description of the experiment).}

Prior instructions to the confederates:
In a moment, you will be shown two lines; then you will be asked to choose which one is longer. No matter what you think, choose the shorter line.

Instructions during the class:
In a moment, you will be shown two lines; when asked, choose which one is longer.

This very same experiment was done in 1955 by social psychologist Solomon Asch. 75% chose the wrong line at least once; 5% conformed every time.

Other experiments: people continued giving shocks (they thought) to other people (the Milgram experiment); people were influenced when guessing the number of beans in a bottle (Arthur Jenness)

? Why is peer pressure such a big problem?

Tonight, we are going to talk about some ways not to get caught in the peer-pressure game.

[Read 2 Kings 5:1-12]
? How would you describe Naaman?
How do you typically react to a person like this?
How would you expect Naaman's servants to react to his outrage?

Let's see... **[Read 2 Kings 5:13-14]**
? How do they react?
What do you think are some ways they prepared themselves to talk with Naaman?
- Respectful
- Logical

- Did not cut him down, kept relationship
- Confident

? Where did their confidence come from?
- Knew what was right, they had seen prophets work

My challenge for you is to be determined not to let peer pressure influence you in a negative way.
1. Think through how you will react to negative pressure; how you can stand up for what is right without tearing the person down or being stuck up.
2. Grow in knowing what is right.
3. Start acting righter.
4. Get your confidence from being righteous and let that influence you and others.

Most people do what is natural when they are under pressure. Make righteousness your natural behavior—you do that by constantly doing what is right.

? How many of you were told to vote for number two no matter what?
Some of you were influenced by that peer pressure. If you do the four steps above, you can beat the pressure. You set the standard for righteousness.

One last thing...

? What stands out to you in verses 13 and 14?
- "Servants," plural; it was the servant girl who told Naaman's wife, but it was the servants who talked to him after he was angry.

Realize that you need each other, so work together in confronting peer pressure.

#94. XXX: Three Characteristics of Sin

? What is something that disturbs you?
{Could be personal, family, school, world events, news items, etc.; not "I don't like broccoli"!}
Why is it happening?
What can you do about it?
How do you think God feels about it?

This lesson comes from a time of thinking about things that bug me: terrorism, nasty people, people with a lack of integrity, and judgmental people.
What do all the things that bug you and me have in common?
- Sin

? What is sin?
- Literally means miss the target, which is God's character

Tonight, I want to talk maturely to you and teach you about sin and a few of its characteristics. Sin is:

1. X-Rated. [2 Samuel 11:1-5]
? What was David's sin?
Extramarital whackness

? What do you think of David's actions?

[Read James 1:13-14] The Bible describes sin as evil.
? Which sins?
- All of them

If you miss the mark, you've missed. Does it matter by how much? No, maybe in a game of horseshoes or grenades or atomic bombs but not with sin. Illustration: an Atlanta radio station did an experiment where the DJ posed as a 13-year-old girl on the internet. Within 30 minutes the DJ was able to get a guy to call the station hotline. He talked with the station producer who sounded like a 13-year-old. Within a couple of minutes, he was asking whether or not she was alone and how big her chest was. (Yes, right on the radio!) Sin is X-rated and it is disturbing!

Don't think that it isn't. If you do, it will get you.

2. Exponential. [2 Samuel 11:6-17]
? How did David attempt to deal with sin?
What does exponential mean?
- Growing at an increasing rate

Sin breeds sin. David slept with another man's wife and got her pregnant, then he did all he could to cover it up. He tells one lie after another until he murders.

[Read James 1:15]
Sin likes to grow. "Be afraid; be very afraid" of what you start, i.e. gossip, lies, anger, hatred, lust, criticalness, etc., for it may take you to places you don't want to go. Understand the nature of sin. It wants to consume you. Here are two areas where I think you need to be afraid:
1. Instant messages: you play around with conversations you shouldn't have, act like someone you are not. Remember the radio station experiment, where the DJ posed as a middle schooler.
2. Lust: You allow yourself to think thoughts that you shouldn't or look at things you shouldn't. If you keep it up, you will find yourself with regrets.

3. Excruciating. [2 Samuel 12:1-10]
? How would you feel if you were Bathsheba?
How did God feel?

Sin always leaves a mark. Name an actor in a movie who has tattoos all over. Did you know they are fake? Off screen, most actors have no tattoos. Sin's tattoos, however, are real. If you gossip about someone, or lie, or slam someone, or disrespect them, there are marks—marks on the person, on you and on God.

{Read the following poem.}

Six humans trapped by happenstance
In bleak and bitter cold;
Each one possessed a stick of wood,
Or so the story's told.

Their dying fire in need of logs,
The first man held his back,
For of the faces around the fire,
He noticed one was black.
The next man looking across the way,
Saw one not of his church
And couldn't bring himself to give
The fire his stick of birch.
The third one sat in tattered clothes;
He gave his coat a hitch.
Why should his log be put to use
To warm the idle rich?
The rich man just sat back and thought
Of the wealth he had in store,
And how to keep what he had earned
From the lazy, shiftless poor.
The black man's face bespoke revenge
As the fire passed from his sight,
For all he saw in his stick of wood
Was a chance to spite the white.
The last man of this forlorn group
Did naught except for gain.
Giving only to those who gave to him
Was how he played the game.
Their logs held tight in death's still hands
Was proof of human sin;
They didn't die from the cold without;
They died from the cold within.

I teach this lesson in hopes that it will help you understand some things about sin and, maybe, something about yourself, so that you will go about your time at school or at play or with your family and friends and not be fooled by sin's deceitfulness.

#95. Becoming A Box Office Hit

Opening activity: As kids arrive, provide a nametag and a black or red marker. Have the kids write their names on a nametag. They can choose which color marker. Until you split up for the lesson, have all the workers pay "special" attention to the people whose nametags are written in black. Give gum out only to those people, talk with them, hug them, etc. Treat people with red nametags as lower-class citizens.

To begin the discussion, give each person a 3x5 card and ask them to think of the job on a movie set that best represents them in reference to their relationships with people in the middle school group. This could be actor, singer, director, producer, sound guy, makeup, cameraman, film editor, etc.

? What did you write down and why?
What makes a great team?
What could you do to make this group a better team?
{Make sure when they give their answer they say "*I can...* or *I will...*" It needs to be first-person kind of talk.}

[Read Galatians 2:11-14]
Tell me what was happening here.
Describe the team that Peter and Paul were on.
- They were on God's team, which has all kinds of people.

? How did Peter cause disunity within this team?
- Caused a clique or a faction

Making a team takes effort. It doesn't happen naturally. In fact, our nature is to create cliques.

[Read Galatians 5:19-20]
Factions, disunity, CLIQUES are an act of your flesh—what it is in your nature to do. To make a great team, you must do the opposite of your sinful nature.

? What are some basic things you must have to make a blockbuster movie?
- Supporting role, great plot, etc.

Tools to Help Preteen and Young Teen Leaders and Parents

Let's come up with a few basics to building friendships, just like a supporting role and a great plot.

[Read Proverbs 17:17, 18:24]

? What basic element of friendship are these scriptures talking about?
- Supporting role

Your role is to be devoted to the friendships you already have in here. Don't be a friend only when it suits your pleasure. Support each other. Watch each other's back. That's building each other up according to your needs. Be there for your friend even if you lose face.

[Read Proverbs 18:1]

? What element of friendship is this scripture talking about?
- Great plot

Be friendly. Build the plot in this room with new friendships. Invite someone you don't know very well to come over or go to the movies or just hang. Thicken the plot by pursuing their interest instead of yours. You may be surprised to learn to like something new and enjoy yourself. Once this person has become a friend, don't forget to support them as well.

? What's the goal of every movie?
- To be a blockbuster, box-office hit

List the top 5 grossing movies of all time.

? How will this team {meaning the group} be a box office hit?
- By creating a place where
  1) you can be accepted for who you are (supported)
  2) great friendships are made (great plot)

? What clique did we create earlier tonight? How did it make those of you with red nametags feel? How many of you would like some help to keep people from feeling that way?

I will help you with this by pointing out ways you can be better friends and reminding you to support each other and to build new friendships.

> There's a story of a man who had a neighbor who was trying to put a TV antenna on his roof in time so he could watch the television premiere of his favorite movie, but he was having a terrible time. The man decided to give his neighbor a hand. He went over and took with him his best tools and soon had the antenna up. His neighbor asked him what he made with such fancy tools. The man replied, "Friends, mostly."

The scriptures we've looked at tonight are tools that, if you actually use them, will help you to make great friends, will help this group become stronger, and will keep some of you from feeling what the red-name-tagged people felt. It will help us become a blockbuster, a box office hit!

Challenge: Before you leave give a ticket to one person that you've never had to your house.

#96. Exact Time & Place

Opening activity: Give out the worksheet (below) to small groups and have them fill in the blanks.

Worksheet answers (based on the 2016 study found at http://www.100people.org/statistics_detailed_statistics.php):

60 Asians
10 Europeans
14 from the Western Hemisphere
16 Africans
50 would be female
50 would be male
70 would be nonwhite
30 would be white
69 would be non-Christian
31 would be Christian
78 would have shelter from wind and rain
11 would be undernourished
14 would be unable to read and write
7 would have a college education
11 would live on less than $1.90 USD/day
6 people would possess 59% of the entire world's wealth (all from the US)

? What are your thoughts after learning this?

[Read Acts 17:16-34]
? What is the main thrust of Paul's message in this passage? How does it relate to you?

? Do you realize that you were appointed a certain place and a time in history by God?

? Looking at the statistics above, how does it make you feel that God would put you where you are?
Why would he do such a thing?

- To perhaps reach out for him

What would it communicate to God if you didn't take that chance to reach out to him?
How can you show you will make the most of the time and place God has set for you?

» If you woke up this morning with more health than illness; you are better than the million who will not survive this week.
» If you have never experienced the danger of battle, the loneliness of imprisonment, the agony of torture, or the pangs of starvation, you are ahead of 500 million people in the world.
» If you can attend a church meeting without fear of harassment, arrest, torture, or death, you are more blessed than three billion people in the world.
» If you have food in the refrigerator, clothes on your back, a roof overhead, and a place to sleep, you are richer than 75% of this world.
» If you have money in the bank or in your wallet, and spare change in a dish someplace, you are among the top 8% of the world's wealthiest people.
» If your parents are still alive and still married, you are very rare, even in the United States and Canada.
» If you can read this message, you are more blessed than over two billion people in the world that cannot read at all.

God has placed you in an amazing station in life. Don't let your ETA (Exact Time of Arrival) slip by because you take it for granted. You could have been born in any other place. Take every opportunity to learn about life, about God, about yourself, and about other people. Who knows, it may be the very thing that saves your soul and someone else's.

WORKSHEET

If the world were made up of 100 people, how many would be:

___ Asians
___ Europeans

Tools to Help Preteen and Young Teen Leaders and Parents

___ from the Western Hemisphere, both north and south
___ Africans
___ Female
___ Male
___ Nonwhite
___ White
___ Non-Christian
___ Christian
___ Have shelter from wind and rain
___ Unable to read
___ Would be undernourished
___ A college graduate
___ Live on less than $1.90 USD per day
___ In possession of 59% of the entire world's wealth

CONSTRUCTION AREA II
Bible Reliability

#1. Change Is Good but Not God

Game: Twenty-One. Divide into teams and provide a dealer (an adult) for each team. Each team will have the rules of 21 explained one time at the beginning of the first round.

Beginning Rules: Dealer deals each player two cards. Each player has the option to ask for ONE additional card. The closest to 21 without going over wins a point (ties okay). Play the round for two minutes and give a prize to the person with the most points. After each round, the dealers rotate to the next team. In each of the next three rounds the dealer changes the rules to the following without telling the players what the changes are:
Round 2: Closest to 25 w/o going over wins a point (ties ok)
Round 3: Any player with a face card wins a point (ties ok)
Round 4: Closest to 21 w/o going over, but ONLY black cards count (ties ok).
Give a prize for the person with the most points for all four rounds, if you would like.

? What was happening in this game?
- Rules changed in each round.

How is this like life?
- Life is very dynamic...never know what to expect.

? What are some things that are constantly changing?
What are some things that never change?

[Read Malachi 3:6a, James 1:17] {Have two kids ready to read}
? What does this tell you about God's character?
Why would that be important for you?

[Read Mark 13:31, Psalm 119:89] {Have two kids ready to read}
? What does this tell you about the Bible?

There was a study done on the power of peer pressure in which a group of six people were asked to look at a piece of paper with three horizontal bars on it of three differing lengths. They were then asked to raise their hand whenever the instructor pointed at the longest bar. Five out of the six people had been told beforehand to incorrectly pick the second bar when in fact the third bar was the longer one. 75% of the time the person who wasn't told which one to pick refused to raise their hand when the instructor pointed at the third bar. Their reasons ranged from "unsure" to "did not want to stand out."

{If you would like and have time, you could actually do the above experiment by getting four volunteers to be the "untold" person and see what results you get.}

We all are influenced (changed) by the world around us!

? What role can the Bible play to help you not be pushed around by everyone else?
What emphasis should you put on the trusting the Bible?
What can you do to trust the Bible more this year?

This lesson is to act as an introduction to a 4-week series on the trustworthiness of the Bible and God, i.e. Is there a God? Is the Bible God's word? How was the Bible created? Is the Bible reliable? What in science, history or archeology supports the Bible, etc.

#2. A Unique Standard

What are some topics that you would like to discuss in here? {Make a list for your future use}

Opening activity: Taste Test. Make a sandwich with bread and tuna only—no condiments. Cut it into small pieces. Have some volunteers eat a piece and tell the group what they think it is. Do not tell them what it is until the very end of the lesson. Some will guess tuna; others will guess something else. Once you are done or run out of pieces, continue with the following questions:

? We have differing opinions on what it is; what would we need to do to know?
- Send it to a lab and have it tested and compared to a standard

{At this point, tell the group that you called and made sure that everything was alright and nothing would harm them. Tell them the pieces of sandwich have tuna flavored cat food on them. After all the fuss, continue with the lesson.}

? What is a standard? What would make a great standard for our lives and the topics you have chosen to talk about?

[Read John 12:44-48] You will be judged by this standard just as the sandwich would be.

? What would you want to know about the Bible before you made it a standard for your life? {It might be good to make a list and come back to this throughout this series or at a later time.}

{Share some of the interesting facts below regarding the Bible. You don't have to share all of them but enough to help them see that this book is amazingly unique and true! The rest are for you. Enjoy! (All the information below was taken from Josh McDowell's *Evidence That Demands a Verdict*, Volume 1, 1979.)

Unique in Its Continuity:
1. Written over a 1,500-year span of 40 generations by over 40 authors from every walk of life including kings (David/Solomon), a herdsman (Amos), a general (Joshua), fishermen (Peter), a doctor (Luke), a prime minister (Daniel), a tax collector (Matthew), a rabbi (Paul), a cupbearer (Nehemiah), etc.
2. Written in different places: Moses in the wilderness, Jeremiah in a dungeon, Daniel on a hillside and in a palace, Paul inside a prison, Luke while

traveling, John on an island, others in the rigor of a military campaign.
3. Written on three continents: Asia, Africa and Europe.
4. Written in three languages: Hebrew (Old Testament), Greek (New Testament), Aramaic.
5. Written to include a host of controversial subjects (Can you name any?); yet biblical authors spoke of them with harmony and continuity.
6. Written with one harmonious theme: God's redemption of man.

Unique in Its Circulation:
1. Read by more people and published in more languages than any other book. For example, 30 years ago, to meet demand, the British and Foreign Bible Society had to publish one copy every three seconds day and night—you figure the math!

Unique in Its Translation:
1. One of the first major books to be translated.
2. By 1966, translated wholly in 240 languages and partially in another 739.

Unique in Its Survival:
1. Through time: has more manuscript evidence than any 10 pieces of classical literature combined.
2. Through persecution: in AD 303 an imperial edict was passed to burn every known Bible...and yet!
3. Through criticism: no other book has endured the level of criticism, e.g., at one time it was said that there was no way Moses wrote the Pentateuch (first five books of the Bible) because writing was not invented during Moses' time. Yet the "black stele" was discovered, which dated writing as being before Moses' time. So much for the critic!

Unique in Its Teachings:
1. Of prophecy: no book tells so much of the future relating to individual nations, to Israel, to all peoples of earth, to certain cities and the Savior, Jesus.
2. Of history: no other nation can claim such an accurate and detailed writing of its history as Israel.
3. Of personalities: no other book deals so frankly as to the lives of people and yet is consistent in its teachings. The Bible not only is the truth but tells the truth!

Unique in Its Influence on Surrounding Literature:
Cleland B. McAfee stated, "If every Bible in any considerable city were destroyed,

the Book could be restored in all its essential parts from the quotations on the shelves of the city public library."

Conclusion: Oh, by the way, the sandwich was actually tuna—yet some of you will walk away not sure if I am telling the truth. Unlike the tuna/cat food, the Bible is something of which you need to be sure. It will pay to make sure, considering that one day you will be judged by it! In the next lesson we will learn how accurate and well-documented the Bible is.

#3. A Reliable Standard*

Opening activity: Play the Telephone Game using tongue twisters: "A skunk sat on a stump and thunk the stump stunk," "Shy Shelly says she shall sew sheets," "A noisy noise annoys an oyster," etc.

Play Art Relay: have the kids sit in a straight line so that they are facing the back of the person in front of them. Show the person in the back of the line (the one who has no one looking at his back) a simple picture (i.e. a square or smiley face). He is to draw the picture on the person's back in front him, who in turn draws it on the person's back in front of them and so on and so on. This continues until the drawing reaches the first person in line (the one with no one on whose back to draw). That person draws the shape on a piece of paper. See how close they come to the original.

? How do these games relate to our ability to communicate with someone else?

? What would make communication more reliable especially between two parties that could not see each other?
- Write what you want to say, talk directly

? How does either one of these games relate to the reliability of the Bible?

? The Bible is God's direct communication to you…what are some of the factors that could challenge the reliability of an ancient writing like the Bible?
- Copying mistakes, careless translation errors, forgotten parts, etc.

[Read 2 Timothy 3:16, 2 Peter 1:19-21]
? What do these two scriptures say about the origin of the Bible?
- It is a product of God himself.

Tell me what you know of how the Bible came about.

The process is known as the canonization of the Bible. The word "canon" means "reed," which was a standard unit of measure; therefore, the word "canon" became synonymous with the word "standard." The early Christians had to decide which books to include in the Bible.

? How would you go about deciding which books to include?

Tools to Help Preteen and Young Teen Leaders and Parents

It is important to understand that the early church did not create the canon or books included in Scripture. Isn't that what the two scriptures we just read said? Instead, their job was to recognize which ones were inspired by God.

? Why do you think the early Christians felt a need to create the Bible?

Three reasons:
1. A heretic, Marcion (around AD 140), developed his own Bible, so they wanted to determine what the real deal was.
2. Many books were in circulation, so they wanted to know which ones were inspired.
3. The Edict of Diocletian (AD 303) declared the destruction of the earliest copies of the Bible. Who wanted to die for a religious book? They needed to know if it was truly inspired!

Old Testament {Have them turn to the index in their Bible.}
- There are 39 books in the OT which were written by prophets—men of God.
- Your OT is the same one as the Jews have been using and recognize as inspired by God for the last 2,000-3,000 years.
- We order the books differently (by topic) and break some in two; otherwise it is the same.
- Christianity just accepted what books have always been accepted, and that is how we got our OT.

Next, we will look at the New Testament and how they decided which books were inspired by God, and we'll look at how we can determine the reliability of the Bible.

New Testament
- There are 27 books in the NT which were written from AD 40-100.
- There were five principles which determined if a book was to be included in the Bible:
    1) Is it authoritative—did it come from God?
    2) Is it prophetic—was it written by a man of God?
    3) Is it authentic? The early church had the policy of "if in doubt, throw it out."
    4) Is it dynamic—did it come with the life-transforming power of God?
    5) Was it received, collected, read and used—was it accepted by the people?

» Since the year 393 there has been no challenge to the 27 books of our NT.

? If it were up to you, how would you determine if the books of the Bible are reliable?

One way to test a manuscript is called the bibliographical test. This test was used to determine how the text was handed down from generation to generation. Since we don't have the original manuscripts, this test determines how reliable the copies are, based on the number of copies of a manuscript and the time interval between the original and the earliest copy.

According to this test, no other text comes close to the Bible (New Testament). The Iliad by Homer is a distant second. See the chart below for other examples.

Manuscript	When Written	Earliest Copy	Time Span	No. of copies
New Testament	AD 40-100	AD 125	25 yrs.	Over 24,000
Iliad by Homer	900 BC	400 BC	500 yrs.	643
Plato	427-347 BC	AD 900	1,200 yrs.	7
Sophocles	496-406 BC	AD 1000	1,400 yrs.	193

Practices of early scribes that were followed to ensure the accuracy of the texts:
1. Counted and verified the number of words and of letters in each copy.
2. Calculated and verified the middle word and the middle letter of each text.
3. Each copy was from an authenticated copy known as an exemplar.
4. No letter could be copied by memory; it was verified by sight first.
5. Had to be written with a certain known ink recipe on an approved paper.

We don't have time to look at two other tests used; if we did there would be an enormous amount of evidence. God meant for his words to not only be from his own lips but for them to be passed on to you as if he whispered them in your own ear yesterday. He wanted this so the communication between you and him would be direct and correct in regard to having a relationship with him. God has spoken well...are you listening?

* All the information was gleaned from Josh McDowell's *Evidence That Demands a Verdict*, Volume 1, 1979.

#4. One Smart God

? What important scientific discoveries can you name?
How could science make the Bible more trustworthy?
If the Bible was full of claims that science could prove to be mistakes, how would this affect your trust in the Bible?
Let's look at a few biblical claims and see what science has had to say:

1. Biological Claim: {hold up a container of antibacterial soap}

? What is this? What is it used for? When was it created?
- Cleansing agent containing a chemical that kills bacteria, became commercially available in the 1980s

? When was bacteria discovered?
- Around 1675 by Antony van Leeuwenhoek; however, it wasn't until the late 1800s that people believed they cause disease

? [Numbers 19:16-18] Who wrote this book?
- Moses, over 3,000 years ago

? What do you think they knew of germs and biology then?
- Nothing, in fact, there were some strange ways to cure people of disease then, e.g. bloodletting, crushed flies spread on wounds, etc.

God told people to use ash and hyssop along with water. The ash combined with the oil from the hyssop made soap. The hyssop plant coincidentally contains in its oil about 50% carvacrol, an organic compound that is the equivalent of one found in this container of soap I am holding today. Imagine that!

2. Medical Claim: {hold up a Band-Aid}

? What is this? Why do we use it?
- Helps the body stop bleeding until blood clotting agents come

? [Genesis 17:12] God says not to do this surgery until the baby is eight days old. Why do you think this so specific?

First of all, babies don't remember the pain and they heal quicker, but more amazingly, the eighth day is when a baby produces the optimum amount of vitamin K, which is vital for making prothrombin, the main blood-clotting protein. Vitamin

K is produced by bacteria in the body. A baby doesn't have enough bacteria until the eighth day—studies show that vitamin K production peaks at 110% on the eighth day. Do you think Moses knew this?

3. Geological Claim: {show a map or a globe of the earth}
When was it discovered that the earth was round?
- First known claim by Pythagoras in 525 BC

[Isaiah 40:22] This was written around 750 BC, 225 years before the first theory.

4. Meteorological Claim: {present an umbrella}
What is meteorology?
- Study of the weather

How is rain created?
- Evaporation, condensation, distillation—the rain cycle

[Read Job 36:27-29] God explains the process that man could not. This process is known as the hydrological process, and only in the nineteenth century did it become widely accepted.

5. Cosmological Claim: {display a picture of the known universe}
How was the universe made?

"Today, due to the discoveries of the Hubble telescope, it is generally accepted by all astronomers that the universe began by the detonation of the 'primordial atom' of unthinkable mass" (*US News & World Report Special Edition*, "Mysteries of Outer Space," November, 2003).

[Read Hebrews 11:1-3] What does this mean?
- That God made what is seen out of what is unseen.

There so many more things we could talk about that the Bible says and science confirms. How does this help you to trust the Bible?

[Read 1 Thessalonians 2:13]
If the Bible were the words of men, especially men of such great scientific ignorance, then there would be many scientific inaccuracies; however, the evidence suggests otherwise—that, indeed, this book was written by an all-knowing and amazing God! Isn't it worth our trust?

In the next lesson we will look at archeological claims.

#5. A Tale of Two Cities

{Hide $5 in the room and have the kids search for it.}

How did you feel looking for the $5?

That's how an archeologist feels while on a dig. Tonight we are going to look at how archeology has given proof to the validity of the Scriptures.

What is archeology? {Define.}
Does it prove the Bible is from God?
- No, but it confirms that the historical information in the Bible is true and accurate; therefore, the rest should be as well.

What famous biblical archeological findings do you know about?

Here are a few exciting findings that have been unearthed and how they refute a widely held criticism:

Criticism	Archeological Evidence
The first five books of the Bible could not have been written by Moses because writing did not exist during that time period.	Ebla Tablets: over 17,000 writing tablets were unearthed predating Moses by 1,000 years.
The walls of Jericho could not have fallen outward—all walls fall inward when a city is attacked.	The excavation of Jericho in 1930-36 found the walls to have indeed fallen outward allowing the Israelites to walk into the city as described in the Bible.
No census was taken under Governor Quirinius as described by Luke regarding the birth of Jesus.	An inscription was found confirming Quirinius was governor, and a papyrus was found referring to a census and the procedure mentioned to return to one's place of origin.

Many more findings confirm biblical statements and facts; just in the book that was used during my preparation for this lesson, over 50 such findings were referenced.

What kind of archeological find would be the most amazing to you; what would make you say, "Yes, the Bible is true and accurate beyond any doubt"?

I'll tell you a tale of two cities: the cities of Tyre and Babylon and how history and archeology has proven true what the Bible wrote about each them.

Tyre
[Ezekiel 26:3-8, 12-14] {written around 586 BC—have the kids underline the following phrases or write them on an easel for everyone to see.}
- v.3   many nations
- v.4   bare rock
- v.5   out in the sea, place to spread fishnets
- v.12   throw your stone, timber and rubble into the sea
- v.14   never be rebuilt

King Nebuchadnezzar was in power three years after this prophecy—ruler of the known world.

Tyre was arrogant and ungodly, on the edge of the ocean. "Nothing can get us… we are safe."

King Nebuchadnezzar put Tyre under siege, which lasted 13 years.

Ask: What is a siege?

» At the end of 13 years, Tyre relented and when Nebuchadnezzar broke down the gates, most of the people relocated to an island a half mile off the coast. The mainland city was destroyed in 573 B.C. The city of Tyre (out on the island) remained a powerful city for couple hundred years.
» 240 years later, Alexander the Great wants to access the city as a port; Tyre says no so he lays siege to it; he uses Tyre's mainland rubble, stones and timber to make a causeway out to the island. Tyre tries to stop him, but with superior naval forces Alexander overcomes the city and kills 8,000 and enslaves 30,000 more.
» 50 years later another king attacks what little of Tyre is left.
» In the 11th, 12th and 13th centuries, crusades were fought in the region, and finally after 1,600 hundred years Tyre is no more.
» Great location for a city, yet no city has ever been built there to this day.
» In fact, the local fishermen dry their nets on the rocks of Tyre.

What amazes you about what the Bible says about Tyre and what was found?

Babylon
[Isaiah 13:19-22] written around 700 BC
» Known as the Wonder City of the Ancient World around 600 BC
» Surrounded by a wall 56 miles around, 311 feet high (30 story building), 87 feet thick (11 cars side by side), 100 gates of solid brass, 250 watch towers 400 feet tall (one every quarter mile)

- » Outer wall was surrounded by a 30-foot moat
- » Euphrates river ran through the middle of the city with high walls on either side
- » One bridge ½ mile long with a drawbridge that was removed each night and a tunnel under the river 15 feet wide and 12 feet high
- » Inner wall was 80 feet thick
- » Considered to be impregnable by ancient standards

? How would you suggest attacking such a city?

Here's what happened:
- » Around 520 BC, King Cyrus of Persia put a siege on the city; the Babylonian king and its people were very confident of not being overtaken.
- » During a feast to one of the Babylonian gods where everyone got drunk, Cyrus, with the help of two Babylonian deserters, diverted the waters of the Euphrates and came through the tunnel under the river.
- » The city came to a slow ruin and many nations conquered it to the point that it was more feasible to build other cities.
- » Babylon was rediscovered in the early 1900s; for 2,000 years people walked over the city, nobody ever built there. Legend was that the land was haunted so nobody camped or grazed there or even used the rocks on the land.
- » Most travelers to the area take note of the various kinds of wildlife that exist, especially that of owls and jackals, as author Austen Layard states, "Owls start from the scanty thickets and the foul jackal skulks through the furrows."

? How do these two stories help your trust in the Bible?
How do these stories help you with the direction the Bible gives you?

God is serious about his honor and his Word. What he says will happen, will happen; and eventually findings, whether historical or archeological, will prove him to be right. If what he says about cities and stones and other insignificant matters is true, then how about heaven, hell, his feelings toward you, his promises regarding your life, and the issues of your heart and character? There is no room for doubt—God's way is true and reasonable!

CONSTRUCTION AREA III
Character Studies

#1. Building a Great Foundation

? Why do you want to study?
What do you think will be the most difficult thing for you in studying the Bible?
What fears do you have about studying the Bible?
What have you been studying in your quiet times lately?
What are your expectations from studying the Bible?
What do you expect from me?
Do you want any input/advice?
Would you like to be encouraged?
How often would you like to study?

[Read 1 Corinthians 3:9-10]

? What do you know about the construction of a house and what takes the longest?
- Foundation

? What are some things that would be important for us to study so that you will have a solid foundation at such a young age?
- Jesus (we may study him for a few weeks: typical day, purpose, heart, was he real, how is he a hero, etc.)
- Jesus' character {introduce the character studies}
- Scriptures that will help you be more like him. {Great time to talk about how any study we do is a real study—address the "real studies" issue}

When do you see yourself being baptized? {Assumption is that they know what this is—especially if studying with a believer's kid.} I have no idea—the Bible will tell us. am not going to rush building your foundation, but I still want you to be urgent. You need to be serious about what we study and put into practice what you learn, but not hurry the day of your baptism. It will come.

? If you were leading this study, what expectations would you have of yourself?

Here are my expectations of you:
- » Have quiet times
- » Come to studies w/notebook and questions
- » Obey the Bible
- » Be open, honest, real; it's okay to question the Bible as long as you are seeking understanding. God likes questions and seekers!

? When do you want to get together again?

#2. The Character of Jesus

Purpose of the study:
- » Spark an interest in the Bible
- » Shatter misconceptions about Jesus
- » Motivate to read the Bible

? What are some misconceptions about Jesus?
- Pale, weak, thin, effeminate, boring, quiet, "doormat"
- "Love the children and animals, lamb in arms" tone
- Spacey, dreamy look on face and in eyes

? Why so many misconceptions?
- Listening to what others say
- Watching poor media coverage
- Don't read about Jesus for ourselves

The Real Jesus
Examine the gospels to find the real Jesus: his heart, attitudes, priorities, relationship with God, how he spent his time, how he reacted, how he treated people.

[Read Mark 1:16-20]
? Why did they follow him?

? Crowds always around him [1:33, 1:45, 2:1-2, 13, 3:7, 20] Charisma? Confidence?

Name some people in modern times who have or had charisma to attract others to follow—in good ways and bad ways.
- Martin Luther King, Jr.; Nelson Mandela; Hitler; Osama bin Laden

Must be more than charisma. Read on...

[Read Mark 1:21-28]
? How did he teach?
- With authority (and with conviction)

? What does it mean to teach with authority?
- Not afraid of what others think
- Confident
- Knows the topic

Tools to Help Preteen and Young Teen Leaders and Parents

They came back to hear his teaching! More than just charisma. Look at how he treats this man possessed by an evil spirit.

? How would most people react to a person "possessed by an evil spirit"?
- Afraid
- Cross the street
- Back off

How did Jesus treat him?
- Sternly
- Boldly

Not how we picture Jesus. These people remembered this event.

[Read Mark 1:35-37]
? What was his priority?
When was the last time you got up before dark, left the house and prayed?
What does this show about Jesus, especially after the day that he had the day before? (Look back through the chapter.)
- Shows his relationship with God

[Read Mark 1:40-42]
? How did he react to and treat people?
What is the result of leprosy?
- Grotesque physically
- Social stigma

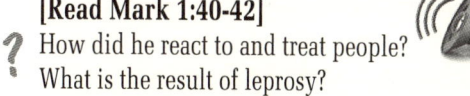

? How would most people treat this man?
- Afraid, like AIDS today—afraid it's contagious

? How does Jesus treat him?
What is compassion?

? Why do you think he touched him?
- Sometimes words aren't enough.
- Maybe no one had touched him in years.

Could have healed him from afar ("Ok, you stand over there, keep your distance—ok, you're healed now.")

? What does this say about Jesus?

[Read John 2:13-16]

? What is the Passover?
- A time to bring animals to sacrifice

? Why is what they're doing wrong?
- Making a profit off it
- Not sincere

Like buying a birthday gift at the last second, no pre-thought put into it.

? How does Jesus react?
- Doesn't lose his temper—takes time to make a whip out of cords

Imagine this! Must have made the Jerusalem news ("Jesus Clears Temple!").

? What does this say about Jesus' character?
- Takes a stand on what is right/wrong, not afraid to cause controversy, takes a stand even when outnumbered.

Note the exclamation points. Strong words! Not wimpy.

[Read John 8:2-11]

? What speaker would you get up at dawn to listen to?

Imagine the scene: Jesus quietly teaching the people, the Pharisees wanting to make him look bad, the woman caught in the act of adultery thinking she will be stoned, Jesus put in a Catch-22 situation.

? How does Jesus handle this pressurized situation?
- Calm, logical, not overwhelmed, keeps his cool as the younger guy

? Why is his answer so good?
- Turns it back on them

Wisdom! With one sentence, he clears the crowd.

? How does he treat the woman?
- Able to forgive her in her failure, gives her a chance to change

Challenge: Read the gospels, starting in John, and find out WHO JESUS IS!

{Give them the book *Jesus the Same* by Charles Edward Jefferson (available at www.ipibooks.com).}

#3. Dig Deep in Your Heart

[Read Luke 8:1-15]
Read the Parable of the Sower and talk about the different types of hearts.

- Which heart is yours? Why?

- Which heart would you like to be? Why?

- What does it take to be the good soil?
  - Dig out the weeds—sinful nature, weak character areas

[Read Hebrews 4:12-13]
- What does "it judges the thoughts and the attitudes of the heart" mean?

- What has to happen before the Bible can judge your thoughts and attitudes?
  - YOU have to be aware of them and be willing to admit them.

Talk about last week's study and what your concerns are. The purpose of character studies is to help you change things in your character. You can't change something you don't know or won't admit.

It takes maturity and a willingness to do this.
- Which is keeping you from it? [Refer back to Luke 8:14.]

- What is keeping you from maturing?
- What can we do this week to help grow consistently?

#4. Generosity

? What does it mean to be generous?
What are ways to be generous?

[Read 2 Corinthians 8:1-15]
There is a lot of parallel to us in this passage. Put verse 12 into practice—give what you can, willingly. Generosity takes away problems of money and deadens the love of money. Go beyond in generosity. People should not give who cannot give according to their faith.

Things that stop us from giving:

1. Money Demons
[Read Acts 5:1-10]
Not how much you give but the attitude with which you give it

2. Selfishness
[Read Matthew 6:19-21, 24]
No one can really serve two masters. Money => Mammon => god of wealth. Can't love the world and God.

3. Lack of Faith
[Read 2 Corinthians 8:2]
Faith is contagious. Stop thinking of it like an investment—the kingdom grows because we share our faith without worry of return; it is the same way with giving our money. If you don't believe there will be a great place to worship all over the world, then don't give.

? Have you thought about your time, your words, your attitude, your money in regard to being generous?

We give to be like God.

#5. Grace

[Read Titus 2:11-12]

? What is grace?
- Undeserved forgiveness
- "In-spite-of" kind of love
- Real love
- Acceptance w/out perfection

? Where does grace come from?
- Jesus—takes punishment for sins
- After baptism, blood of Jesus covers over sins [1 John 1:7]
- From God's heart, his desire to have a relationship with us

Our Part: sin, imperfection, filthy heart
God's Part: forgiveness, perfection, sinless heart

Too good to be true, but it is! The goal is to see the real God who loves you and how valuable you are to him. He valued you at the cost of his only Son, whom he gave up so that your sins could be forgiven and your relationship with him restored.

[Read Psalm 103:8-10]

? What are some sins in your life?
What do you deserve for them?
- Punishment (grounding, jail, etc.)
- Not being trusted by people

God sees everything you do and knows everything you think, and he knows what you deserve; yet he gives us grace—forgiveness rather than punishment.

[Read Ephesians 2:8-9]

? How many times do you need to obey your parents to receive one grace point?
- No such thing as grace points
- Nothing you can do to earn grace

? Why is there no boasting when grace is involved?
- It is a gift.

God gives grace. You cannot earn it. Our role is to be grateful for it.

? [Read 1 Corinthians 15:9-11]
What is Paul because of grace?
- Forgiven man
- A Christian

? What effect did God's grace have on Paul?
- He worked hard for God.
- He lived his whole life for Christ [Philippians 1:21].
- He was a very grateful man.

Grace completely changes our lives.

? What should God's grace produce in you? Does it?
How should you respond to God's grace? Will you?

Decide you will live for God BECAUSE of his grace, not to earn it.

Write a one-page letter to God expressing your understanding of his grace (using a personal example from your life) and your gratitude for his grace.

#6. Great Convictions

? What does the word "conviction" mean?
- State of being convinced
- Fixed or strong belief
- Convince => to conquer

? Can you name anyone you would consider to have great conviction?
Why is it important to have godly convictions?

[Read Jeremiah 1:1-6]
? In verse 6, why was Jeremiah afraid?
- Too young
- Have to say tough things

[Read Jeremiah 1:7-19]
? How did God respond to Jeremiah's excuse?
- "Do not say…"
- "Do not be afraid."
- You are my messenger.
- "I am with you and will rescue you."

? What did God call Jeremiah to do?
- Preach to Israelites about truth, their sins, judgment

? How would you feel if God asked you to do what Jeremiah had to do?

? What are some convictions you would like to have? Need to have?

[Read Jeremiah 20:9]
Jeremiah is much older now.

? How did Jeremiah develop convictions to have this attitude?
- Conquered doubt
- Believed God is real
- Believed God's words were true

Let's talk about one conviction I believe you need to have.
_____ {Insert scripture that fits the need of the person.}

? What conviction do you think I believe you need to have?
How can you develop your conviction about this?

#7. How Jesus Shared His Faith

[Read Luke 19:10]
What does Jesus say his purpose is?

We're going to look at some examples of Jesus sharing his faith. I want you to notice who he shared with, how he shared with people, and what he did to go the extra mile in giving to people.

[Read Luke 19:1-9]
Tax Collector
Why did Jesus choose Zacchaeus to talk to out of the crowd?
Who was Zacchaeus? What kind of person?
How does Jesus go the extra mile?
- Stayed with him at his house, spent time with him, connected

[Read Mark 1:40-42]
Leper
What kind of life did this leper have?
How was he treated by society?
What does it mean to have compassion?
- The deep feeling of sharing the suffering of another that results in giving aid or support
- Showing mercy
- Emotionally and empathically connecting

How does Jesus go the extra mile?
- He touched him
- Gave him something he had not had in a long time: connection

[Read Matthew 14:13-21]
The Crowd
How do you think Jesus is feeling here?
How does Jesus go the extra mile?
- He gave even though he was going through a hard, emotional time

[Read John 4:1-42]
Samaritan Woman
Who is this woman?
What kind of relationship existed between Jews and Samaritans?
What kind of attitude would we be tempted to have toward her?
How does Jesus go the extra mile?
- Pushed through his tiredness—and as a result many people were saved

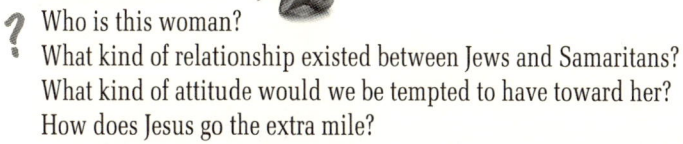

[Read John 8:1-11]
Adulterous Woman
What kind of situation was this?
How does Jesus go the extra mile?
- Peer pressure, uncomfortable situation, he could have chosen to not deal with it

After reading these passages, what are some of the things that characterize Jesus' sharing his faith?
- Compassion
- Self-denial
- Boldness
- Time
- All kinds of people
- All kinds of circumstances
- Did things no one else would do

How were you like Jesus this week?
Celebrate that.
How were you not?
Improve that.

#8. Humility

? What is pride?
- Being stubborn
- Thinking you are better than others or above others
- Thinking your ideas are best and that things should always go your way
- Not admitting wrongdoing or apologizing

? What do you think humility is?
- Listening to input and getting help from God and others
- Taking correction well
- Apologizing for sin
- Confidence and security in yourself

? What are negative ideas that people have about humility?
- Means you let people walk all over you
- Means you let people tell you what to do
- Means you have no opinions

The goal of this study is to help you see your own pride and to help you understand what it means to be humble.

[Read Philippians 2:5-8]
? How was Jesus humble?
- He was God, but became a man.
- He became a servant when he could have been king over the whole earth.
- He died for others!

To be like Jesus is to be humble.

[Read Ephesians 4:2-3]
? How does God want us to get along and be unified with others?
- Be completely humble and gentle (no selfishness)
- Deal patiently with people
- Focus on our love for others so that we can bear with their faults

To get along with others, we must put ourselves aside—that is what Jesus has done for us.

[Read 1 Peter 5:5-7]

? How can humility be like clothing?
- You have to put it on every day before you go outside.
- It is not a natural part of us—it has to be put on (thought about).
- It should be the first thing people see about us.

? What is in store for the humble person?
- Grace
- "Lifted up"—growth and blessing
- Relief from burdens and anxieties because God will carry them instead of you having to
- Better relationships (as God opposes the proud, so do other people)

The humble person is on God's team.

[Read Isaiah 66:2b]

God is fired up about the humble person.
To be humble when you sin:
- » Accept full responsibility
- » Make no excuses
- » Don't be defensive
- » Apologize humbly and be fired up that you are pleasing God and being like Jesus

When others sin against you:
- » Tell them in a respectful way
- » Focus on your love for them and not on what they have done to you
- » Forgive them and forget about it, moving on to being even better friends

Write a one-page description of how you see your pride and how you can turn it into a humility that will make you ready to become a Christian.

#9. Jonah Study

? What are some of the most unbelievable stories in the Bible?
- Red Sea, plagues, Samson, Jonah, etc.

? Why are they in the Bible?
- To serve as examples [1 Corinthians 10:11]

Look at one of those stories, that of Jonah, learn what happened, and apply it to your life.

[Read Jonah 1:1-3]

? Why would Jonah try to hide from God?
- Not willing to obey
- Didn't want to be disliked

? How do you hide from God? Run from God?
- "I don't understand."
- Retreat to sinful nature and actions
- Sleep
- Hang with old crowd

[Read Jonah 1:4-10]

? What affect did Jonah have on the sailors?
- Scared them—boat was going to sink, going to die

? Who are the sailors in your life?
- Parents
- Best friends
- Leaders
- God

? What affect can you have on the sailors in your life?
- Fear
- Anxiety
- Unhappy
- Confidence
- Peace
- Joy

[Read Jonah 1:11-16]

? What did Jonah decide had to be done?
- He must die for the seas to be calmed and the sailors saved.

? How must you die to bring calm and save lives?
- Stop running
- Die to selfishness
- Repent and turn to God

{Discuss specifics of what must be done, including a discussion on the consequences that may result from lack of repentance.}

[Read Jonah 1:17]

? How did God save Jonah?
Was this a part of Jonah's decision?
- No, he thought his life was over...he fully counted the cost of changing.

[Read Jeremiah 29:11]

God does want us to make tough decisions sometimes, but he never leaves us and always has a plan for us. Just like Jonah, there is a big fish to save you. You may not be able to see how the story will end, but you must seek God with all your heart and see how running affects the people in your life. {Help build their trust in God's love and dreams for them.}

#10. Openness

[Read John 18:20]
Jesus "said nothing in secret."
Can he say that about you?

[Read Luke 12:2-3]
Everything will be made known.
How do you think that made them feel?
What are the reasons you aren't open?
What topics are hard for you to talk about?

[Read James 5:16-17]
What is the result of confessing sin?
- We can be healed—not so people can rebuke us!

[Read Proverbs 28:13]
What happens if we don't confess sin?
- If we aren't open, then no healing.

[Read Acts 19:18-20]
These people openly confessed their evil deeds.
The outcome of confessing publicly was that they grew.

[Read 1 John 1:8-10]
When you are not wanting to be open, ask yourself: "Who am I fearing more—men or God?"

[Read 2 Timothy 3:10-11]
Paul writes that his friends know everything about him.
Can you say these words about any relationship in your life?

[Read Psalm 66:18-19]
How does unconfessed sin affect your relationship with God?

[Read Psalm 32:1-7]
This sums up the preferred attitude and the result when we are open.

#11. Prayer

? What is one of the most defining characteristics of Jesus?
- Man of prayer

? How much do you pray?
Why do you think Jesus prayed?
What do you pray about?
What do you think Jesus prayed about?
When do you pray?

Look at a snapshot of Jesus' prayer life:

[Read Luke 6:12-13]
? What did Jesus pray for? Why?
- Big decisions; needed God's help.

[Read Luke 9:28-36]
? Why did Jesus take Peter, James and John?
Whom have you prayed with?

[Read Luke 18:1-8]
? Why did Jesus tell them this parable?
What spiritual qualities does prayer help with?
- Your faith
- Closeness to God

How to pray: **[Read Luke 11:1-4]**
{Teach about a pattern of prayer.}

[Read Luke 11:5-10]
? How does Jesus want you to pray?
- Boldly

#12. Purity

In the Bible, the term "purity" is most often associated with sexual purity; however, it also refers to being free from contamination by worldliness. Contaminated water is undrinkable, just as a contaminated heart is unacceptable to God.

? Have you, or anyone you know, had food poisoning?
Do you know what happens?
- Body rejects contamination

? What are some ways you and your peers are impure in everyday life?
- Lustful thoughts/fantasies
- Flirting
- Second looks
- Sexual immorality
- Movies/TV/porn mags
- Masturbation
- Listening to or telling dirty jokes
- Raunchy music

The goal of this study is to help you take hold of God's conviction on purity of the heart and life, and also to help you see that God's plan is fulfilling in the long run. Being contaminated and poisoned by the world will damage your soul.

[Read 1 Thessalonians 4:3-8]
? What are some things you need to do to stay pure?
- Get conviction about obeying God
- Avoid sexual immorality [Hebrews 13:4]
- Control your own body

God has high standards for us—he expects us to be totally different from people in the world. Have the same expectations as God does. It is not impossible; when you are impure, you hurt God, yourself and someone else, if they are involved.

[Read 2 Timothy 2:22]
? What are evil desires of youth?
- Sensual pleasures: sex, drugs, alcohol
- Reckless abandon
- Greed for latest things

Tools to Help Preteen and Young Teen Leaders and Parents

? Why do you think God says these evil desires have to do with youth?
- New experiences—appeals to curiosity
- Your body is changing sexually
- "Young, wild, free and indestructible" mentality

? What does it mean to "flee" from something?
- Desperately run away, usually from danger

? What does it mean to "pursue" something?
- Go after it with all your heart

You have the right to choose where you spend your energy. God calls you to run after godly character, not worldliness.

[Read Ephesians 5:3-5]
? How much is "not a hint"?
- None, zilch, nada

? What does God say to replace impurity with?
- Thanksgiving

? What does it mean to have no inheritance?
- Cut out of the deal

God takes purity seriously!

? How are you different from your friends in the world?
Are you willing to change your life, thoughts, and habits to be radically pure all the time?

Practical application:
1. Read Psalm 119:9 – Have scriptures ready to battle impurity.
2. Read James 5:16 – Confess sin. Get advice about movies, etc.
3. Write a one-page letter to God about how you were convicted and how you are going to change.

#13. Relationships With the Family

? What are your greatest strengths and weaknesses in your relationships with your family?

[Read Proverbs 23:22-26]

? What do you think will bring the greatest joy to your parent(s)?
- Listening to them
- Living by the truth
- Changing how you live at home

The goal of this study is for you to change the dynamics in your relationship with your family. The results will bring greater joy to your family and to you.

[Read John 19:25-27]

? As Jesus was dying on the cross, what are some words you would use to describe how he looked after his family?
- Compassion
- Love
- Care

The point: if Jesus shows that kind of care for his family—especially making sure his mother was taken care of—while dying on a cross, then we need to daily care about our own families by being righteous and loving toward them.

[Read 1 Thessalonians 5:12-13]

? Whom should you respect?
- Those who work hard
- Those who care for you in the Lord (your parents fit in this category)

? How will your parents know that you love them?
- By how well you listen and obey
- Frequent verbal expressions of love and respect

You've been given so much by your parents. Give back to them with your love and respect.

[Read Ephesians 4:29-5:1]
How do you get along with each sibling? {Go through each one.}

? In your relationship with your sibling(s), what should you get rid of?
- Bitterness
- Rage
- Anger
- Any bad feelings

? How should you treat your sibling(s)?
- With encouragement, kindness, compassion

In God's eyes, there is no such thing as sibling rivalry. You must treat all your siblings with as much love as you would want from them.

? What needs to change the most in your relationship with your family? How will you go about changing these things starting today?

Practical application:
1. Apologize specifically to each of your siblings for the way you have treated them.
2. Write a one-page letter to your parent(s) about how grateful you are for them and how you will specifically change to show greater love and respect for them.

#14. Reliability

? What do you think about studying the Bible so far?
Do you feel like we've really studied?
Why?

[Read 2 Timothy 2:2]
? What does it mean to be reliable?
Why does Paul tell Timothy to teach to reliable people?
What is he entrusting to Timothy?

? What are areas in your life that you need to be reliable in?

? You are struggling with life right now, struggling to be reliable. Why?

[Read Luke 16:10-11]
? What is Jesus teaching here?
- Need to focus on what is in front of you already

1. School
2. Being responsible at home (your room, chores, etc.)
3. Responsible with friendships
4. QTs (if you want)

#15. Respect

? What does respect mean?
- Look up to
- Admire
- Listen to

The goal of this study is to learn how important respect is to God and to teach you who needs to be respected.

[Read Mark 12:28-30] Respect for God
? How do you show respect for God?
How do you love God with all your heart and soul (emotions)? Mind and strength (actions)?
- Sharing your heart with him in prayer
- Doing all God asks of you
- Serving God (serve others)
- Finding out, by studying, how to be with God in heaven
- Constantly thinking about God and what Jesus would do

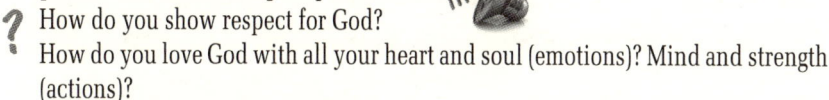

Show respect for God by honoring him by who you are, what you say, and how you live. Your respect for God will directly cause you to respect others, as he commands.

[Read Ephesians 6:1-3] Respect for Parents
? How should you honor and show respect for your parents?
- Obey right away without complaining.
- Listen—look in their eyes.
- Love them unconditionally.
- Be open with them.
- Appreciate them.

The point is that any disrespect for them needs to change. The result of respect is that it brings joy to God and family

[Read 1 Peter 2:17] Respect for Others
? Who are some others you need to respect?
- Siblings
- Teachers

- Policemen and the like
- Leaders in church
- Coaches
- People running clubs, etc.

[Read 1 Thessalonians 5:12] Respect Spiritual Leaders
Why should you respect spiritual leaders?
- Given responsibility; make it a joy for them
- Builds your character to respect others
- God says so

[Read Romans 13:1-7] Respect Rules, Laws, Regs & Guidelines
Why wouldn't you follow these?
- Rebellious
- To get unfair advantage

Why should you follow these?
- God expects you to
- Builds spiritual character
- Contributes to order
- To not be a disgrace

What rules, regulations, etc. should you follow at home, school, etc.?

What attitudes must grow after studying this?

[Read Romans 12:10] Respect shows your spiritual maturity.

Would God say he feels like you respect him?
To whom are you most tempted to be disrespectful?
How will you repent?
What laws, rules, regs, etc. are you most tempted not to follow?'
How will you repent?

Write a one-page description about what you've learned and what you will do to change.

#16. Righteousness...No Matter What

[Read Matthew 6:33]
What does Jesus say should be a high priority in your life?

Righteousness is one of the least pursued qualities of Jesus.

How do you describe "righteousness" in your own words?
- Doing the right thing
- Obeying God and parents
- Obeying laws

Righteousness = being like Jesus.

Write down your top five situations during which it hardest to do what is right?
- Possible situations:
    o During peer pressure
    o Don't feel like obeying
    o When things are hard
    o Don't understand

The goal of this study is to help you understand biblical righteousness and see your need to be righteous in every situation...no matter what!

[Read 1 John 3:7]
Who is righteous?
- Those who do what is right
- Those not led astray
- Those who imitate Jesus

[Read James 2:21-22]
What made Abraham righteous?
- Offered Isaac
- Obeyed God
- Obeyed with faith

To be righteous is to do what is right and to obey God's commands.

[Read Matthew 26:38-39]
? How was Jesus feeling?
? How did Jesus respond?
- Open about his feelings in prayer
- Willing to do God's will
- Made a decision to obey...no matter what

You must do right even when you don't feel like obeying God.

[Read Acts 5:28-29]
? Why were the apostles persecuted?
- Filled city with words of Jesus
- Made people feel guilty about hurting Jesus

? How did they handle persecution?
- They were bold.
- They obeyed God...no matter what.
- They did what was right or righteous.

Even in the face of persecution, you must obey God.

? Is righteousness a daily goal in your life?
? In what area are you most tempted to be unrighteous?

[Read Matthew 6:33]
Start every morning by seeking God first:
1. Pray to be righteous
2. Be open about areas of weakness
3. Ask what Jesus would do

#17. Run to Get the Prize

? Which kind of race is the Christian life like: a sprint or a marathon? Why?

In every marathon, there are two types of runners: one type runs to finish the race; the other type runs to win the race.

[Read 1 Corinthians 9:24]
As a disciple, we can choose between these two perspectives in our spiritual race. In this verse, Paul encourages us to run to win the prize. That's what I want to encourage you to do: to have great dreams for God, to run to win for God.

You are at the very beginning of your race; you need to understand that it is a marathon, a lifelong decision.

? When an athlete is preparing for competition, how often does he train?
- Daily

An athlete must make sacrifices to train well daily.

Three things involved in TRAINING:

1. Ready Your Feet (work hard)
- Can't run a race unless you prepared—physically, mentally, emotionally
- Have to set your mind and heart on what you are going to do

Being a disciple is all about being ready—ready to serve, ready to encourage, ready to share your faith, ready to be trained.

[Read 2 Timothy 4:2]
? What does it mean to be prepared in season and out of season?
- Whether you feel like it or not
- Whether it's easy or not
- Whether it's comfortable or not
- Whether it's convenient or not

Recommit yourself daily to following Jesus, this will train your heart to respond to and obey God and his commands.

? How often do you think about being a disciple?

2. Untangle Yourself from Sin (remove distractions)
- An athlete has to remove all distractions to train effectively (sometimes they go to a specific place to train, away from families, etc.)
- Must be able to focus

[Read Hebrews 12:1-4]

? What does this passage tell you about sin?
- It will entangle us.
- Winning the race involves a daily decision to resist sin.

? How can you resist sin?
- Confess

Just as an athlete endures pain each day, we must be willing to endure the pain of confessing our sin each day.
- Practice

Just as an athlete repeats the fundamentals all the time, we must be willing to go over and over the ways of Jesus: his mindset, his daily activities, his instructions.

? When you are running in a race, where do you look?
- Straight ahead

Have the same attitude about being a disciple—keep your eyes on Jesus, don't get distracted.

? What things distract you?

3. Nurture Your Spirit (care for physical needs)
A true athlete is concerned about the care and nurture of their body. They eat properly and exercise regularly.

[Read Hebrews 5:11-14]

? What do you need to nourish yourself with spiritually?

What will this help you to be able to do?

Tools to Help Preteen and Young Teen Leaders and Parents

- Distinguish good from evil.

Just as an athlete would be weak if they only ate quick snacks and junk food, if your Bible study and prayer is quick and junky, you will be weak spiritually; you will be timid and faithless.

[Read Galatians 6:9]

Obviously, in a marathon, if you don't persevere you won't even finish, much less win. There will be times you will want to quit.

? What happens if an athlete quits training for competition?

[Read Ecclesiastes 5:1-7]
- » Your decision to become a disciple is very serious.
- » Be serious about starting and serious about finishing.
- » Doesn't mean you won't have lower-than-expected split times, i.e. times in your life when you struggle. Struggling doesn't mean you quit on your vow; in fact, it means the opposite.
- » It's all about making a vow to run to the very end!

Ready your feet.
Untangle yourself.
Nurture your spirit.

R.U.N. to get the prize!

#18. Seeking God

[Read Acts 17:16-21] {Give an overview of the situation in Athens.}

[Read Acts 17:22-28]
Why did God create and bring you to this very place and time?

Why do so few people seek God?
- We create our own gods.
- The whole perception of God has been watered down and changed.
- We don't see a need for him or for reconciliation and atonement.

[Read Jeremiah 29:11-14]
What is something you have done with all your heart?
- Heart = seat of passion and longing

[Read Acts 8:26-40]
The Ethiopian was a busy man, but he still found time for God.
How did he go about seeking God?
- He was humble, asked
- He was hungry, used his "down" time

[Read Acts 17:10-12]
God commends the Bereans as noble.
How did they go about nobly seeking God?

[Read John 1:18]
Where do we begin in seeking God?
- Bible: It is the manual for a relationship with God.
- Jesus: If you know him, you know God.

[Read John 20:30-31]
By believing in Jesus you will have true life—and later eternal life.

[Read Hebrews 1:3]
Jesus is the exact representation of God.

What kind of heart is God looking for you to have as you seek him?
How can you get to know Jesus?

[Suggest they read *Jesus With the People* (available at www.ipibooks.com).]

#19. Tale of Two Sons

[Read Matthew 21:23-27]
The chief priests and elders confront Jesus because they don't understand who he is.

? What other ways could have Jesus answered these questions?
- "I am the Son of God. God gave this authority to me. Can't you believe because of the miracles I've done?"
- Got up in their grill: "Who are you to question me?"
- "Go away. Don't bother me with your questions."
- Ignored them.

? Why did Jesus answer their question with a question?
- He kept the attention on WHAT is important not on WHO is important. By answering in this manner, he kept the focus on their heart.

? What did this question reveal about their character?
- More concerned with themselves than with God's honor

I have a question for you {tailor this question to address the person's specific need and/or area of change and growth}:

? Coarse joking and talking about girls with friends—is it ungodly or okay?

? Answer carefully, giving consideration to the affect your answer has on yourself and your friends if they were here to hear it.

[Read Matthew 21:28-32]

? Why did Jesus tell this parable to the chief priests and the elders?
Which son are they more like?
Why do you think I am studying this passage with you?
Which son are you being like?
Why would the tax collectors and the prostitutes believe John before the chief priests and elders? Weren't they more up on the law and stuff?
- They didn't worry about what people thought of them and didn't get caught up in their own self-righteousness.

? What did he tell the chief priests and the elders they needed to do?
- Repent

You've got to repent (change your mind and direction) of _____ {whatever you are addressing}.

{May consider before or during this study, a study about repentance—specifically that it is not a term of damnation and judgment but of growth.}

#20. Train Yourself to Be Godly

Are you involved in anything that takes training? Tell me about it.

? What is specifically involved in training?
- Repetition
- Learning the basics
- Becoming as good as or better than your coach/teacher

? How can you train yourself to be godly?
- Reading and studying the Bible

? What does this accomplish?
- Sharing your faith

? Why? **[Read Philemon 6]**
- Self-control

? What does this have to with the purpose of training?

The goal of this study is to help you see that your spiritual progress depends on your willingness and effort and that it requires self-discipline and seriousness.

[Read Philippians 2:12-13]

? Who is responsible for your salvation?
- Ultimately, you

? What does it mean to "work out your salvation"?
- Obedience to God, even when alone
- Personal attention to your spiritual welfare
- Fearing God

? Anything specific for you?

God puts the responsibility to work out your salvation on you, then when you start working, he works in you to help you live out your purpose.

[Read 1 Peter 2:2-3]

? What does it mean to crave?
- To have an intense desire
- Can't wait to get it

? What is meant by pure spiritual milk?
- Bible study and prayer
- Christlike examples
- Godly advice
- Wisdom that comes from experience {khokhmah—skill, applied knowledge—mentioned throughout Proverbs}

What we desire, we pursue. Cultivate an appetite for a godly character by "tasting" the goodness of the Lord.

[Read 1 Timothy 4:12]

? What example can you set for other teens?
- Bible study and prayer
- Daily evangelism with faith
- Home life (Christianity starts at home)
- Serving without hesitation
- Speaking to others (build up)
- Acting maturely in church
- Being real and sincere in motivation to become a Christian

? Even though you are young, be inspiring!

? What areas do you see that you need to mature in?
Are you willing to take responsibility for changing in these areas?

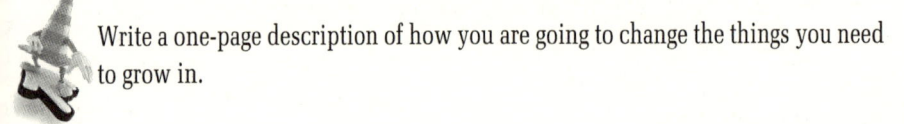

Write a one-page description of how you are going to change the things you need to grow in.

#21. What's Your Dad Like?

{Before doing this study, have the person with whom you are studying write down their view of God and bring it with them.}

{This study in no way is to throw the person's dad under the bus; keep the dignity of their father while teaching them that their view of him can permeate and influence their view of their heavenly Father.}

? Pretend I have never met your dad. How would you describe him?
{Helpful questions} What does your dad love to do? Hate to do? What are some of his best and worst characteristics? How do you know how he feels about you? When is he most proud of you? What makes him mad?

[Read Luke 15:11-24]
? What is the son like before he leaves and when he is on his own?
- Selfish—took dad's money before he was dead
- Very sinful—reckless, wild, sensual

? Even though the son was mean to his father when he left, how did the father respond when the son returned?
- Excited
- Gave him gifts
- Called people together for a party

God is a compassionate and loving father who desperately wants to be with us. He is not judgmental, waiting to zap us for every mistake. He is not uncaring, laughing at our pain. He wants to welcome each one of us home to a relationship with him.

Side note: Jesus is the exact representation of God [Hebrews 1:3], so he is a great example even though he is not a dad per se.

[Read John 8:1-9]
? What was Jesus' reaction to this woman's embarrassing, humiliating sin?
- Sensitive to her embarrassment
- Treated her sin like any other—not, "Oh, I can't believe she did that!"
- Totally forgiving, even though that sin was punishable by death

Forgiveness is part of God's character. Understanding our need for forgiveness and God's willingness to totally forgive helps us to draw closer to him, to love and appreciate him more.

[Read Hebrews 12:5-11]

? How does this passage say it feels to be disciplined?
- Like hardship
- Painful
- Unpleasant

? Why does God discipline?
- For our good (to keep us from evil paths)
- So we can learn lessons in order to make better decisions in the future
- So we can be secure that he loves and cares for us

[Read Jeremiah 29:11]
This passage sums up how God takes care of us when we seek him.

? Do you want to be closer to God?

{Read their essay and see if their view of God is the same as what the Bible says.}

? What relationship do you see between how you view your earthly father and your heavenly Father?
Are you willing to open wide your heart to God and let him be the perfect Father to you that he wants to be?

Practical application:
1. Write a one-page description about what you learned from this study and why you think this concept is important for drawing close to God.
2. Pray every day to see God as the Bible describes him.
3. Praise and thank your earthly father for ways he teaches and loves you.

#22. What Must I Be?

{This study can be helpful especially with someone who has grown up in the church or a strongly religious environment.}

? Why do you want to study?
What is the purpose of studying?
- Build relationship with God and Jesus
- Know what to obey {illustration: ride from a stranger vs. ride from family or parent}

[Read Mark 10:17-18]

? Why did Jesus say, "No one is good except God alone"?
Is this how we think? Why not?
How do you think about yourself?

You study because there is a need to study! No God, no hope.

? How do you see your need to study?

[Read Mark 10:19]

? What are some of the good things the rich young ruler has done?

[Read Mark 10:20]

? What do you think of his response?
Could you say the same about yourself?

The purpose of the law was to show that no one could be perfect. You're are not perfect; you need a relationship with God.

[Read Mark 10:21-23]

? Why didn't he do what Jesus said?
- No relationship

? Why did Jesus ask more of him than the law required?
How are you like this man?
What would Jesus say is the one thing you lack?

Studying the Bible and becoming a disciple is about developing a lifelong friendship with Jesus—out of that relationship comes the love and devotion to be like him and obey him.

[Read Mark 12:28-31]
It is not about what you do, it's about who you are—your heart.

? So, what do you want be?

#23. Who Are You Living to Please?

? Whose approval is important to you? Who do you want to please or get approval from?
- Yourself
- Parents, teachers
- Teen leaders and older disciples
- Friends

? Why?
- To be accepted, liked, popular
- To feel good about yourself
- Because it feels good to be praised

The goal of this study is to help you to see the importance of pleasing God and seeking praise and approval from him.

[Read John 5:41-44]

? What is Jesus teaching in this scripture?
- We need to follow his example by focusing on getting praise from God, not people.
- We will try to please those whom we love.

These people knew the truth but did not follow it because of peer pressure. They cared more about their reputation with people than doing what was right before God.

[Read Galatians 1:10]

? What does Paul tell us about the difference between pleasing people and pleasing God?
- They are opposites!

? When are you tempted to do the God-pleasing thing but with people-pleasing motives?
- Going to church
- Obeying parents because they say so, not because we want to make God happy
- Serving because we want recognition from friends, parents, leaders—not to please God

- Reading the Bible

When we strive to please God, we may not be popular with the world, but keep in mind that man's approval is temporary, while God's approval is eternal!

[Read 2 Corinthians 5:9-10]

Why should we care about trying to please God?
- We will all be accountable for our lives (everyone, whether we believe in God or not).
- Jesus died for us, and we need to live to please him.

It doesn't just happen—it has to be a set goal.

Personal heart-check questions:
Can you relate to the people-pleasing Pharisees in any way?
Have you counted the cost of studying the Bible?
What do your lifestyle and priorities say about how much faith you have in God?

Practical application:
Make three columns on a page. In the first column, list all the activities you are involved in—everything. In the next column, write the reason you think you participate in it. Ask others who know you well to tell you why they think you are involved. Allow them to point out the areas where they see that you "love human praise more than praise from God," and write down their insights in the third column. Be honest and encourage honesty! This will help you to see whom you are living to please and decide to please God instead.

Column 1:   Activities you are involved in
Column 2:   Why you think you involved in it
Column 3:   Why others think you are involved in it

Possible activities:
Studying the Bible, being in sports, hanging with friends, going to church, teen ministry activities, household chores

Write a one-page essay about why you really want to study the Bible. Include whom you are trying to please by studying and why.

CONSTRUCTION AREA IV
Heroic Character

#1 Obedient: Noah

[Revelation 20:11-12] {Break into groups of 4 or 5 and discuss what characteristics would be found in a person whose name was written in the Book of Life. Make a master list and refer back to it at the end of the Heroic Character series.}

Noah

? What do you know about Noah?
- Name means "comfort"
- Father was Lamech
- Had children at the ripe old age of 500
- Sons were Shem, Ham, and Japheth
- Some consider him to be the father of winemaking
- One of the five great Islamic prophets

[Read Genesis 6:5-9]

? How did God describe Noah?
- Favored
- Righteous
- Blameless
- Walked with God

[Read Genesis 6:10-7:16]

? What characteristic of Noah led to the qualities listed above?
- Obedience [vv. 6:22, 7:5, 9, 16]

? What does obedience mean to God? Not what it means to you, but to God.
- Better than sacrifice [Psalm 40:6-8]

? What does this verse say to you?
- Obedience shows love and overcomes corruption [1 John 5:3-4]

? Based on what you learned today, why would obedience be a heroic quality?

Once an English earl visited a tribe on the Fiji Islands and was critical of the chief's obedience to the Bible. "You're a great leader, but it's a pity you've been taken in by those foreign missionaries. No one believes the Bible anymore. People are tired of the threadbare story of Christ dying on a cross for the sins of mankind. They know better now. I'm sorry you've been so foolish as to accept their story." The old chief responded with a gleam in his eyes, "See that great rock over there? On it we smashed the heads of our victims. Notice the furnace next to it. In there we formerly roasted the bodies of our enemies. If not for the Bible, you'd never leave this place...you'd be our supper!"

Heroes are often defined by their momentary display of courage or sacrifice in the face of danger or adversity; however, the ability of a hero to act in such a manner when needed was refined and developed over many prior days as he trained his faculties in preparation for such a time. This took obedience: the capacity to surrender one's will to an overriding presence. One day, maybe tomorrow, you will be called upon for your heroic moment: I wonder...will you have imposed enough obedience on yourself to rise to the moment?

#2. Trustworthy: Abraham and Isaac

Opening activity: Everyone pair up and each pair get a banana. Peel the banana and cut it into slices. Now you put the bananas back together with tape and toothpicks.

? What do you know about Abram?
- Name means "exalted father" and was changed to Abraham or "father of many"
- Considered the founding patriarch of Jewish, Christian, and Muslim religions
- Lived around 2,000 BC

? What do you know about Isaac?
- Abraham's son who was offered as a sacrifice and yet saved at the last minute

Abraham
[Read Genesis 12:1-9]

? What do you notice about Abram from the start?
- Obedient...characteristic #1, left at age 75

[Read Genesis 15:1-6]

? What stands out regarding Abram's response to God?
- Believed him, trusted him

Example of this:
» Abraham and his nephew, Lot, separate; Lot lives near Sodom [Genesis 13:12]
» Lot gets captured; Abraham rescues him [Genesis 14:14-16]
» God is going to destroy Sodom [Genesis 19:12-13]
» Abraham let God deal with it...he trusted God [Genesis 19:27-29]

Isaac
[Read Genesis 22:1-13]

? How old do you think Isaac is?

Actually, he is an adult; Josephus says around 25.

Tools to Help Preteen and Young Teen Leaders and Parents

? How did Isaac respond to this situation?
- Never cried out

Why? **[Genesis 18:18-19]**
- Abraham directed him how to trust.

? After all that you have read and seen in Abraham and Isaac, what makes trust such a heroic quality?
- It allows you to know God and for him to know you.

Blondin lived from 1824-1897 and was a famous French tightrope walker and acrobat. His highest fame came in 1859 when he accomplished one of his greatest feats for the first time: walking on an 1,100-foot tightrope suspended 160 feet above the waters of Niagara Falls. Blondin went on to walk across the falls several times, each time with a different theatrical flair. On one such high-wire walk Blondin crossed over the falls pushing a wheelbarrow. When he reached the other side he asked the spectators if they believed he could do it again. Everyone cheered. Blondin then asked if they believed he could again cross the tightrope with someone in the wheelbarrow. Everyone cheered, trusting that he could do it and wanting to see this incredible stunt. Blondin then asked for a volunteer to ride in the wheelbarrow. No one stepped forward. It was one thing to believe Blondin could do what they had all seen him do, and another to trust their life in his hands.

Once trust is broken it is hard to put back together—like your banana; however, when intact it can be the difference between an act of righteousness and an act you may regret your entire life. May it be said of you in your time of trust, "Now I know that you fear God."

#3. Righteous: Joseph

{Look at the list from lesson 1 of this series and review the characteristics talked about so far: obedience and trustworthiness.}

[Read Matthew 6:33]
? What does Jesus say is top priority?
- Seek his righteousness

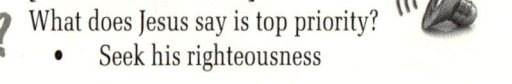

? How would you describe righteousness to a brother from another planet?

[Read 1 John 3:7]
? According to this scripture, who is righteous?
- Those who do what is right
- Those not led astray
- Those who are like Jesus

Pair up; create a top-five list of situations where it is hardest for you to be righteous according to this passage.

? What do you know about Joseph?
- Name means "shall add" and is the eleventh son of Jacob and first son of Rachel

{Review the story of how Joseph came to be in Potiphar's house.}

[Read Genesis 39:1-6]
- From slavery to head of house; a lot to lose

[Read Genesis 39:7-10]
- He refused—righteous no matter what!

? Who can tell me what happened to Joseph?

{Finish the story of Joseph's life.}

? Joseph's character never broke down. Why?

[Read Acts 5:28-29]

? The apostles' lives were under threat and yet what did they say?
- Must obey God rather than you

> The Great Wall of China is a gigantic structure that cost an immense amount of money and labor. When it was finished, it appeared impregnable. But three times the enemy breached it—not by breaking it down or going around it. They did it by bribing the gatekeepers. Dr. Harry Emerson Fosdick, in referring to this historical fact, had this to say: "It was the human element that failed. What collapsed was character, which proved insufficient to make the great structure men had fashioned really work."

You are building a great wall of character. Every time you fail to do the right thing or are led astray by others or your own temptations, your wall is weakened. At some point, the enemy will want to attack. Will your character be up to the task of defending your heart?

#4. Humble: Boaz and Ruth

[Read the book of Ruth]
As you read, highlight the verses about Boaz and Ruth. Ask listeners to be prepared to say what stands out to them about their character.)

? What stands out to you about Boaz and Ruth?
- Patience
- Committed to law and Lord
- Follows advice
- Respect for kinsman, elders, community
- Treats women with respect
- Takes care of poor/needy

? What does each one of these acts and attitudes have in common?
- Not much "me" and "I"

[Read Titus 3:1-2]
? So, what is true humility?
- Lack of self-promotion, coolness when things aren't going your way

? What is so powerful about humility?
- It allows God to be God; it's the foundation for faith.

[Read 1 Peter 5:5-7]
The context is suffering. Is this not what we saw in Boaz and Ruth? They were cool, patient, and self-reserved even though they could have done it their way.

> *Leonard Bernstein was once asked which instrument was the most difficult to play. He thought for a moment and then replied, "The second fiddle. I can get plenty of first violinists, but to find someone who can play the second fiddle with enthusiasm–that's a problem. And if we have no second fiddle, we have no harmony."*

Many characteristics are needed at certain times, like an armory of weapons that are called upon in certain battles; however, humility is one characteristic that will serve you in every circumstance.

Humility is what kept Boaz committed to God, to the Law, to the welfare of the needy, to the respectful treatment of women, to his integrity with his family, and to being a man of noble character.

Humility is what kept Ruth committed to a new God, to her mother-in-law's advice, to authorities, to being content, and to waiting patiently. Humility is what allowed them to be the great-grandparents of Israel's greatest king, David, and the great-great-great ancestors of Jesus, who would become the savior of the world only through humility.

Humility is what will keep you spiritual; it is what will get you to heaven; it is what will bring harmony to a harsh world.

#5. Repentant: Jonah

Game: Toss It! Divide into two teams; draw a line down middle of the room; put crumpled of pieces of paper on the line; each team has 1 minute to toss as many pieces to the opposite team as possible.

Game: Repent! Choose one player to be it; put him on one side of the room and everyone else on the opposite side lined up arm-in-arm facing "it." All together, the group starts walking toward "it" until the leader yells "repent" at which time they all run back to the starting point. "It" must keep still until "repent" is yelled, at which time they may chase down and tag someone from the group—this person now becomes "it." Repeat until there is one person left who is declared the winner.

? What was the point of these games?
- Get rid of sin, change

? What word describes this?
- Repentance

? What is repentance?
- Going one way then turn in exactly the opposite direction

[Read Jonah 1:1-3]
? Why was Jonah hiding?
- Not willing to obey, selfish, didn't want to be disliked

[Read Jonah 1:4-10]
? What affect did Jonah have on the sailors?
- Scared them—boat was going to sink, going to die

? Who are the sailors in your life?
- Parents
- Best friends
- Leaders
- God

? What affect can you have on the sailors in your life?
- Fear

- Anxiety
- Unhappiness
- Confidence
- Peace
- Joy

? What happened to Jonah?
- Threw him off the boat [v. 15]

? Who made that decision?
- Jonah did [vv. 11-12]

? Then what happened?
- Swallowed by a fish

? And what happened inside the fish?
- He repented [Jonah 2:9]

> *July 8, 2005, ISTANBUL, Turkey: First one sheep jumped to its death. Then stunned Turkish shepherds, who had left the herd to graze while they had breakfast, watched as nearly 1,500 others followed, each leaping off the same cliff, Turkish media reported Friday. In the end, 450 dead animals lay one on top of the another in a billowy white pile, the daily newspaper Aksam said. Those that jumped later were saved as the pile got higher, cushioning the fall, the newspaper reported. "There's nothing we can do. They're all wasted," Nevzat Bayhan, a member of one of 26 families whose sheep were grazing together in the herd, was quoted as saying by Aksam. The estimated loss to families in the town of Gevas, located in Van province in eastern Turkey, tops US$100,000, a significant amount of money in a country where the average annual salary per person is around $2,700. "Every family had an average of 20 sheep," Aksam quoted another villager, Abdullah Hazar, as saying, "But now only a few families have sheep left."*

I wonder what would have happened if just one sheep had turned around.

? What will you do in your moment of decision? Be heroic and repent or jump to your death.

#6. Open-Hearted: Jeremiah

Opening activity: Bible Books Puzzle (below)

What methods do we use to get to know each other?

[Read Jeremiah 1:4-10]
What was Jeremiah's mission?
Based on the scripture, what was Jeremiah to use to fulfill his mission?
What challenges would you face if you only had your mouth to communicate?
How would only having a mouth affect your relationship with God?

{Watch Nick Vujicic video.}

A relationship with God is based on communicating with God; letting him know what you really think.

No prophet exposed his feelings more than Jeremiah. His relationship with God was streaked with quarrels, reproaches, and outbursts. He told God he wished he were dead [Jeremiah 20:14-18]. He accused God of being unreliable [Jeremiah 15:18].

What keeps you from being real and open with God?

[Read Matthew 7:21-23]
The question I leave you with is, what does God know about you by what you say to him?

BIBLE BOOKS PUZZLE

Can you find thirty (30) books of the Bible in the paragraph below? Actually, there are thirty-one (31) Bible names if you can find the variant of one Old Testament prophet.

This is a most remarkable puzzle. It was found by a gentleman in an airplane seat pocket, on a flight from Los Angeles to Honolulu, keeping him occupied for hours. He enjoyed it so much, he passed it on to some friends. One friend from Illinois worked on this while fishing from his john boat. Another friend studied it while playing his banjo. Elaine Taylor, a columnist friend, was so intrigued by it she mentioned it in her weekly newspaper column.

Tools to Help Preteen and Young Teen Leaders and Parents

Another friend judges the job of solving this puzzle so involving, she brews a cup of tea to help her nerves. There will be some names that are really easy to spot. That's a fact. Some people, however, will soon find themselves in a jam, especially since the book names are not necessarily capitalized. Truthfully, from answers we get, we are forced to admit it usually takes a minister or a scholar to see some of them at the worst. Research has shown that something in our genes is responsible for the difficulty we have in seeing the books in this paragraph. During a recent fundraising event, which featured this puzzle, the Alpha Delta Phi lemonade booth set a new record. The local paper, The Chronicle, surveyed over 200 patrons who reported that this puzzle was one of the most difficult they had ever seen. As Daniel Humana humbly puts it, "The books are all right here in plain view hidden from sight." Those able to find all of them will hear great lamentations from those who have to be shown. One revelation that may help is that books like Timothy and Samuel may occur without their numbers. Also, keep in mind, that punctuation and spaces in the middle are normal. A chipper attitude will help you compete really well against those who claim to know the answers. Remember, there is no need for a mad exodus; there really are 30 books of the Bible lurking somewhere in this paragraph waiting to be found. God Bless.

#7. Learner: Joshua

Opening activity: Divide the group into even teams and give each team a small, unassembled pup tent. Tell each team they have five minutes to erect the tent. Since you are indoors, provide a roll of duct tape to replace the pegs, which are normally hammered in the ground. Give a prize to the fastest or most complete.

? When did you have to do something but didn't understand why you were doing it?

[Read Exodus 33:7-11]
Explain that this is after Moses had led two million once grateful but now whining, hardheaded, and complaining Israelites out of Egypt. Moses had this tent put up so people could talk to God and take their issues directly to him. Meanwhile, there was a young aide, Joshua, who had to stay in the tent while all this was taking place.

? What could Joshua have been feeling?
Why was Joshua left in the tent?
- He got to watch and learn

? What were some things Joshua could have learned while in the tent?

Could you imagine being in the tent when Moses came in? Joshua got to watch Moses and God talk face to face. I don't think he got to ask a question or say anything, but he watched and learned. He got to watch Moses' relationship with God; he got to grow in his faith and see God's character; he got the chance to learn patience—you know he wanted more than anything to go out there and help Moses with the people, and yet here he was stuck in this tent.

[Read Joshua 1:1-6]
? Why do you think God chose Joshua after Moses died?
- Because of all that he learned while in the tent

? What does it take to be a great learner?
- Imitation, patience, humility, questions

[Proverbs 13:20]
? Who are you watching and learning from?

- **?** What do you think you need to learn from this person?
  Why should you be a good learner?

- **?** What will you be if you hang with a fool?
  - A fool

- **?** What will you be if hang by yourself?
  - A fool

So your only choice is to be with the wise, if indeed that is what you want to be. Otherwise, you will be found a fool.

Bottom line, whose tent will you be found in this week, this month, this year, this life? You don't have to answer that...your life will.

#8. Persistent: Caleb

Opening activity: Have the kids work on the puzzles below. Give them enough time to get frustrated, if possible, and urge them on to see who will not give up.

How did you feel working these puzzles?
- Frustrated, exasperated, discouraged

Tell me some situations where you might encounter this same feeling.
- New sport, moving, trying to learn something, trying to persuade someone of something

What is your natural tendency when you get in these situations?
- To give up, let someone else do it, never do it again

[Read Numbers 13]
What was Caleb trying to tell the people?
What was their response? [Numbers 14:3-4]
How could have Caleb responded to the people's reaction? [Numbers 14:5-10]
What value is there in never giving up?
In what situations would it be beneficial to having a persistent attitude?

You will be challenged in many ways and have many things go against you. The question is not when its going to happen, but when. It is up to you to respond.

[Read Joshua 14:6-13]
Caleb decided to answer by never giving up, and look what his reward was!

_____ **PUZZLES** _____

1. What is the next letter in this sequence?
S S E N T T T T T T T T T T T T T T T T T T T T T

2. What do the following numbers have in common?
3 7 10 17 11 12 73 77

3. A man walks into a bar and asks for a cup of water. The bartender pulls out a shotgun and points it at him. The man says thank you and leaves. Why?

4. What do these two words have in common?
   a. SUBCONTINENTAL
   b. UNCOMPLIMENTARY

#9. Courageous: Deborah

{Place paper around the room with each of the quotes below, one per page.}

Describe a time when you felt most afraid.

? What would have helped or did help you during that time?

Take time to walk around the room and read the quotes on courage. Be ready to discuss what you believe courage to be.

? What struck you as you read these thoughts on courage?

The word "courage" derives from the Latin cor, which means "heart"; however, it is more a matter of intellect, a battle between the neocortex and limbic brain—reason versus emotion.

[Read Judges 5:6-8]
Deborah was a brave woman who led Israel to victory in a time when courage was needed.
{Recap what happened, how the people of Israel were being bullied, and how Sisera died.}

? In what situations do you need courage the most?

Go stand in front of the quote that describes what you will do to face the situation you just mentioned.

One day Hugh Lattimer delivered a sermon before Henry VIII. The king was greatly displeased by Lattimer's insolence and ordered him to preach again on the following Sunday to make amends for the offence he had caused. Sunday soon arrived, and Lattimer, after reading his text, began his sermon: "Hugh Lattimer, do you know before whom you are this day to speak? To the high and mighty monarch, his most excellent majesty, who can take away your life, if you offend him. Therefore, take heed that you speak not a word that may displease him. But then consider well, Hugh, do you not know from where you come–upon whose message you are sent to deliver? Even by the great and mighty God, Who is all-present and Who beholds all your ways and Who is able to cast your soul into hell! Therefore, take care that you deliver your message faithfully." Then he proceeded to give the very same message from the previous week with much more enthusiasm.

Don't give in to fear. Face it and it will make you stronger.

———— QUOTES ————

"Courage is not the absence of fear, but rather the judgment that something else is more important than fear." – Ambrose Redmoon

"Courage is resistance to fear–mastery of fear–not the absence of fear." – Mark Twain

"Courage is being scared to death, but saddling up anyway." – John Wayne

"Life shrinks or expands in proportion to one's courage." – Anais Nin

"Courage is the price life extracts for granting peace." – Amelia Earhart

"You gain strength, courage, and confidence by every experience in which you really stop to look fear in the face. You are able to say to yourself, 'I have lived through this horror. I can take the next thing that comes along.' You must do the thing you think cannot do." – Eleanor Roosevelt

"When a resolute young fellow steps up to the great bully, the world, and takes him boldly by the beard, he is often surprised to find it comes off in his hand, and that it was only tied on to scare away the timid adventurers." – Ralph Waldo Emerson

"Most of our obstacles would melt away if, instead of cowering before them, we should make up our minds to walk boldly through them." – Orison Swett Marden

"Courage and perseverance have a magical talisman, before which difficulties disappear and obstacles vanish into air." – John Quincy Adams

"The highest courage is to dare to appear to be what one is." – John Lancaster Spalding

#10. Perfect Hero: Jesus

Describe the perfect hero.
What makes a hero so attractive?

{Recap the heroic characteristics.}

Today we are going to do some Bible hopping and see what kind of character Jesus has.

- Obedient [Read Luke 2:51, Philippians 2:8]
- Trustworthy [Read John 17:1-5]
- Righteous [Read John 8:29]
- Humble [Read Philippians 2:7]
- Direct [Read Luke 13:1-3]
- Open [Read Luke 22:39-44]
- Learner [Read Luke 2:46]
- Resolute [Read Luke 9:51]
- Courageous [Read Hebrews 7:27]
- Loving [Read Hebrews 7:27]
- Prayerful [Read Hebrews 7:27]

{Read excerpts from *Jesus the Same* by Charles Edward Jefferson about the character of Jesus.}

CONSTRUCTION AREA V
Rising Preteens

A Note from Jeff and Jennifer Rorabaugh

Thanks for teaching our up-and-coming middle schoolers. This nine-week section of the curriculum is designed to prepare the kids for two things: entering the Sunday service and getting used to a typical middle school midweek service.

Each lesson has an agenda, which matches a typical middle school midweek service: a combination of an adult midweek service and a Bible talk. The lessons are full of questions and activities. Please read and come each Sunday prepared. Maybe have a quiet time on the lesson so that you will be fully prepared both mentally and spiritually. You may need to adjust how many of the lessons you use, depending on how many weeks remain until your group is to officially go into the middle school ministry. Please try to complete all the lessons regarding the worship service at the least.

The atmosphere is one of fun, controlled chaos, if your facility allows it. Bring a radio. Be out of yourself. How you greet them sets the tone. If you are unsure about the atmosphere, maybe a visit to your sector's middle school group at midweek is in order.

Have expectations; yet keep it real and real fun! Flea trainers have observed a predictable and strange habit of fleas while training them. Fleas are trained by putting them in a cardboard box with a lid on it. The fleas will jump up and hit the lid of the box over and over again. As you watch them jump and hit the lid, something very interesting becomes obvious. The fleas continue to jump, but they are no longer jumping high enough to hit the top. Apparently, an Excedrin headache forces them to limit the height of their jump. When you take the lid off, the fleas continue to jump, but they will not jump out of the box. Why? The reason is simple: they have conditioned themselves to jump just so high and no higher. Once they have conditioned themselves that is all they can do!

Many times, this age group does the same thing. They restrict themselves and never reach their potential. Just like the fleas, they fail to jump higher, thinking they are doing all they can. You must train them to jump higher. If they are not answering questions, then talk about it in a respectful, non-degrading manner and expect them to do it. If they are being silly, that's okay. After all, they still young! There is a time for silliness. Just help them to understand when to and when not to be silly. What you create and teach them is what they will become.

Thanks for your hard work and preparation for these kids. They are worth it! And one day they will thank you as we do. We love you!

#1. R.E.S.P.E.C.T.

Welcome / Introductions of new friends / Prayer (1 guy & 1 girl)

Singing {2 or 3 kids help lead}

Good News {get one of the kids to lead off}

Opening activity: Have several teachers dress up and lip sync "R.E.S.P.E.C.T." by the Pointer Sisters

Today we are going to talk about respect. I know many of you treat this word like a cuss word, but without it in your life you will be miserable. By way of skits and discussion, we will see what God thinks and how it will relate to you going into the middle school ministry and Sunday service.

Perform Skit #1: Two kids in a class totally disrespect a teacher trying to give the lesson. Feel free to ham this up. Make it fun, obvious, and educational for the kids.

[Read 1 Thessalonians 5:12-13a]
What does "who care for you in the Lord and who admonish you" mean? Why should you respect them?
- Because of their work

Your parents care for you above and beyond the obligations of parenthood. They care for you voluntarily. Your middle school leaders and church leaders do what they do because they want to. Many don't get paid to do it, and those who do could be making big bucks doing something else. Be grateful and learn from them.

Perform Skit #2: Two kids playing a video game get into an argument.

[Read 1 Peter 2:17]
Who are some of the others you need to respect?
- Siblings
- Friends
- Adults

Why does it say "proper" respect?

Tools to Help Preteen and Young Teen Leaders and Parents

From this point in your life, you will be with and interact with other people. While in service on Sunday or midweek, this is key to making it a great time. Learn to respect everyone in the proper way. You will find various ways of showing respect depending on who the person is. Your job is to show the right kind of respect.

Perform Skit #3: Children in a classroom setting are attentive, alert and behaving appropriately by being quiet, raising their hand before speaking, saying "yes, sir" and "no, sir," and volunteering gladly to participate in the class lesson.

? What did you like most about the last skit?

Break up into small groups and have each adult lead a short discussion on the following questions:
? To whom are you most tempted to be disrespectful? How will you change? Would God say he feels like you respect him?

Close out by praising one or two of the kids for their respectful attitudes. End with a game.

Group Game: The Bible Name Game
Split the kids up into 3 even groups. Each group will have two teachers (probably a married couple in each group). The game starts by selecting a student and asking that student to come up with the name of anyone in the Bible (it must be a person's name, not a city name or a person's title). The second student must then say the name announced by the first student and add another name that they come up with. This is repeated indefinitely with each consecutive student repeating every name that has come before them IN ORDER and adding their chosen biblical name (one that has not yet been used) to the end of the list. Ways to get "out": a) forget any name in the order, b) mess up the order of names, regardless of whether or not they are all correct, or c) repeat a name at the end that has already been used. The winner is the last student in the circle who can repeat the names and continue adding names without messing up. The fat brain of the group!

#2. The Weakest Link

Welcome / Introductions of new friends / Prayer (1 guy & 1 girl)

Singing {2 or 3 kids help lead}

Good News {get one of the kids to lead off}

Opening activity: Start by asking for volunteers (as many as you want to use). Have them come stand in a semicircle in front of you; the rest of the class is in a large circle around you. All the leaders put on long black trench coats and glasses, to look like the host of the TV show. Speak with a British accent for added affect.

Tonight, we're going to play The Weakest Link. How many of you have seen shows where people are voted off their team? OK, so you know the rules, here we go...

Ask each individual a trivia question (Bible/Kingdom/Music/Sports/TV) for round one. At the end of the round, each contestant is asked, "Who's the weakest link?" The person voted off leaves and returns to the audience. (Remember to tell them, "You ARE the WEAKEST LINK, goodbye!") Continue in this way until you're down to two contestants. Ask each contestant a trivia question until they miss one. If they do, go to the next contestant, and if they answer correctly, they're the winner. Give them candy as a prize and ask them to return to audience.

What are some things you like/dislike about that show?
- Not fun being considered weak
- Put on the spot
- The host is rude

Think about this.... are YOU the weakest link in your family? Are you the weakest link in your peer group? Are you the weakest link in this class? That's what we're going to talk about today...

You ARE the WEAKEST LINK if you are...

Not giving and friendly **[Read James 2:1-4]**

Tools to Help Preteen and Young Teen Leaders and Parents

? What was the situation here?
- Preferential treatment
- Excluding others

? How could someone be like this today?
- Not wanting to associate with someone "uncool," etc.

? Think: when you came in today, did you sit with/talk to/hang out with the same people you always do? Or did you get to know some others? Do you know everyone's name in this class and maybe ONE thing about them, like their hobbies, etc.?

? What is a clique?
- An exclusive group that looks down on others

? Why are cliques bad?
How does it feel if you're not included?
How did Jesus feel about cliques?

Not a grateful person **[1 Thessalonians 5:15-18]**
? How can you tell someone's thankful?
- Does things in return
- Says "thank you" a lot

How many of you have said thank you to someone today (other than someone at a store or fast food restaurant when you get your change)? What are some things you said thank you for? {Go around the room and have them tell.}

? Are you thankful for the kingdom? A thankful kid isn't one who's dragged to church or to camp! (Imitate: "Mo-o-om...please don't make me go make friends and learn about God.") When was the last time you thanked your leaders or camp counselors? Are you thankful for your room, your bed, your clothes, and your stuff? A thankful kid isn't one who is constantly reminded to make their bed or clean their room. Do you thank your parents for the things they give you?

Challenge: The challenge isn't just to NOT be the weakest link wherever you are, but to be the STRONGEST link—in your family, in class, in whatever group you're in. Make it your goal to be the strongest link in giving and gratitude.

Next week: come in and tell us about a situation in which you were the STRONGEST link.

#3. Worship

Welcome / Introductions of new friends / Prayer (1 guy & 1 girl)

Singing {2 or 3 kids help lead}

Good News {get one of the kids to lead off}

? Who can tell me what the word "worship" means?
Whom do we worship?
Why do we worship them?
Would you like to be worshipped? Why or why not?
If you were to be worshipped on a regular basis, what would you expect from your worshippers?
Why do you think we have church services?

[Read Matthew 4:7-10]
{Explain context of Satan tempting Jesus.}
? Why did Jesus tell Satan this?
What do think you think God expects from you as you worship him?

Why Sunday [Read Acts 20:7]
- The Bible mentions meeting as a body on the first day of the week.
- Jesus was raised on the first day of the week, which was Sunday.

? How do we show honor and respect to God in the worship service?
- By giving God ALL of our focus and attention
- By setting aside this time in our week every week for God and God alone
- By following the example that God gave us of the first-century church {sometimes called the blueprint of the first church}

[Read Acts 2:42-47]
? What examples do you see that we should follow?

Just because people come to church does NOT mean that they are really worshipping God.

? What are some ways that people can come to church but NOT show God honor and respect?

- By not paying attention
- By sleeping
- By not living up to the expectations of worship {remind them of what they would want if they were worshipped}
- By talking and distracting other people who are trying to worship God
- By making church boring because you are not giving

[Read 2 Samuel 6:12-23]

David was willing to look silly because he wanted to give to God. He did not worry about what people thought, even his own wife. In just a while, you will be given the privilege of attending worship service. Some think that you are too young or may be too immature. I, however, believe you can make the service better; you can sing, pray, listen, take notes, and be a great example to other more "experienced" worshippers. After all, it is what you want!

Group Game: The Bible Name Game

Split the kids up into 3 even groups. Each group will have two teachers (probably a married couple in each group). The game starts by selecting a student and asking that student to come up with the name of anyone in the Bible (it must be a person's name, not a city name or a person's title). The second student must then say the name announced by the first student and add another name that they come up with. This is repeated indefinitely with each consecutive student repeating every name that has come before them IN ORDER and adding their chosen biblical name (one that has not yet been used) to the end of the list. Ways to get "out": a) forget any name in the order, b) mess up the order of names, regardless of whether or not they are all correct, or c) repeat a name at the end that has already been used. The winner is the last student in the circle who can repeat the names and continue adding names without messing up. The fat brain of the group!

#4. Spotify: Sunday Edition

Welcome / Introductions of new friends / Prayer (1 guy & 1 girl)

Singing {2 or 3 kids help lead}

Good News {get one of the kids to lead off}

Opening activity: Call people beforehand and have them tell you their favorite song. Set up a Spotify playlist and play each person's song. Have each person (or as many as you have time for) come up while their song is playing and tell why they like it so much. Be sure the music is clean and appropriate.

Who can tell me what the word "worship" means?
What are some things we do in our worship on Sundays?

Today we are going to talk about singing.

Why is singing important?
How many of you are uncomfortable when we sing?
What makes singing uncomfortable?
What makes singing your favorite song okay?
What is the difference? Should there be a difference?

[Read Ephesians 5:19-20]
What does this scripture teach about singing?
- Singing helps us to be grateful to God.

How many ungrateful and unhappy people do you see singing?
How could your singing dishonor God?
- Mumbling the words
- Laughing during songs
- Not being giving
- Not thinking about the words

[Read Psalm 33:1-3]
What did the author mean by "It is fitting"?

Music is a way to express many feelings. It is right to be open with God. Singing is a form of communication with him.

Finish out with some singing. Get some of the kids to come up with a song and lead it. Get in a circle and have fun.

#5. Communion

Welcome / Introductions of new friends / Prayer (1 guy & 1 girl)

Singing {2 or 3 kids help lead}

Good News {get one of the kids to lead off}

Opening activity: Make a setting like a Middle Eastern feast. Have pillows on the floor and have the kids take their shoes off (P.U.! You may want to combine this with a lesson about how Jesus washed the disciples' feet!) Have unleavened bread and something in which to dip it. Have grape juice. Shoot, just have brunch for them! Teach that this is how they ate together in NT times. Give the lesson from this position.

Last week we discussed singing as a part of worship. What are some other parts?

Today we are going to talk about the Lord's Supper, also called communion. The definition of communion is the act of sharing or participation in something as a group. Communion in church is the act of coming together to participate in the Lord's Supper. The Lord's Supper itself is not communion. The Lord's Supper, or the Last Supper (as it is sometimes called) that Christ had on earth before he died is about sacrifice and is a representation of Christ's death on the cross. To understand the Lord's Supper and the purpose Jesus had behind it, we are going to teach about sacrifices in the Old Testament and what Jesus' sacrifice meant according to the Law and the traditions of the time.

[Read John 1:29] Why did John call Jesus the Lamb of God?

John the Baptist was Jesus' cousin, but he was also a prophet whose purpose was to prepare the way for Jesus by alerting the Jewish people that the Messiah, their prophesied Savior, was coming soon. When he saw Jesus coming down the road, he called out to the people that Jesus was the Lamb of God. {Explain the importance of this saying: lamb carried to temple on shoulders of people, lamb is innocent but had to die, etc. Reference Leviticus 4:32-35.} A lamb was used for Old Testament sacrifice and atonement for sins—once a year the Jews would take a lamb and go into the temple area and sacrifice a living lamb to God for the forgiveness of their sins for that previous year. They were not forgiven of their sin until they had made this sacrifice, which also meant that they had to sacrifice every year, because each sacrifice only lasted one year. It was a repeated event for their whole lives.

[Read Matthew 26:17-30]
They were in a setting much like we are now. This passage describes what the communion represents for us. (Explain BRIEFLY what the Passover was and why it was so significant that Jesus was sacrificed during this feast.) Like the lambs, because of Jesus' blood, we are passed over and our sins are forgiven, but not in a yearly sacrifice, as they were accustomed. Jesus was to be the last sacrifice that would last forever.

[Read 1 Corinthians 11:23-29] What kind of attitude should someone have when they take the Lord's Supper?

The Lord's Supper is not be participated in out of habit or just tradition, but from the heart, understanding the sacrifice that was made so we could have a relationship with God and possibly be saved and spend eternity with God in heaven.

[Read Acts 20:7] Who are "we" in this passage?
- Disciples

We take the Lord's Supper weekly to remind us of Jesus' sacrifice. We as humans are not perfect and do not have perfect memories, so we need to be reminded of important things so that we don't forget them. Jesus knew this, so he instituted the Lord's Supper for us to give us something that would always last and always serve as our reminder of the time he took his last meal and prepared to die as a sacrifice for everyone's sin, just like a lamb. In school some material is repeated because without constant reminding, you would forget it; we are the same way throughout our lives, which is why it is so important to have something like the Lord's Supper to remind us of this important event.

Group Game: Blind Floor Volleyball
With a sheet and two chairs, a "net" is set up in the middle of the floor with "court" boundaries taped off. Each side serves to the other, as in real volleyball. Each side, when the ball has been served to their side, has two hits to get it back over the net in bounds to the other team, or the other team gets a point. Points are awarded to a side only when that side is serving. EVERYONE MUST STAY SEATED DURING PLAY—if a teammate lifts their behind off the floor to hit the ball, then it is either a point to the other side, or a "sideout," depending on which side is serving.

#6. The Good Soil

Welcome / Introductions of new friends / Prayer (1 guy & 1 girl)

Singing {2 or 3 kids help lead}

Good News {get one of the kids to lead off}

{Set up four stations, one for each of the different soils in Mark 4:13-20, complete with a sample of each soil type; divide kids so that there is one group per station.}

Answer the questions regarding the example of the soil in front of your group:
1. What observations can you make about this soil?
2. How conducive is this for growth?
3. Would you recommend this soil to a farmer? Why or why not?
4. If this soil represented a heart, demonstrate what their heart would be like.
{Have each group present their answers.}

[Read Mark 4:1-20]
{Instruct each person to go sit at the station that describes their heart.}

? Why did you choose this station?
What will it take for someone:
In soil #1 to get to #4?   In soil #2 to get to #4?   In soil #3 to get to #4?

The goal for you is to get your heart soft, ready to grow. Don't be surprised if God allows things to happen to prepare your heart for growth, either spiritual or character growth. Don't be surprised if your heart is not where you want it, if you are not doing something about it.

When you get into the middle school group and into the worship service you will hear lessons like this. They are taught to help you learn about yourself. Jesus
? used parables to teach the people. Why?
Learn to take notes and to ask yourself some key questions.

? What kind of questions would be good to think about after hearing this lesson?
What would the middle school leader expect you to do with these questions?
What role can your parents play when you hear lessons like this?

Get used to telling them what you learn at midweek. They can help you put the Bible into practice. {End with a game or two.}

#7. Baptism

Welcome / Introductions of new friends / Prayer (1 guy & 1 girl)

Singing {2 or 3 kids help lead}

Good News {get one of the kids to lead off}

In earlier lessons, we talked about singing and the Lord's Supper.
Have you ever noticed that sometimes people cheer during the service? Why is that? At what point in the service does this happen?
- People cheer after baptisms.

Let's see why...

[Read Acts 2:36-38]

? What is the definition of baptism?
- To immerse, or place under water

Its origin is not necessarily religious. It does not mean to sprinkle or dip, but to get completely under the water.

? Who can tell me what the word "repent" means?
- To change or turn around

? Why does someone get baptized?
- God says so, for the forgiveness of sins, and to have God's spirit inside you.

Who can get baptized? **[Read Matthew 28:18-20]**
- People who have become disciples can be baptized (anyone can, really, but simply being baptized does not mean you are a disciple).

A disciple is not someone who goes to church every week or has gone through all of the Bible studies, but is someone who has changed, decided to live a life that obeys the Bible, and wants to be like Jesus.

Who can baptize new disciples? **[Read Acts 2:41]**

- Anyone. It does not have to done by a minister or preacher or a man. With 3000 being baptized, I doubt that only the apostles baptized people. (They would each have had to baptize 250 people if they divided them evenly!)

? Why do you think baptism is so important? **[Read 1 Peter 3:18-22]**
- God commands it.

Baptism is the point in time when people become saved and can go to heaven.

A person ready to get baptized has studied the Bible and come to believe that Jesus is the Son of God. They've changed and stopped doing sinful things and are ready to be a follower of Jesus the rest of their lives. Cool, huh?

	THAT IS WHY THE CHURCH CHEERS AFTER A BAPTISM!!

One day they will cheer for you!

Group Game: Blind Floor Volleyball
With a sheet and two chairs, a "net" is set up in the middle of the floor with "court" boundaries taped off. Each side serves to the other, as in real volleyball. Each side, when the ball has been served to their side, has two hits to get it back over the net in bounds to the other team, or the other team gets a point. Points are awarded to a side only when that side is serving. EVERYONE MUST STAY SEATED DURING PLAY—if a teammate lifts their behind off the floor to hit the ball, then it is either a point to the other side, or a "sideout," depending on which side is serving.

#8. Bible Games

Welcome / Introductions of new friends / Prayer (1 guy & 1 girl)
Singing {2 or 3 kids help lead}
Good News {get one of the kids to lead off}

Opening activity: Bible Baseball, Jeopardy, or Bible Bowl
Use the following questions and/or add your own for whichever game is chosen.

1. Who can recite the first five books of the New Testament?
   - Matthew, Mark, Luke, John, Acts
2. Who can name Moses' brother AND sister?
   - Aaron [Exodus 4:14] and Miriam [Exodus 15:20]
3. Who knows and can recite the shortest verse in the Bible?
   - John 11:35, "Jesus wept."
4. Who wrote the Book of Revelation?
   - The Apostle John [Revelation 1:2]
5. What book and chapter tells about the beginning of the first-century church?
   - Acts 2
6. How many times is the word "Christian" in the Bible?
   - Three [Acts 11:26, Acts 26:28, 1 Peter 4:16]
7. Which prophet was Jesus' relative?
   - John the Baptist [Luke 1:36]
8. What did John the Baptist's diet mainly consist of?
   - Locusts and wild honey [Mark 1:6]
9. Name six of the apostles.
   - [Matthew 10:2-4]
10. Who was King David's best friend?
    - Jonathan [1 Samuel 20:17, 41-42]
11. Who was Jonathan related to? How?
    - He was King Saul's son [1 Samuel 14:1]
12. What sea did God part?
    - The Red Sea [Exodus 13:18]
13. Name five of the 10 plagues.
    - [Exodus 7-11]
14. How many years did the Israelites wander in the desert?
    - 40 years [Numbers 14:34-35]
15. What foods did God provide the Israelites as they lived in the desert?
    - Quail and manna [Exodus 16:13, 31]

16. How many psalms are in the Book of Psalms?
    - 150
17. What did the Israelites make when Moses went up on Mt. Sinai?
    - A golden calf [Exodus 32:2-4]
18. How many of each animal did Moses bring on the ark?
    - None—Noah brought them. [Genesis 7:9]
19. Who was Ananias' wife?
    - Saphira [Acts 5:1]
20. What mountain were the Ten Commandments written on?
    - Mt. Sinai [Exodus 31:18]
21. How old was Jesus when he began to preach?
    - About 30 years [Luke 3:23]
22. How long was Jonah inside the belly of the fish?
    - Three days and three nights [Jonah 1:17]
23. What was the name of the demon-possessed man?
    - Legion [Mark 5:9]
24. How long did the water flood the earth?
    - 150 days [Genesis 7:24]
25. What sin does God hate most?
    - Pride [Proverbs 8:13]
26. What were Jesus' last words on the cross?
    - "It is finished." [John 19:30]
27. Who is the oldest person in the Bible?
    - Methuselah [Genesis 5:27]
28. Who closed the door to the ark?
    - God [Genesis 7:16]
29. Who was taken to heaven in a whirlwind?
    - Elijah [2 Kings 2:11]
30. Who betrayed Jesus?
    - Judas [Matthew 26:49-50]
31. Who was king when Jesus was born?
    - Herod [Matthew 2:1]
32. What is God's sign to never again flood the earth?
    - Rainbow [Genesis 9:13]
33. What is the greatest commandment?
    - Love God with all your heart, soul, mind, and strength. [Mark 12:30]
34. What was God's first creation?
    - The heavens [Genesis 1:1]

TIE BREAKER: Without looking, what is the last book of the Old Testament? Malachi

#9. Who's Got Game?

Welcome / Introductions of new friends / Prayer (1 guy & 1 girl)

Singing {2 or 3 kids help lead}

Good News {get one of the kids to lead off}

{Set up the room for a party and team games. Use the following tournament instructions, a combination of any of the games in the series, or choose your own games. Split the group into teams and rotate through the games or have everyone play one game at a time. Give out prizes. Have food and music. Give award certificates at the end signifying that they are prepared to go into the worship service and the middle school ministry. Make this a fun end-of-the-summer-ready-to-promote time!}

Tournament introduction
At the beginning, each team will choose a team name. Each team will also have a scorecard that they will carry with them from game to game. The judges at each game will log the points scored by each team. At the end of the five games, the team scorecards will be given to the gamemaster, who will tally each team's scores for a grand total for each team. The team with the highest grand total score will be declared the winner of the tournament. {The five games are described below. There is also an alternate game that can be substituted if one of the following games is deemed unsuitable.}

1. Who's got "ups"?

INSTRUCTIONS
This is a straight-"up" dunk contest. Place two adjustable rims in the room, one at each end of the room. Each team chooses 10 dunkers for each rim. One rim will be placed at 7 feet and the other at 8 to 9 feet, depending on the skill level of the kids.

OBJECTIVE
Gather the most points for your team from the judges.

SCORING
There will be three judges per rim. One will judge style. One will judge power. One will judge creativity/originality. When the round is finished, each team captain will collect scorecards and take them with them to the next game.

EQUIPMENT
2 Adjustable basketball rims suitable for dunking
Rubber basketballs
Band-aid and athletic tape in case of any minor injuries. Blisters can sometimes form on the fingers for those who are uninitiated to the world of dunking.
Some creative minds.

PERSONNEL
6 judges and 2 refs

2. Who's got the "brain"?

INSTRUCTIONS
This is a mental competition that will pit the teams in a battle of concentration. The group forms two teams. The members of each team line up along the opposite sides of the room. The teams face each other. The ends of the lines need to bend toward each other so that one big circle is created in the middle of the room. At this point, everyone except the team members at the ends of the lines turns and faces outside the circle. Then, everyone sits down. The opposing team members at the ends of each team line are the only ones facing each other. One of the referees now designates one end of the lines as the BEGINNING and the other end of the lines as the END. Each team member now clasps hands with the teammate next to them, forming a human chain. The opposing team members at the ENDS of this human chain face each other with the target between them. The target is a soft ball, like a Koosh ball or tennis ball. The members that make up the center of each team chain continue to face the outside of the circle. A coin is flipped between the opposing team members at the BEGINNING of each team line. With all the other team members facing outside the circle, the two opposing team members at the BEGINNING of the lines will be the only ones able to see the outcome of the coin toss. Once these two see heads, they will initiate a nonverbal signal that will be passed through the human chain of their teammates to the member of their team at the END of the line. Once that person receives the signal, they are to pick up the target. The first one to pick up the target will place it back where it was and move to the BEGINNING to become the first member of their chain. When the coin toss lands on tails, a signal should not be sent and therefore the target should not be picked up. If the target is picked up when the coin lands on tails or if there is any false signal that causes the target to be picked up, the opposing team is allowed to advance a player from the END to the BEGINNING.

OBJECTIVE
Each team is attempting to move as many of their team members as possible from the END of the chain to the BEGINNING of the chain.

SCORING
The team that passes the most members through the first position in the time allotted leaves this game with one point.

EQUIPMENT
Coin for flipping and a soft ball that can be gripped easily

PERSONNEL
2 referees and 2 monitors

3. Who's got the "look"?

INSTRUCTIONS
This game is based on the game Assassin. Each team member receives a designation as they arrive in the room that they are to keep to themselves. Three members of each team will receive a card marked with a dot. The other members will receive an X. The kids will sit in a circle. Teammates will not be allowed to sit beside one another, therefore the teams will count off, 1, 2, 1, 2, etc. The assassins who are designated by the dots are to assassinate members of the opposing team by winking at them, but they must try not to let anyone but their "victim" see them do it. Once a member of either team is winked at they must immediately put their head down and submit. They are out at this point. The objective is to expose the assassins. This is done when someone still in the game raises their hand and announces that they know who the assassin is. At this point, one of their teammates has to be willing to support their accusation. This person must state, "I support the accusation." Once the accusation is made and supported, the referee, who will be aware of who the assassins are, will determine whether the accusation is accurate or not. If accurate, then points are gained for the accuser's team and an assassin is eliminated. If the it is incorrect, then both the accuser and their ally are eliminated from the game. The game continues until all the assassins are exposed or all of their competitors have been assassinated. If time expires, the victory goes to the most skilled team. Any team member deliberately looking away from the circle or that the referee determines is only trying to survive by not making eye contact is eliminated. Any discussion or communication as to who the assassin is among teammates is prohibited.

OBJECTIVE
Each team is trying to expose the assassins on the opposing team. Each team's assassin is attempting to eliminate as many of the opposing team members as possible.

SCORING
One point will be awarded for each player assassinated. 5 points will be awarded for each assassin that is discovered.

EQUIPMENT
Eyes, Eyelids. Small index cards. A Marker.

PERSONNEL
2 referees and 2 monitors

4. Who's got "touch"?

INSTRUCTIONS
Divide the group into two teams. The teams line up on opposite sides of the room. The lead player on each team will be facing each other with the other team members teams trailing behind them in a straight line. These opposing teams will be roughly 10 feet apart. To each team's right will be a square box that has a PVC pipe standing vertically in the center of the box {attach it with wide masking tape}. The PVC pipe will be wide enough to receive a metal washer that is tossed into it. Each team will toss washers across the 10 feet of floor space toward the box and the PVC pipe next to the line of the opposing team. Each member will throw two washers. As the washers are landing in or around the box, or in the pipe, they may be picked up immediately and thrown back across the room toward the other box and pipe to score points. This will be done in rapid fashion. The contest will play out like a relay, with the competitors rotating to the back of the line as soon as they have made their tosses. Just prior to beginning the game each team's line will step far enough to the left so that they will be standing directly across from the box and pipe to which they will be tossing their washers. This way none of the opposing team members will be standing in the line of fire as the washers are tossed.

OBJECTIVE
Just like horseshoes, getting a ringer (getting the washer into the mouth of the pipe) will score maximum points while missing the box will score no points. The objective is to pick up and toss the washers as quickly yet as accurately as possible.

SCORING
In the pipe = 5 pts
Leaning = 2 pts
In the box = 1 pt
Outside the box = 0 pts

EQUIPMENT
6 large washers (2 for replacements)
2 pieces of PVC pipe wider than the washers
2 wooden boxes
Wide masking tape

PERSONNEL
2 scorers, 2 referees, 2 traffic controllers

5. Who's got "survival skills"?

INSTRUCTIONS
This game is similar to Bombardment or Dodgeball. Make a tape line across the center of the room (the midcourt line). Tape off two goals at each end of the court, one with red tape and one with blue tape. Mark one ball clearly with red tape and one ball with blue.

The group divides into two teams, which take opposite sides of the court. Kickballs are thrown at opponents to get them out. If a ball is caught when it is thrown, then the person who threw the ball is out. Those who are out must go to jail. Each person sent to jail scores points for the opposing team. If a player crosses the midcourt line while throwing, hitting an opposing player does not put them out, but if the ball is caught, the thrower is out. The goals at each end of the court must be hit with special balls marked with their corresponding tape color. If the ball hits one specific goal, then all of that team's prisoners are released (don't make this goal too large!). If the ball hits the other goal, the team receives the point value for that goal. There will also be a "BALL-O-DOOM." A large ball is placed on the field of play. This ball is passed from one team to the next, much like a "hot potato." If the ball is on your side when a whistle is blown then your team receives a penalty.

OBJECTIVE
The teams are attempting to score points by throwing a ball at their opponent and sending them to jail while attempting to avoid being hit. Extra points can

be earned by throwing at goals that are placed at each end of the field of play. A special goal is designated to release prisoners from jail.

SCORING
Hitting an opponent = 5 pts
Hitting Goal #1 = 15 pts
Hitting Goal #2 = 25 pts
BALL-O-DOOM =15-pt penalty

EQUIPMENT
10 kickballs, 6 Hula Hoops, One VERY LARGE Beach Ball
Red tape, Blue tape
XL Red T-Shirt (for a ref), XL Blue T-Shirt (for a ref)
3 XL Black T-Shirts (for the ump and jailors)

PERSONNEL
1 umpire, 1 red referee. 1 blue referee, 2 jailers

LIST OF EQUIPMENT FOR ALL GAMES

2 Adjustable basketball rims suitable for dunking
Rubber basketballs
Band-aid and athletic tape
Coin for flipping
Soft ball that can be gripped easily
Small index cards
Marker
6 large washers (2 for replacements)
2 pieces of PVC wider than the washers
2 wooden boxes
Wide masking tape
10 kickballs
6 Hula Hoops
One VERY LARGE Beach Ball
Red tape
Blue tape
XL Red T-Shirt
XL Blue T-Shirt
3 XL Black T-Shirts
Party streamers and other party decorations

CONSTRUCTION AREA VI
Spiritureality

#1. Spiritual Elements

Opening activity: Divide the group into four smaller groups by having them count off using the words "heart," "soul," "mind," and "strength."

Have the word "SPIRITUREALITY" written on poster board and placed on a wall. Give each group a piece of poster board and a marker. See how many words they can derive from "spiritureality."

? What is the transitive property of equality in math?
- If A = B and B = C, then A = C.

[Read Romans 7:14]   Spiritual = Law

[Read Mark 12:28-34] Law = love God with heart, soul, mind, and strength
Therefore, being spiritual = loving God with all your heart, soul, mind and strength

These are the elements, the essential tools that you have been given to be spiritual.

Over the course of our Sunday school time together, we will be discussing what it means to be spiritual throughout the real situations in which you find yourselves.

This week we want to understand what the meaning of each of the elements of spirituality is. Next week we will look at what we mean by "reality"; then you'll take time each week to learn how to use the elements (heart, soul, mind and strength) to handle the real situations you face.

You have been divided into four groups based on the four elements.

Take 5 minutes and discuss what your element is and how you think it is meant to be used.

Heart: the seat of thought and emotion, which focuses thinking and understanding [Mark 2:8]

Soul: the immaterial (and eternal) part of the inner person, often meaning the animate self, which can be translated with pronouns such as me, myself, and I.

Mind: the part of the inner person that uses the outcome of the heart to make choices

Strength: the power to carry out the choices the heart and mind make together

These are the four elements which create your spiritual self and are present to aid you in life.

> *There was once a young teenager and his girlfriend who decided to go for a swim in a neighbor's pool while the neighbors were away for the weekend. As they approached the fence, they saw a sign that warned them to keep out of the pool, but ignoring the sign, they climbed straight over. Ten feet away from the pool there was another sign saying "Keep out of pool." They started to undress right by the sign. The boy in his bravado wanted to show the girl what he was made of, so he ran ahead and cried, "Watch this!" He ran onto the springboard to dive into the pool, and as he leapt into the air, the girl screamed "No!" The boy dived head first into the pool. The pool had been drained. The boy spent the rest of his life paralyzed in a wheel chair.*

Most times these four elements will help keep you not only spiritually safe but physically as well.

#2. What Is Real?

Divide into four teams: 2 girls' teams and 2 boys' teams. See who can name the most reality TV shows (competitions) in 5 minutes.

Possible shows:
The Amazing Race, American Gladiators, American Idol, America's Next Top Model, The Apprentice, The Bachelor, Beauty and the Geek, Big Brother, The Biggest Loser, The Contender, Crowned, Dance War, Dancing with the Stars, Extreme Makeover, Hell's Kitchen, The Hills, I Love New York, Kitchen Nightmares, Last Comic Standing, Project Runway, The Real World, So You Think You Can Dance, Survivor, Top Chef, Wife Swap

Bonus question: How many reality TV shows have aired on TV?
- 750 as of 2015

What is reality?
What are ways that people deal with reality?
- Entertainment
- Drugs/alcohol
- Ignoring
- Anger/Ridcule
- Being a control freak
- Escape

Why do they choose these ways to deal with reality?
- To escape dealing with it
- To force change
- To be in control

What are real situations you face? {Have each person write a list to turn in. Take time to set this up by asking each one to be gut-level honest; tell them not to hold back, because you want to meet their needs in the situations they really do face.}

[Read Colossians 2:17b] Reality is found in Christ.
What does this mean?

Written by a guy: It's that guy sitting in front of you in class doing the crossword instead of taking notes. It's the people who play video games for hours at a time instead of doing their homework. It's the insecure person who has to drink his own weight in alcohol before he can get up the nerve to ask a girl on a date and then forgets he did it the next morning; whatever the scenario, we as humans cannot get rid of our incessant desire to escape from reality. Constantly seeking some change from our routine schedules, US citizens try as hard as possible to do anything but the things they have to do. Either procrastinating until the day before or just neglecting things totally, we do manage to accomplish absolutely nothing in the process. Sure, video games are fun, but no matter how high the score gets, it just isn't real. We sit around for hours at a time watching reruns of Saved by the Bell, but to no avail. Zach is still going to have to take the test he keeps putting off, too. So, why is this? Why have we decided that our nine-to-five lives don't cut it, and we have to be entertained by Tarantino covering an entire set with blood and letting Uma stand over it with a Samurai sword? We escape, most likely, because frankly, reality sucks. People die every day in huge numbers. Billions of people are starving, and we can't do anything about it. Nature is going to keep ticking by without giving a single care in our direction whether we are doing homework or playing Jenga and listening to Raffi. Even the inevitable gut class you are enrolled in is a great example of you escaping reality. Think about it. Eventually you have to get a job, stop living off Dad and somehow start contributing to society. So, how have you decided to prepare for this?

Written by a girl: Was there something you always wanted to be as a child? Some children want to be doctors, or firemen, or teachers. I always wanted to be an actress. Growing up in New York, I dreamed of escape. I was the oldest of six children and the caretaker—my mother was often ill and slowly developed a drinking problem. My father worked all day and would walk in through the front door and out the back to the basement, where he worked on hobbies and drank beer. As the oldest girl, everyone leaned me on for support. I cleaned, shopped and changed babies, was my mother's friend and my father's wife. Lacking the parental support that most children receive while growing up, I craved love and attention. By the time I was sixteen I started to drink and smoke cigarettes and marijuana. I aggressively sought escape from my reality. After finishing high school, I became a regular drinker at a bar in a very small town, beginning a phase of promiscuity that lasted for years. Nothing mattered to me except running and escaping. I danced in a bar for two months to make some quick money for my move to California. I was going to be an actress. It was what I'd always dreamed of. I took some acting courses, but my drinking became a stumbling block. I moved in with a man that I thought I loved, and we traveled up and down the California coast growing marijuana in our renovated school bus as we went. We became regulars at swap meets where I eventually sold everything I had—my car, jewelry, even childhood trinkets. I was completely dependent on him. I had promised myself that I would never let a man hit me. After a few drunken episodes, this man I thought loved me beat me up. I flew back to New York. I had dreamed of acting, marriage, and children, but I ended up back where I started, alone at home now with a black Shih Tzu named MaiTai.

#3. A Delightful Path

Opening activity: At one end of the room, set up a target with a Bible sitting in front of it. Move all chairs, tables, etc. to the side except for four chairs are in a row on the opposite room from the target and facing the target. Ask for four volunteers and have them sit in the chairs.

We are going to play a game where each of our volunteers must get from their chair to the target once they are told "go." The target represents spirituality and the space between the volunteers and the target represents life.

Before each round have a volunteer leave the room; the other three volunteers sit and watch.

Round 1, Volunteer 1: Everyone sits or stands against the wall so there is a clear, unobstructed path to the target; when ready have the volunteer enter the room and sit in their chair, and then say go. There is to be absolute silence when the volunteer enters the room and during their journey to the target. If all goes well, the volunteer should just get up and walk easily to the target.

? If what we just saw represented your life, how realistic is this?
What would make it more real?
- Some obstacles

Round 2, Volunteer 2: While the volunteer is out of the room, set up a maze of people, chairs, tables, etc. that the volunteer must navigate in order to get to the prize. When ready, have the volunteer enter the room and sit in their chair, and then say go. There is to be absolute silence when the volunteer enters the room and during their journey to the target. The volunteer should make it fairly simply to the target with some easy decisions and maneuvering.

? If what we just saw represented your life, how realistic is this?
What would make it more real?
Do you know everything you need to know about being spiritual and godly?

Round 3, Volunteer 3: Keep the maze of people, chairs, tables, etc.; maybe change it a little. While the volunteer is outside, have someone blindfold them and then, when ready, have them enter the room, sit in their chair, and then say go. Have everyone be silent until they begin their journey and then have everyone start talking and making noise. The volunteer may not move or try to get through and find it very difficult; watch and observe their reactions.

? If what we just saw represented your life, now how realistic is this?

Round 4, Volunteer 4: Keep maze of people, chairs, tables, etc.; maybe change it again. While the volunteer is outside, have someone blindfold them and tell them that there will be some people talking to them to help; when ready, have them enter the room and sit in their chair, and then say go. Have everyone be silent until they begin their journey and then have everyone start talking and making noise. Choose one person to represent each of the following: the voice of anger, the voice of lying, the voice of manipulative emotions, and the voice of pleasure; have them talk to the volunteer as they try to make it to the target—they must stay in character (angry, liar, emotional, enticing) the whole time telling the volunteer they are trying to help them.

? If what we just saw represented your life, how realistic is this?

The people talking to the volunteer represented some of the items you put down as real situations.

? What point are we trying to make with this activity?
- Every one of us has some obstacles in our way to spirituality.

? What would have made it easier for volunteers 3 and 4 to succeed?
- Simply taking the blindfold off

[Read Psalm 119:33-37]
When you train your heart, mind, soul, and strength to follow the Bible, your eyes are opened so that you can tell when real obstacles (anger, lies, emotions, temptations) are trying to block you. One little decision can keep you from the right path.

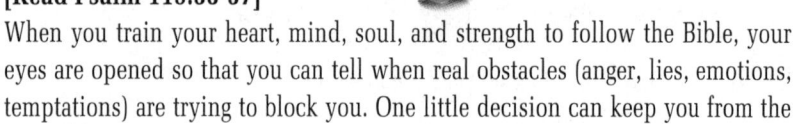

> In the 1880s a little lady lived in a little house. The little lady woke up very early one ordinary morning. There had been little rain that summer. This morning there was a little wind blow-

ing. It was still dark, so the little lady picked up her little lamp with a little oil in it. She picked up a little match and lit with the little fire the little lamp that produced a little light in the darkness. She walked out to her little barn and walked their little cow into its little stall. The little lady got a little corn and a little hay and put it in front of her little cow. She took her little milk bucket and started milking a little milk from the little cow. There were a bunch of little flies flying around the little cow. So the cow used its little tail to SHOO off the little flies. The cow's little tail knocked over the little lamp, and a little oil ran onto the little bit of dry hay and the little flame ignited a little fire. The little lady didn't think too much of the little fire. She ran to get a little bucket of water and it took a little while; when she returned her whole little barn was on fire. The barn caught the little house on fire, and that little house caught the next house on fire. Before long the little fires combined to make what is known as the great fire of Chicago, Illinois. The great fire burned over a square mile of homes and businesses. Many died and much property was totally destroyed. THE GREAT FIRE WAS A COMBINATION OF MANY LITTLE THINGS COMING TOGETHER TO CREATE A NIGHTMARE IN HISTORY.

#4. Guard Your Treasure

Opening activity: Divide the class into groups of three, each with one 6th grader, one 7th grader, and one 8th grader. Instruct the 8th graders: Come up with things for which a guard would be needed or used. Be ready to mime your answer. If another person takes the one you were going to mime, you must choose something different from your list, so come up as many different things as you can.

Have the 8th graders mime and the group guess.

? Who remembers the four elements of spirituality?
- Heart, mind, soul, and strength

[Read Matthew 6:19-21]
? What does Jesus say we must guard?
- The heart

Think of all the things you came up with that required a guard. Of all the things, Jesus chose the heart.

In your groups of three, discuss why he would choose the heart.

? If you were Satan and you wanted to steal someone's treasure, based on this scripture where would you go?

There are two questions you must answer now that you know where the enemy is going to attack and rob your spirituality:

? What do you treasure?
How do you plan to protect it?

? What are some ways you can protect your treasure (heart)?

Now that you have some ideas on how to guard your treasure, my encouragement is that you focus a great deal of attention on understanding what it is you treasure. The answer to the first question defines the level of commitment to the plans of the second.

I have three treasures. Guard and keep them:
The first is deep love,
The second is frugality,
And the third is not to dare to be ahead of the world.
Because of deep love, one is courageous.
Because of frugality, one is generous.
Because of not daring to be ahead of the world, one becomes the leader of the world.
– Lao-tzu (604-531 BC)

#5. Salt of the Earth

Activity: {Bring a bag(s) of salt and have the kids guess what it is. Put some salt in a glass or jar of water and let it dissolve as you talk; mix it every so often.}

What is salt?
What are its uses?
How important is salt today?
What was salt's importance in Jesus' time?
- Very expensive
- Preservative
- Sacrificed to the gods
- Used as payment for wages; the word "salary" comes from the word for salt

[Read Matthew 5:13]
Jesus calls the disciples the "salt of the earth."
What did he mean by that?
What might the salt represent in your life?
What can cause you to lose your saltiness?
- Anger
- Lying
- Gossip
- Making fun of people
- Lust
- Sexual sin
- Materialism

What happens to your convictions or the truth when they get watered down?

{Refer to the glass or jar of salt; the salt should have dissolved—like their convictions, it disappears. This makes for a good visual aid. Read Matthew 5:11-16 so they can see the context.}

I think this is a time when people are looking for lights on a hill, for some taste to their food, meaning we've got to stand up and see that there are many opportunities to do good.

- » Your family can be a great source of comfort to your neighborhood, but NOT if you lose your saltiness and are disobedient.
- » You can be a great friend and bring honor to all that is good, but NOT if you lose your saltiness and are disloyal and a gossip.
- » You can be a hero to your younger siblings, but NOT if you lose your saltiness and are unkind and abusive.
- » You can be an example of faith and maturity to adults, but NOT if you lose your saltiness and are disrespectful and a nuisance.

Keep your saltiness. Don't let someone's immature comments, or being made fun of, or your own selfish desires cause you to lose your saltiness!

You are the salt of the earth! You are one of the few people in the entire world who are being taught and exposed to the truth of God's word. Show the world what you are really made of! Show them that you are worth your salt!

Camp Swamp

Besides your home—the safest place on the planet!

As a global 501(c)3 organization offering an "unrivaled camp culture" to the young and young-at-heart, we:

- Organize weeklong summer camp sessions for kids ages 9-18
- Provide Youth & Family Retreats for all ages
- Conduct camp staff training and mission work worldwide
- Extend an exceptional rental facility for retreats and events
- Host laser-tag gaming with state-of-the-art taggers

Best known as Camp Swamp, we are located in the rural setting of Penfield, Georgia just two hours east of Atlanta and 45 minutes south of Athens, Georgia on 188 acres of wooded land and open fields. In operation since 1993 and at this location since 1998, we offer experiences unlike any other. Visit the website below for all the details and FAQs.

www.campswamp.com

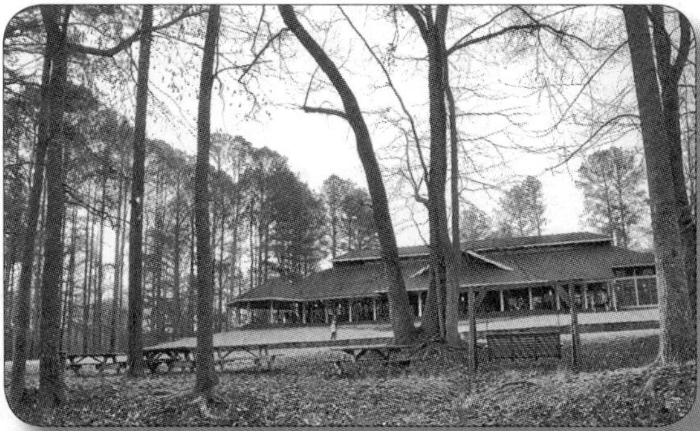

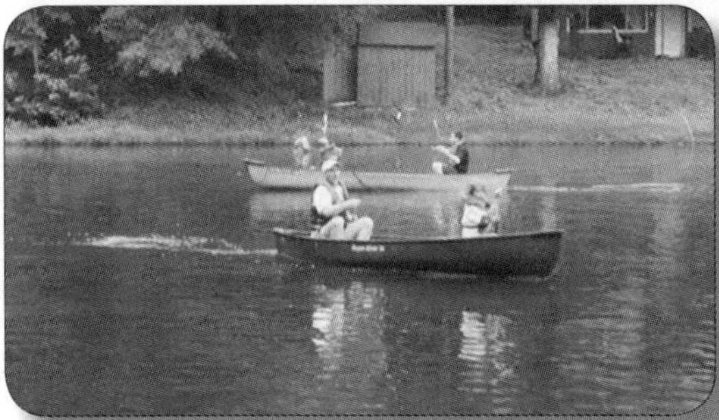

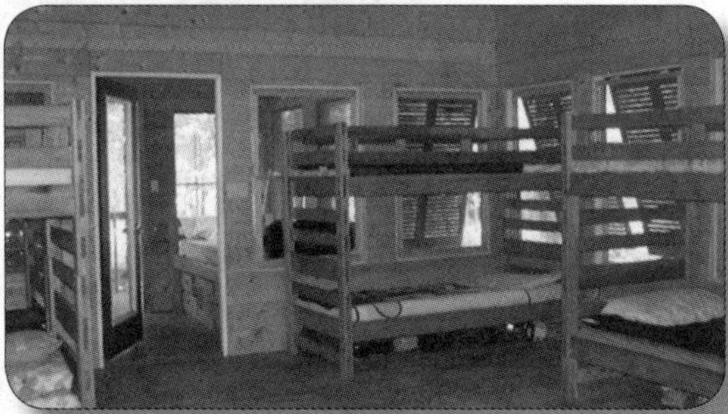

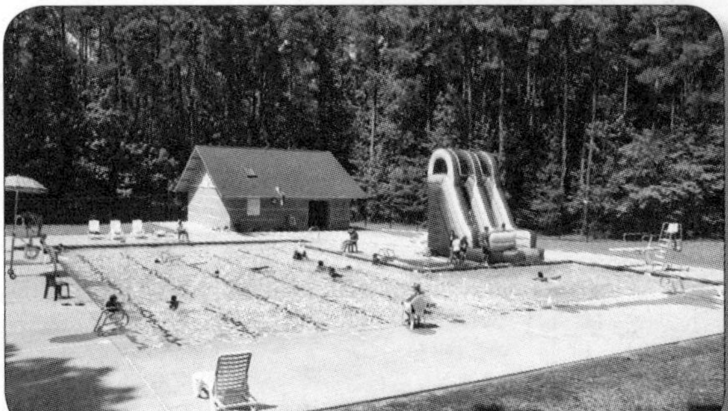

www.ipibooks.com